Figural Space

Global Aesthetic Research

Series Editor

Joseph J. Tanke, Associate Professor, Department of Philosophy, University of Hawaii

The Global Aesthetic Research series publishes cutting-edge research in the field of aesthetics. It contains books that explore the principles at work in our encounters with art and nature, that interrogate the foundations of artistic, literary and cultural criticism, and that articulate the theory of the discipline's central concepts.

Titles in the Series

Early Modern Aesthetics, J. Colin McQuillan
Foucault on the Arts and Letters: Perspectives for the 21st Century, Catherine M. Soussloff
Architectural and Urban Reflections after Deleuze and Guattari, Edited by Constantin V. Boundas and Vana Tentokali
Living Off Landscape: or the Unthought-of in Reason, Francois Jullien, Translated by Pedro Rodriguez
Between Nature and Culture: The Aesthetics of Modified Environments, Emily Brady, Isis Brook and Jonathan Prior
Reviewing the Past: The Presence of Ruins, Zoltán Somhegyi
François Jullien's Unexceptional Thought: A Critical Introduction, Arne De Boever
Figural Space: Semiotics and the Aesthetic Imaginary, William D. Melaney

Figural Space

Semiotics and the Aesthetic Imaginary

William D. Melaney

ROWMAN & LITTLEFIELD
Lanham • Boulder • New York • London

Published by Rowman & Littlefield
A wholly owned subsidiary of The Rowman & Littlefield Publishing Group, Inc.
4501 Forbes Boulevard, Suite 200, Lanham, Maryland 20706
www.rowman.com

6 Tinworth Street, London SE11 5AL, United Kingdom

Selection, Editorial Matter, Introduction, Chapter 3, Chapter 4, Chapter 8, and Conclusion Copyright © 2021 by The Rowman & Littlefield Publishing Group, Inc.

This volume contains revised versions of the following material, reproduced with permission:
Melaney, William D. "Revolutionary Kristeva: Conflict, Mimesis, Rimbaud." In *Proceedings of the Eleventh International Symposium on Comparative Literature*, edited by Salwa Kamel, 845–53. Cairo: University of Cairo Press, 2014.
Melaney, William D. "Spenser's Poetic Phenomenology: Humanism and the Recovery of Place." In *Analecta Husserliana XLIV*, edited by Anna-Teresa Tymieniecka, 35–44. Dordrecht: Kluwer Academic Publishers, 1993.
Melaney, William D. "Rancière's Proust: A Rebirth of Aesthetics." *Res Cogitans: Journal of Philosophy* 13, no. 1 (2018): 52–62. Odense: University of Southern Denmark.
Melaney, William D. "Blanchot's Inaugural Aesthetics: Visibility and the Infinite Conversation." In *Analecta Husserliana CX*, edited by Anna-Teresa Tymieniecka, 467–83. Springer International, 2014.
Melaney, William D. "Semiotics Mythologies: Jean Rhys and the Postcolonial Novel." In *Semiotics 1995*, edited by C. W. Spinks and John Deely, 31–40. New York: Peter Lang, 1996.

All rights reserved. No part of this book may be reproduced in any form or by any electronic or mechanical means, including information storage and retrieval systems, without written permission from the publisher, except by a reviewer who may quote passages in a review.

British Library Cataloguing in Publication Information Available

Library of Congress Cataloging-in-Publication Data

Names: Melaney, William D., 1953- author.
Title: Figural space : semiotics and the aesthetic imaginary / William D. Melaney.
Description: Lanham : Rowman & Littlefield, [2021] | Series: Global aesthetic research | Includes bibliographical references and index.
Identifiers: LCCN 2020053235 (print) | LCCN 2020053236 (ebook) | ISBN 9781538147856 (cloth) | ISBN 9781538179888 (paperback) | ISBN 9781538147863 (epub)
Subjects: LCSH: English literature--History and criticism--Theory, etc. | Literature--Philosophy. | Literature--Aesthetics. | Semiotics and literature.
Classification: LCC PR21 .M45 2021 (print) | LCC PR21 (ebook) | DDC 820.9--dc23
LC record available at https://lccn.loc.gov/2020053235
LC ebook record available at https://lccn.loc.gov/2020053236

This book is dedicated to Zhiping and Yongyi

Contents

Acknowledgments		ix
Introduction: An Opening of Figural Space		xi
1	Kristeva and Hegel: Subjectivity Reconfigured	1
2	Spenser's Renaissance: Ideality and Discourse	19
3	Image in Wordsworth: Space/Time and Semiotics	35
4	Shelley's Double Vision: Figural Counterworlds	57
5	Proust and Aesthetics: A Narrative Sensibility	73
6	Space in Blanchot: Orphic Testimonies	99
7	Revisiting Jean Rhys: Postcolonial Aesthetics	117
8	Ishiguro's Imaginary: Figures of History	133
Conclusion: Negotiating the Figural		149
Bibliography		171
Index		179

Acknowledgments

I am grateful to the American University in Cairo (AUC) for having provided me with a research grant to pursue the study of Proust and the French novel at the Regenstein Library at the University of Chicago in August 2013. Through funding provided by the same institution, two papers formed the initial basis for chapters that appear in the present work. "Ishiguro as Historical Witness: Memory, Aesthetics and Critique" was read at the International Convention of Asian Studies, Leiden University, Leiden, Netherlands, on July 19, 2019. "Wordsworthian Tales: Myth, Nature and History" was read at the Mythological Panorama Conference in the Senate House, University of London, King's College, on October 4, 2018.

The following publishers and editors have allowed me to develop articles into chapters for this book: "Rancière's Proust: A Rebirth of Aesthetics," *Res Cogitans: Journal of Philosophy* 13:1, ed. Søren Harnow Klausen, Odense: University of Southern Denmark, 2018, pp. 52–62; "Revolutionary Kristeva: Conflict, *Mimesis*, Rimbaud," *Proceedings of the Eleventh International Symposium on Comparative Literature*, ed. Salwa Kamel, Cairo: University of Cairo Press, 2014, pp. 845–53; "Blanchot's Inaugural Aesthetics: Visibility and the Infinite Conversation," *Analecta Husserliana* CX, ed. Anna-Teresa Tymieniecka, Springer International, 2014, pp. 467–83; "Semiotics Mythologies: Jean Rhys and the Postcolonial Novel," ed. C. W. Spinks and John Deely, *Semiotics 1995*, New York: Peter Lang, 1996, pp. 31–40; "Spenser's Poetic Phenomenology: Humanism and the Recovery of Place," *Analecta Husserliana* XLIV, ed. Anna-Teresa Tymieniecka. Dordrecht: Kluwer Academic Publishers, 1993, pp. 35–44.

Introduction

An Opening of Figural Space

The importance of context to whatever can be identified as knowable was often foregrounded in the past century as crucial to the attainment of truth, broadly conceived. Pragmatism, phenomenology, hermeneutics, and critical theory, as well as certain strains of analytic philosophy, beginning with the late Ludwig Wittgenstein, were differently concerned with demonstrating how context, far from comprising an incidental feature of knowledge, is inextricably linked to the pursuit of truth and cannot be detached from epistemological outcomes. In many cases, the role of context acquires deeper significance when it is emphasized at the expense of an outcome that otherwise might be limited and "abstract" in the sense of testifying to a denatured or impoverished conception of human cognition. This emphasis would be misunderstood if it were taken to be a mere supplement to a process that could be essentialized as constituting a separable core of intellectual inquiry. Moreover, context becomes crucial to the pursuit of knowledge when it challenges a traditional notion of truth as invariable and stable, that is to say, as "metaphysical" because it can be arraigned against the element of time that is inherent in all experience and cannot be cognized as prior, original, or unified before it appears in one setting or another.

Nonetheless, this apparent innovation in knowledge theory can be traced back to sources that are by no means epistemological, if this word is taken in its dominant usage, but overlap with the history of aesthetics and, in another way, evoke literary traditions that employ *figural expressions* to draw the subject (or reader) into the quest for meaning, if not ultimate truth. Beginning with aesthetics, we might identify Immanuel Kant's *Critique of Judgment* (*Kritik der Urteilskraft*, 1790), as an attempt to *re*contextualize the laws of nature and moral freedom in his own philosophy by arguing how the mind necessarily includes a noncognitive component in the quest for universal satisfaction in the mode of the beautiful. This noncognitive component might be said to comprise a context that needs to be evoked if aesthetic apprehension can be thematized as psychologically compelling. Such an argument, however, might be criticized as irreconcilable to a belief in the possibility of absolute truth that emerges in the aftermath of Kant's aesthetic innovations. At the same time, as an aesthetic theorist, Kant can be read as rehabilitating appearance itself, instead of demoting it in the style of the philosophical tradition that derives from Plato, when read primarily as a metaphysician, thus clearing a productive "space" in which aesthetic judgments can be assigned extra-aesthetic, and far-reaching, meanings. For instance, in arguing that the beautiful is a *symbol* of morality, Kant separates aesthetics from ethics but also suggests how the two realms can be bridged, even though the notion of the symbolic may not solve the problem of how the sphere of aesthetics can be used to enforce the basically foundationalist claim that is made for the ethical. This problem is heightened when Kant defines aesthetic as a sphere of nonknowledge, thus undercutting the possibility of employing it as a discipline that might found the legitimacy of ethics.

However, the successors to Kant were also unwilling to refurbish the aesthetic in a way that might recall his rationalist predecessors, focusing instead on the broader problem of how the aesthetic, as a form of nonknowledge, reopened philosophical questions that wove it more strongly into cultural and, even, political experience. On the one hand, particularly in the letter series, *On the Aesthetic Education of Mankind* (*Über die ä sthetische Erziehung des Menschen*, 1795), Friedrich Schiller strove to redefine the aesthetic as an implicitly *political* regime in developing the possibility of a third sphere that provided a hypothetical alternative to both Thomas Hobbes's state of nature as the sphere of internecine conflict and the Kantian sphere of moral law, which in Schiller's account bore many of the harsh traits that it was designed to surpass. In this way, Schiller sought to overcome a remote and perhaps mythic past as well as the moralism of the modern age in opposing both of these realms to a newly constructed public sphere that generated the political *out of the aesthetic*, rather than merely alongside of it. As inadequate as this effort may seem to be from the standpoint of later thinkers, especially those who would question the idealistic nature of Schiller's enterprise, we should not be surprised to discover that G. W. F. Hegel's own position as an aesthetic theorist drew on this effort at crucial junctures because the latter's argument against Kant also stemmed from a persistent dissatisfaction with dualism, which generally fell back on a generalized agnosticism, whether in the domain of knowledge, art, or morality. Indeed, not only in his strong response to Schiller's aesthetic thought but also in his methodological reflections on this reconceived aesthetic project, Hegel roughly adopts the "space" of the aesthetic in Schiller's sense when he elaborates on how the three phases of art (i.e., symbolic, classical, and romantic) allow us to envision a movement from substance to spirit and how the attainment of classical integrity in the Greek phase of art is articulated in increasingly *semiotic* terms during postclassical times.

From one standpoint, the projects of Schiller and Hegel seem to be completely unlike one another. The aesthetic chronologies of the two theorists seem to have little in common. Schiller appears to be the more optimistic of the two, endowing the aesthetic sphere with a political potential that invites us to envision a future that resolves conflicts that were enshrined in nonaesthetic regimes, thus initiating a dialectic that may not be progressive in time but at least opens a more promising future, assuming that we are able to appropriate the aesthetic as a challenge to preexisting systems. Hegel, in contrast, provides an image of increasingly limited aesthetic fulfillment when he argues that the fusion of spirit and substance, as it appears in the art of Greco-Roman antiquity, undergoes protracted dissolution, culminating in the romantic apotheosis of sign over symbol to guarantee the irreversible decline of art as a home for thought during the late modern period. Moreover, Hegel's argument is also couched in terms of a movement from aesthetic presence to semiotic motility, constituting in this way a passage from static achievement to dynamic play under the conditions of modernity itself. Hence, although Schiller conceives of this play in optimistic terms, as the political realization of a futural project, Hegel as an aesthetic theorist responds to Schiller as a quasi-dialectical thinker, even when the former seems to be arguing that "art does not progress" to the degree that it ultimately becomes incapable of encoding a satisfactory adequation of substance and spirit. At the same time, we might say that Hegel's "end-of-art" thesis is not so much a pronouncement on the demise of art in modern times as an affirmation of the aesthetic as the only category appropriate to the apprehension of art in its conceptual unfolding.

Hegel's contribution to aesthetics, therefore, is part of the modern tradition that was initially formalized by Kant and then developed, sometimes quite differently, in the period that follows Kant's breakthrough. One way of understanding this tradition is to say that, instead of simply dealing with the question of how art objects are made, the aesthetic tradition took up the question of how art is to be identified as art. In the postclassical aftermath that does not begin until the late eighteenth century, the status of representation is placed under critique when the categorical framework through which art is approached as art is placed in the center of aesthetic reflection. This can only occur, however, because the older approach to art that is shared by both classical mimetic theories and early modern rationalism is disbanded when representation is no longer taken to be the touchstone for defining either the work of art or aesthetic experience. A nonclassical reading of Hegel demonstrates that his own contribution to this tradition participates in the insight that aesthetics is the scene of an extended crisis, that is to say, the crisis in representation that requires a new understanding of art as art, which for Hegel means that aesthetics as a "method" of interpretation cannot be assimilated to classical paradigms. Whereas Kant strongly opposed the subordination of aesthetic judgment to rationalist conceptuality, Hegel offers a more historical scheme for the development of art, arguing that the classical phase in the art of the ancient world has been superseded by the increasing disjunction between substance and spirit. Although these two types of opposition to "classicism" are not to be confused, both Kant and Hegel indicate in different ways how the aesthetic introduces a basic rift in the way that art can be *thought* on the level of the how it categorizes the objects that it arranges.

We can see the difference that aesthetics makes to the apprehension of cultural objects through the example of how figuration in art acquires a new significance only when the older rhetorical tradition ceases to regulate criticism. The approach to tropes that is enshrined in classical rhetoric generally stems from Plato and continues in modern rationalism, which subsumes the figure under conceptual meanings. This approach is still alive in the response to figures that animates the postclassical tradition that begins with Tertullian and arguably ends with Erich Auerbach. This tradition adopts biblical hermeneutics as its point of departure and prefers a forward-looking reading of (literary) figures that is assumed to be already at work in scriptural typologies. And yet, both the Platonic and hermeneutical approaches share a common resistance to allowing the figure to drift away from a controlling factor that is either conceptual or invested in the project of interpretation itself. My argument is that Hegel's contribution to aesthetics is completely misunderstood when it is assimilated to either or both of these approaches. On the contrary, I will suggest that Hegel is only misread when his complex philosophy is reduced to a series of figures that simply disappear under the weight of a progressive dialectic, or worse still, when an arbitrary selection of figures, or perhaps even a single figure, is assumed to constitute the "meaning" of his system as a whole.

Moreover, if the two versions of rhetoric can be said to share a common assumption about the figurative, namely, that its meaning depends on the possible fusion of graphic signifier and abstract signified, the aesthetic tradition that begins with Kant and certainly includes Hegel is strongly concerned with *the figural*, which enables the vehicle through which the figure appears to serve more than a provisional function in any inventory of cultural meaning. Figural, as opposed to figurative, significance is inassimilable to any overarching scheme that would comprehend the figure, especially through an atemporal mode of understanding that prioritizes the eternal over the historical and, therefore, in the long run, subordinates figuration to a nonfigural and basically "metaphysical" order of being. One way of interpreting the figural is to say that it needs to be placed in relative opposition to traditional allegory, which tends to privilege the timeless as the sphere in which the alterity of the figure can be grounded. The figural, on the contrary, as implied in Kant's schematism and Hegel's phenomenology, appears in the "space" in which meaning can be negotiated and is, for that reason, only misconstrued as a sign for truth. And yet, having said this much, we also need to acknowledge the role of the unthought in the process of negotiation whereby the truth of the figure is continually contested. My argument also depends on the contribution of psychoanalysis to clarifying how the figural is to be maintained in its resistance to closure and in opposition to the thrust of reason, which perpetually attempts to clarify what remains hidden and obscure.

In the present study, therefore, I have adopted the work of Julia Kristeva as a starting point for an inquiry into the conditions that render poetic language intelligible to the extent that this language contains the key to both openness and closure as twins themes in figural thought. Kristeva's seminal work, *Revolution in Poetic Language* (*La Révolution du langage poétique* 1974), can be read as a meditation on the importance of *both* dialectics and psychoanalysis to the construction of the poetic, which begins as a semiotic but passes through encounters with Gottlob Frege, Jacques Lacan, and Hegel before entering the domain of Karl Marx, who briefly suggests how the aesthetic as a category might be reopened beyond the specific demands of capitalist production. Moreover, Kristeva's work enables us to place *literature* in the space between aesthetics and semiotics, a space that is *figural* rather than specifically figurative because it constitutes interruption rather than continuity, just as it engages the reader in a quest for norms that are irreducible to the structural features that unify literary texts on a formal level. Hence, although Kant and Hegel suggest how the problem of context is to be interpreted as one that enables the figural as a sphere that is ultimately related to either the ethical or cultural sphere and provides the occasion for a "leap" beyond aesthetics itself, Kristeva invests the literary with quasi-aesthetic significance—to the degree that the aesthetic continues to harbor philosophical meanings—which is even more strongly endowed with linguistic traits. This quest is indeed subjective in the sense of indicating how the reader is provided with a mode of apprehending the riven nature of poetic language, which is *both* instinctive (semiotic) and cognitive (symbolic), inviting reflections on the conflictual origins of cultural expression. This quest also supplies a context within which literature provides the figural traces of quasi-dialectical readings and the rudiments of a noncontinuous history.

Hence, and at the same time, my encounter with Kristeva's later work, particularly the collection of essays titled, *Powers of Horror* (*Pouvoirs de l'horreur*, 1980), demonstrates how the notion of a remainder is present in the experience of abjection, which not only modifies her previous semiotic but also problematizes the canonical reading of Hegel as the idealist philosopher par excellence, inviting us to interpret human institutions as inherently contaminated with elements that are inassimilable to a progressive dialectic. My reading of Kristeva, however, is basically unitary rather than chronologically divided because it argues implicitly that the canonical reading of Hegel is problematic, if not entirely misguided, to the degree that the self that emerges in dialectics is always already inseparable from an invasive alterity that elicits the passage from one philosophical moment to the other and, thus, problematizes any preexisting ground for ego positioning. Moreover, this reading of Hegel also becomes an appropriation of psychoanalysis that would have us recognize the effects of the unconscious on the construction of the ego and the pursuit of knowledge. Kristeva's embrace of aesthetics, particularly in her late work, is haunted by the unique example of Arthur Rimbaud, whose prose poems suggest how interruptions in symbolic understanding call attention to psychic conflicts that refute a ready application of structural principles to the reading of texts. The seven literary studies that follow my discussion of Kristeva differently engage the confluence of Hegel and Sigmund Freud, or dialectics and psychoanalysis, as initially mediated through Kristeva's precarious synthesis.

My study of Edmund Spenser's *Faerie Queene*, Book VI, presumes the author's attempt to recover aspects of the humanistic heritage in the wake of his involvement in the politics of Lord Grey, the colonial administrator who enlisted him in the occupation of Ireland during the late sixteenth century. This chapter depends on Spenser's use of Aristotelean moral philosophy as well as Renaissance iconography in the "Book of Courtesy," which features the movement of its invisible protagonist toward the attainment to virtue. My discussion foregrounds the emergence of Platonism in an anthropological mode that serves a poetic and, perhaps, ideological purpose, but it also suggests how the book's absent center inscribes the problem of discourse when the virtue of courtesy is revealed to be an inherently political one. However, Spenser's epic project, although exemplary of what literature can achieve in one period, is shown to be incapable of fully exploring the aesthetic potential of language, which requires a reorientation from classical mimesis to the liberation of sensuous contents as demonstrated most clearly in the poetry of the Romantic age and in the theoretical revolution that prepares its reception.

The next two chapters, therefore, bring together William Wordsworth and Percy Bysshe Shelley, two nineteenth-century poets whose work was written in the aftermath of the French Revolution and, perhaps largely for this reason, exhibit a basic reorientation that can be articulated as an aesthetic apprehension of figural space. This reorientation implicitly acknowledges the achievements of both Kant and Hegel without arguing that aesthetic theory was employed as a self-conscious resource by either poet. Wordsworth's *Prelude* (1805) is taken up as an attempt to provide the hermeneutics of temporality with an ethical motivation, but the figural dimension that continually surfaces at crucial moments in this poem is sufficiently complex to refute symbolic readings that presuppose the lived experience of a unified subject. But Wordsworth is also shown to engage in the hermeneutical problem that typifies his own century, which upheld the importance of experience to literature while posing the question of its coherence. Without denying that the poet's mind constitutes the subject matter of the poem, my reading of Wordsworth testifies to how aesthetics offers us a basis for gauging the passing of time, which sometimes produces conflicting results but also refers to the intrusion of the historical into the somewhat sheltered world of poetry. Nonetheless, Wordsworth cannot be identified with the eruption of the sublime in any unequivocal sense because the role of the semiotic acquires poetic significance in the sense of time that overlays the encounter between Wordsworth and his younger sister, bringing his great poem to a momentous close.

In a similar way, Shelley's unfinished final poem, "The Triumph of Life" (1822), confronts the problem of the French Revolution in aesthetic terms, improvising a response that clearly distances the poet from the figure of Jean-Jacques Rousseau as the troubled precursor of a movement that was no doubt inspired by Enlightenment influences but who carried these influences in a disastrous direction. By contrasting Harold Bloom's hermeneutical interpretation to Paul de Man's protodeconstructive reading, I am able to suggest how an aesthetic response to the poem would not have to be at odds with historical approaches but instead foregrounds this occasion as a post-Kantian event that both *re*configures Rousseau but also produces a "double image" of the French Revolution as both promise and catastrophe, precarious survival and grievous trauma. The traumatic image of Rousseau himself, who figures history as an ongoing series of calamities, belies the conventional reading of Shelley as a relatively unambiguous advocate of Enlightened reason. My engagement with psychoanalysis adopts the theme of survival as both a remnant of autobiography and sign of history, preventing the reader from interpreting Shelley's poem as a narrative in which before and after are arranged through discrete units.

My chapter on Proust is no doubt a high point in my discussion to the degree that it strongly argues for both an aesthetic apprehension of the great French novelist's masterwork, *À la Recherche du temps perdu*, and redeploys Hegel and psychoanalysis in rethinking the twin problem of self and time. The first part of this chapter is a presentation of Jacques Rancière's reading of Proust, which begins with an inquiry into the role of intense sensations in disrupting lived experience as anticipated in the poetry and prose poems of Charles Baudelaire. For Rancière, this aesthetic disequilibrium is expressed in the difference between Gustave Flaubert and Mallarmé, who prepare the moment when the Proustian narrative acquires a special role in resolving the opposition between art and life or aesthetics and everyday experience. In coming to terms with this event, Rancière argues that the aesthetic revolution initiated by Kant but articulated politically in the theories of Schiller establishes a valid basis for the subsequent development of literature as the contested space of rapprochement between art and life. Rancière convincingly argues that Schiller responded to the threat manifested in the Terror when he transformed Kant's notion of the play of the faculties into an implicitly political challenge to the rigidities of *l'ancien regime*, thus opening a third way that was bound to neither the Hobbesian state of original conflict nor to the legal state of bourgeois modernity. However, I argue that Ranciere's aesthetic reading of Proust needs to be further developed as an exploration of narrative, reconceived as a play between metaphor and metonymy but also in a manner that is no longer restricted to what de Man proposed in his linguistic reading. Hence, the aesthetic reading of Proust, which is shown to engage Kristeva but also Walter Benjamin and J. Hillis Miller, indicates how the structure of traumatic repetition embraces the signs of the unconscious as well as the possibility of a new form of reflectivity, enabling the reader to take up the theme of *writing* on a textual basis.

Although this study might have ended with the chapter on Proust, I further explore the thematic of writing in the criticism of Maurice Blanchot, whose name marks the limits of modernism and a new time in art and literature that cannot be named with complete confidence. Blanchot's critical study, *The Space of Literature* (*L'Espace littéraire*, 1955), is brought into contact with Martin Heidegger's widely discussed essay, "The Origin of the Work of Art" ("*Der Ursprung des Kunstwerkes*," originally 1935–1936). However, Blanchot's criticism is not primarily an exercise in hermeneutical ontology that maps out the dimension of truth and *un*truth inherent in artistic works; instead it sets forth a thematic of writing as crucial to the apprehension of "world" as a verbal commentary on concrete existence, thus challenging an apparent commitment to the artifactual that is expressed in various examples that sustain its argument. From this perspective, Blanchot's criticism engages the virtual in the mythic figure of Orpheus and, in this way, enables the reader to ascribe a nonsubjective meaning to the aesthetic apprehension of literature. Blanchot's critical comments on authors as diverse as Mallarmé, Ranier Maria Rilke, and Franz Kafka are presented as preparatory to a hermeneutic that is no longer classical, in the style of Hans-Georg Gadamer but testifies to the fragmentary and event-like character of art and literature, which reopens the importance of Hegel to contemporary thought. My examination of Blanchot ultimately returns to the question of writing as an aspect of life and literature and argues in favor of a quasi-dialectical appropriation of this contested term, which decenters the traditional Logos without abandoning the concept altogether.

The last two chapters demonstrate that the apparent end of figuration contains within it a trace of the aesthetic, which lies on the horizon of semiotic depletion and challenges the imputation that the sensible world has been reduced or destroyed. The authors considered, Jean Rhys and Kazuo Ishiguro, suggest different ways of coming to terms with the Hegelian legacy as encountered in Wordsworth, Shelley, and especially Proust. First, the early novels of Rhys are briefly explored as autobiographical, while a more extended analysis of her masterpiece, *Wide Sargasso Sea* (1960), becomes an encounter with the theme of repetition in its engagement with the protagonist's family history and the violent world of postslavery Jamaica. While indicating where ethics and politics begin to emerge in this novel on a performative basis, I also suggest how aesthetics acquires post-Kantian significance when it invites the reader to envision a transformation of historical conditions, without specifying the implied link between aesthetics and politics. In my second example, I examine two of Ishiguro's novels in terms of both the problem of aesthetics and ideology as well as inadequacies of ethical formalism, enabling me to uphold the importance of both Freud and Hegel to reading the texts at hand. My discussion of *An Artist of the Floating World* (1986) underscores the great importance of the aesthetic to the political, whereas the treatment of *Remains of the Day* (1989) indicates how ethical issues can be retrieved through a distinctively Hegelian approach to the aesthetic, which runs counter to the aesthetics of disinterestedness that was promulgated by Kant.

The conclusion returns to the thematic originally broached in my discussion of Kristeva's attempt to combine Freud and Hegel in a manner that reclaims some of the major insights of psychoanalysis and dialectical thought. Four issues are discussed in my final remarks. First, I provide an alternative to a chronological conception of origins, as a beginning in time, in discussing how traumatic experience not only makes its appearance in literary texts but also reopens the question of how such experience can emerge at all. In this part of my discussion, I return to the work of Benjamin, who called attention to some of the traumas of modernity in attempting to bridge the distance between Hegel and Freud, mainly through a special use of Marx. Nevertheless, as Kristeva contends, the conflict between semiotics and symbolic understanding continues to be felt so that semiotics emerges as the vehicle of a *possible* world. The second part thus emphasizes how Kristevan semiotics provides an incisive critique of Lacanian psychoanalysis and its tendency toward dualism. This discussion allows me to recapitulate the content of my literary studies, which shows how performance serves different purposes but maintains a complex relationship to concrete life. Nonetheless, the role of figural space in the movement from semiotics to aesthetics remains unclarified in Kristeva's work, so the third section of the conclusion is concerned more specifically with the ethical and political implications of figural space, which does not determine norms but establishes *an open context* within which evaluative procedures can be set in motion. This aspect of my discussion goes beyond the standard reading of Hegel in negotiating a sphere in which creative repetition provides strong challenges to consensual modes of normativity. My final remarks concern how Hegelian aesthetics preserves the tension between sense and world, thus constituting a way of rethinking the classical opposition between the one and the many in terms of poetry, an art of singular importance.

This study as a whole suggests a cautious but appreciative rehabilitation of Hegel, which, unlike previous attempts to revive the philosopher's work, argues against the tendency of many commentators to present as foundational what is perhaps better understood as oriented toward language and time. Moreover, unlike the standard poststructuralist reading of Hegel as a "totalizing" thinker who is always in need of being deconstructed, the reading that has been foregrounded, particularly in my literary analyses, argues that the question of norms is not only recurrent in modern literature but is also generally kept open in signal literary works that are often fruitfully explored through a broadly Hegelian methodology. This method as conceived in the present work need not be insensitive to the more recent modes of criticism that contest the power of dialectics but also allow us to explore new syntheses as antidotes to the unending ironies that often haunt contemporary literature. The conjunction of semiotics and aesthetics that I have sought to advance at different moments in this study is to be interpreted in the spirit of a broad complementarity through which literature itself can be seen to perform a vital role in life as well as in the pursuit of both truth and meaning.

Chapter One

Kristeva and Hegel

Subjectivity Reconfigured

Julia Kristeva's early work in the philosophy of language, as it emerged within the context of French poststructuralism, was not unusual in developing the resources of Hegelian thought in a manner that alternated between resistance and an eagerness to acknowledge and, to some extent, accommodate G. W. F. Hegel's complex legacy. However, among her colleagues, Kristeva viewed Hegel through psychoanalysis in a manner that strongly challenges the tendency of many readers to assimilate her work to mainstream poststructuralism. In this chapter, I examine Kristeva's semiotic position to read Hegel through Sigmund Freud but also to discern how Kristeva attempts to demonstrate that Hegel falls short of Freud's key insights. My exposition enables me to present Kristeva's early work and to examine a major shift that occurs in her thinking when she confronts the limitations of her original project. After turning to the question of aesthetics, I suggest how Arthur Rimbaud's prose poems allow us to clarify this new semiotic as well as the critical stance that emerges in Kristeva's later work. My conclusion argues that Kristeva remains indebted to Hegel, whose principles cast light on how the subject-in-process occupies the nonfoundational space of art and literature.

HEGEL AFTER FREUD

An approach to semiotics that adopts human conflict as its starting point would be different from a discipline that focused on the systematic arrangement of verbal signs within a general taxonomy of linguistic practices. In

Kristeva's *Revolution in Poetic Language* (*La Révolution du langage poétique*, 1974), we learn that negativity and rejection can be considered in terms of both Hegel and Freud as a basis for reconceiving psychic experience. Kristeva argues that Hegelian negativity is not the same as logical negation, just as it should not be confused with a variation of the Kantian idea.[1] If negativity were understood in terms of formal logic, it would operate outside the practical world of everyday life. At the same time, if it were simply defined as a type of judgment, it would involve a relation between representations that compose the act of judgment. For Kristeva, however, negativity appears at a decisive juncture in psychic life; it relates to rejection as an occurrence that is more than an affair of consciousness.[2] Thus, in moving beyond Kantian idealism and in suggesting how dialectics can be invigorated through Freud, Kristeva argues that only a theory of the Unconscious can account for negation as an economy that no longer circulates within the self-contained structure of the subject-predicate relationship. In taking up this position, Kristeva discusses Freud's article, "Negation," as an effort to locate the origin of logic in a domain in which rejection is conceived in conflictual terms.[3]

Through these assertions, we might discern how Hegel and Freud are both joined and separated in Kristeva's analysis, suggesting but also diverging from Paul Ricoeur's hermeneutical interpretation of psychoanalysis. Ricoeur argues that Freud and Hegel are concerned with origins (archeology) and ends (teleology); hence, psychoanalysis and dialectics both require this dual perspective.[4] Kristeva contends in her early work that "the Hegelian conception of negativity already prepared the way for the very possibility of a materialist *process*."[5] At the same time, semiotics need not reduce the movement of the dialectic to a triad that is "progressive" and produces a result that is without a remainder. For Kristeva, dialectics suggests how negativity registers a conflictual state in which heterogeneity can be related to instinctual factors that are expressed in social and material contexts. But in the long run, Kristeva also states that Hegel's concept of negativity cannot account for the role of rejection in psychic life because it attempts to assimilate disunity to speculative unity. Thus, in her brief discussion of dialectical logic, she argues that Hegel subordinates Repulsion to Unicity and, therefore, fails to grasp how expulsion constitutes a limit to symbolization. Freud alone "joins dialectical logic by making expulsion the essential moment in the constitution of the symbolic function."[6]

The notion of expulsion is deployed in terms of Jacques Lacan's model of a split subject that is incapable of providing the basis for truth in representation. The movement of rejection that is an aspect of this model interrupts self-sameness and might be interpreted as a "hermeneutic of conflict" if this phrase can be interpreted anew.[7] The question of meaning reopens the problem of mimesis, but mimesis in Kristeva's thought, as opposed to classical rhetoric and modern realism, is redefined as a likeness that enables "the construction of an object, not according to truth but to *verisimilitude*," so that the subject bears an unstable relation to the semiotic *khōra* that remains an aspect of enunciation.[8] By calling attention to the break that, according to Gottlob Frege, presides over signification, Kristeva questions the absolute nature of a rupture that otherwise would bear no relation to the living subject. Classical rhetoric reduces mimesis to a mirroring of either ideas or actions, whereas modern realism attempts to redefine it through reference. Kristeva, however, places mimesis in a semiotic movement that prevents us from claiming that the object is "true" when it has ceased to be figurative. Only modern poetic language reproduces this movement in abrogating the subject and the production of the thetic, thus, going beyond the categories of denotation and meaning, whereas the poetry that fails to achieve this tends to become theological in concealing the process that produces the break itself.[9]

The key to interpreting this movement in Kristeva's early work is the opposition between symbolic and semiotic functioning, which work together to produce the achievements of language, religion, and human culture. This opposition can be found as well in the work of Jacques Lacan, who not only reads Freud through linguistics but also underscores the importance of the drive as the motor of psychic activity and, in this regard, follows Hegel as a philosopher of consciousness. Lacan's appropriation of Hegel on this issue is ultimately unsatisfactory to Kristeva, perhaps even more during her later phase than in her earlier poetics of language. The promise of art and literature, particularly beginning with the literary avant-garde that makes its first appearance late in the nineteenth century, is inherent in the possibility of reconfiguring symbolic systems. Nonetheless, unless the ego is conceived in a way that permits a free movement between semiotic and symbolic functioning, symbolic codes threaten to confine this movement to a dyadic opposition that enables a basically paternal relation to erase the semiotic as a source of instability and conflict. For Kristeva, Lacan's interpretation of the *stade du miroir*, while providing one model for thinking through the moment of transition from imaginal to symbolic consciousness, runs the risk of closing the gap that Frege's logic allows us to identify and thus fails to show how the semiotic can survive, if only to a limited degree, as an opening beyond the symbolic sphere.

In *Tales of Love* (*Histoires d'amours*, 1984), Kristeva invokes a ternary model in countering Lacan's assessment that narcissism is basically an invariant structure that is locked in a dyadic relationship between imaginal consciousness and paternal law. In contrast to Lacan, who needs to invoke paternal intervention to place a limit on narcissism, Kristeva "must argue for an absolute otherness that arises within the narcissistic structure itself."[10] In this way, Kristeva profoundly modifies the Lacanian model by introducing alterity at the site where the ego separates from the mother, that is to say, in a manner that does not exclude the semiotic from the site of contestation. In Kristeva's revision of Lacan, the maternal is not simply placed on the side of the semiotic as the adversary of the symbolic, or as its reluctant partner, but becomes part of the structure of narcissism that in turn constitutes the space in which the ego can begin to experience, if not fully recognize, the other *as* other. It is within this framework of alterity that love becomes possible for an evolving ego.

Nonetheless, even before this structure has been clarified, Kristeva employs semiotics for investigating *texts* as inherently rifted rather than as metaphysically unified. Texts in this account are not literary objects that can be examined as self-contained entities but archeological residues of cultural life, providing archives of what is other to the same. As a counterpart to the thetic moment in cognitive judgment, sacrifice allows violence to be displaced in the attainment of social coherence but not in a manner that effectively eliminates signs of unconscious conflict from the cultural sphere.[11] A semiotic that adopts conflict (instead of an achieved stasis) repositions the entire effort of analysis, just as it denies the validity of either a bracketing procedure or a residual essentialism that reveals the Platonic origins of modern rationalism. Such an approach, when applied to the reading of literature, corroborates a critique of linguistic orthodoxy and evokes Theodor Adorno's neo-Hegelian remarks on how "the unconscious writing of history" provides an index of the cultural sphere.[12] The analog to this displacement in Hegelian thought is perhaps the event of tragedy, which enters philosophy for the first time when it comes to signify a remainder that is only possible to relate to a dialectical model *insofar as* dialectics depends on moments that punctuate experience when consciousness, on the way to knowledge, succeeds in assuming the burden of the negative.

Certain practices commemorate this sacrifice and, therefore, point to an event that cannot be recovered through empirical reconstruction. This event "breaks through the symbolic order, and tends to dissolve the logical order, which is, in short, the outer limit founding the human and the social."[13] Suggesting the insights of Friedrich Nietzsche, Kristeva reminds us of how the Dionysian festivals that haunt the origin of classical drama signify an outpouring of jouissance that allows the subject to transgress the symbolic and reach the margins of a semiotic khōra on which cultural expression depends. This moment can be viewed historically as suggesting a rupture with Platonizing tendencies that effaced the role of suffering in the production of thought itself.[14] Kristeva's evocation of the unconscious, as anticipated by Nietzsche in advance of Freud, is perhaps equally implicit in her early espousal of the semiotics of Mikhail M. Bakhtin, whose notion of the "carnivalesque" as applied to the novels of François Rabelais in particular might be cited as a later manifestation of the Dionysian impulse, which does not disappear in postclassical art and literature.[15] Bakhtin demonstrates how cultural modalities are polylogues rather than monologues, constituting multiple discourses that need to be investigated as works where a controlling center is no longer constitutive. If Nietzsche was in revolt against the Platonizing tendencies implicit in traditional aesthetics, Bakhtin showed more recently how these same tendencies are operative in the literary tradition when poetry is opposed to prose as a fully unified discourse, thus guaranteeing the triumph of hegemonic and univocal readings over polyvocal ones.[16]

Kristeva does not posit a philosophical subject that is able to master difference but invites us to envision an engaged subject who bears the traces of historical conflict and develops various strategies for expressing what it is marked to endure. If the late nineteenth century is a period when excess emerges in poetic form, this is also a time when political and historical agency is frustrated and when the Platonic aspirations of various poets do not fully exhaust the semiotic possibilities of language. Hence, Kristeva was never primarily interested in a metaphysics of textuality, or metaphysics in general, because the construction of the subject in time always committed her to a *linguistic* approach to lived experience, as opposed to any master discourse that set itself on the side of representation and thereby mistook its own calibrations for reality. The word "linguistic" in this use would not refer to the science of language but would include the semiotic as a sphere of experience that includes imaginal consciousness. Psychoanalysis and the thesis of the unconscious that pertains to it are allies of the resistance to Platonism implicit in this formulation but should not be confused with an unmediated or nonreflective approach to the world.

At the same time, if Nietzsche, Freud, and Bakhtin are names of this linguistic turn, we might also argue that Hegel retains currency in semiotics to the degree that his work specifies how normative decisions are indeed responses to historical situations that are defined in cultural, and, generally, linguistic terms. Indeed, the importance of the linguistic is not fully captured in the way that language overflows with meaning, particularly when specific historical conditions reduce the semiotic options that are operative in times of cultural ferment. It would seem that Kristeva responded to this situation as a thinker who became increasingly aware of how contemporary society tends toward semiotic reduction.[17] Kristeva's response to Hegel as a philosopher of language can be related to this reduction, which is suggested in the movement of *Geist* through errancy and labor to a position of knowledge. The question then becomes: How can the philosophical subject be reconceptualized as a subject on trial or in process that is not only radically decentered but is capable of showing us how the agent proceeds under conditions of constraint and in a *space* that is both limited and free? This question ultimately returns us to a Hegelian thematic. However, we first need to examine how it emerges in Lacanian terms when Kristeva reexamines her view of psychoanalysis as crucial to interpreting the semiotic as a category that is inextricably linked to the emergence of symbolic structures. The result will have political implications that are articulated though the appearance of literature, even when it does not allow us to affirm a specific course of practical action.

DIALECTICS IN DISJUNCTION

Readers of Kristeva have often noted a reorientation that occurs in her writings during the decade following the publication of her first major contributions to the semiotics of literature. However, as the revolutionary possibilities that seemed to be inherent in the early semiotic began to recede, Kristeva does not simply abandon psychoanalysis or return to a more philosophically conservative approach to the human subject; on the contrary, we might argue that her commitment to the idea of a subject on trial or in process becomes more thorough as well as more crucial to the articulation of the semiotic once the possibilities of radical change go into eclipse. In Kristeva's case, this reorientation can be gauged as a further challenge to Lacan, whose work was never uncritically assimilated but whose basic position undergoes further modifications in the three books that Kristeva publishes in the 1980s. On the most general level, we might frame this reorientation as an argument that questions the Lacanian severance of symbolic and semiotic functions, which would drastically curtail the fluidity of mental functioning insofar as the *stade du miroir* (according to this model) would function as the mark of an exclusionary event that banished the imaginary as regressive, as soon as its effects were internalized.

An essential stage in this reorientation is evident in Kristeva's exploration of abjection as a psychoanalytical concept that indicates a sphere of limits that emerges between the ego and the locus of experience. Lacan had argued previously that the real is not to be confused with something that begins when an object imposes on consciousness but that instead testifies to the limits of symbolization. In *Powers of Horror* (*Pouvoirs de l'horreur*, 1980), Kristeva argues that the *abject*, like the object, is opposed to the "I" as the locus of meaning, just as it turns away from meaning-fulfillment and instates a "jettisoned object" that is "radically excluded" from the teleology of consciousness as it "draws me toward the place where meaning collapses."[18] The abject prevents the ego from successfully identifying with an "other" who is then incorporated into goal-directed activity and marks "an Other who precedes and possesses me, and through such possession causes me to be."[19] The ontological valence of the abject, far from constituting identity, is precisely what places identity in question, while also forming an in-between space that prevents my experience of the object world from becoming the source of total mastery, whether practical or theoretical, in which abjection becomes a mere "sign" of what has been surpassed.

Abjection as an anthropological concept can be identified with practices that enable a community to realize itself in language, which "solemnizes the vertical dimension of the sign" when sacrificial rites mark the movement from the thing to the meaning of transcendence.[20] Kristeva remarks on how in sacrifice the object appears in an abject form that precedes the body's differentiation in ego-identity and the acquisition of sexual traits. The abject of sacrifice is "scription—an inscription of limits" that testifies to a maternal authority that has not yet yielded to the structural integrity of the paternal law.[21] The theme of defilement in this case has not yet emerged as complementary to a system of purification that is strongly articulated and is raised to a more conscious level in the theologies of the so-called higher religious. Kristeva argues that literature frequently gives witness to the prestructural aspects of the abject of sacrifice, returning to the maternal situation of which the writer provides the analog and that anthropologists have identified as a semiotic of acts as opposed to symbols.

Abjection is also a limiting category that enables us to rethink any attempt to amalgamate Freud and Hegel, particularly when Hegel is (mis)read as an heir to traditional metaphysics. Kristeva cautions us against overlooking some important differences between Hegel and Kant, while psychoanalysis provides semiotics with a more dependable model for placing the abject in a new framework of knowledge. Hegel, like Kant, views impurity as a problem to be approached philosophically but, in contrast to Kant, moves from the transcendental standpoint to adopt a more historical perspective on how it can be overcome to some degree through institutions. Hence, marriage provides a basis for containing its disruptive features, even when it is haunted by what subsists as the remainder of a (pure) idealism that becomes inoperative in "historical" phenomenology. For Kristeva, this act of philosophical distancing is fundamentally ambiguous: "[Hegel] agrees with his aim to keep consciousness apart from defilement, which, nevertheless, dialectically constitutes it."[22] The result, however, is the production of a space in which discourse is fragmented and in which impurity becomes a "border discourse" that is only unsettled in the analytic session, where silence confronts a counterdiscourse and the goal of purification is replaced with a willingness to accept abjection as an aspect of meaning.

At the same time, Kristeva remarks that the figure of Oedipus in Greek tragedy can be read as a continuing meditation on the Hegelian legacy, while also indicating the strengths and limitations of psychoanalytic interpretation. In contrast to the Oedipus of Thebes, the Oedipus who survives the ordeal of incest and murder has developed a sense of his own mortality and has discovered that Theseus, the foreigner but symbolic son, will assume his political legacy through an act of purification that is the theme of *Oedipus at Colonus*. In Sophocles's other play on the fallen hero, abjection becomes a flaw in the protagonist's knowledge and the "impossible sovereignty" that a democratic future Athens bestows on humanity in the guise of literature even when its political fate remains unclear: "Our eyes can remain open provided we recognize ourselves as always already altered by the symbolic—by language."[23] It is not to the mute, if sublime, figure of Antigone to whom Kristeva pays allegiance in a gesture that goes beyond the founder of psychoanalysis, who tended to privilege Oedipus the King as the site of a universal trauma, but to the aged Oedipus, the broken survivor who "institutes" a future that is no longer bound to the repetition of a primal crime.

MODES OF THE AESTHETIC

Although clearly indebted to Freud, Kristeva argues in her early work that art, rather than psychoanalysis, provides the more effective means for disclosing the semiotic aspects of language. The text is not based on a personalized transference. Rather than merely confirm social and family structures, the text operates in a signifying field that is much wider than what the psychoanalysts interpret in the therapeutic session. The artist, in responding to the event of sacrifice that is specific to all human cultures, introduces a vital practice that repeats a symbolic movement, suggesting what *precedes* sacrifice: "Whereas sacrifice assigns jouissance its productive limit in the social and symbolic order, art specifies the means—the only means—that jouissance harbors for infiltrating that order."[24] Through the use of aesthetic devices, the artist places sacrifice in a new perspective that shows how the denial of the semiotic khōra goes along with the construction of modes of subjectivity that efface the "signs" that have been instituted as identities and values.

Kristeva thus argues that semiotics should be able to disclose the critical potential of privileged texts, enabling us to witness the process of exclusion that results in a reified sense of the world and a congealed concept of the self.[25] While Kristeva's semiotexte is more than a collection of drives or flows, we should not assume that it is a formal construct that can be detached from motility. Kristeva's text is nonformalist on a basic level, calling attention to its own "internal" dynamics in a process that is irreducibly heterogenous and exceeds the confined sphere of official culture. It also enables both critic and reader to theorize an alterity that subverts the description of any cultural object: "The text's principle characteristic and one that distinguishes it from other signifying practices is precisely that it introduces, through binding and through vital and symbolic differentiation, heterogenous rupture and rejection: jouissance and death."[26] This text is not only disunified but inserted in a social system that is always already heterogeneous and plural. The appearance of art as text is a semiotic event that reopens a society that has become self-contained, indicating how matter and spirit are both joined and sutured on the level of image and word.

For Kristeva, the cultural rupture first occurring late in nineteenth-century poetry demonstrates how certain texts connect through verbal means to the semiotic khōra.[27] The avant-garde text bears a relationship to "the specific economy of rejection that produced it," instead of merely testifying to a distortion of everyday communication.[28] It is not a question of discovering in the avant-garde text the signs of an undistorted communication that might have prevailed in an ideal speech situation. On the contrary, the social sphere is constituted through rejection and expulsion "before" the genotext provides a practical model for linguistic research. The avant-garde text, although emerging in a delimited historical situation, casts light on the genotext that exists "prior" to subjectivity and cannot be assessed as a purely verbal structure. Nonetheless, in her later work, Kristeva becomes increasingly concerned with how the semiotic is constrained by systems that prevent it from performing an emancipatory role in specific contexts. The need of semiotics to explore the historical conditions of artistic production is therefore not equivalent to an interest in establishing a linear chronology; on the contrary, the attempt to formalize these conditions allows the limits of the subject to be more clearly defined and is a crucial aspect of the *aesthetic* task itself.

The emphasis in this study will be on how this movement coincides with what might be called "aesthetics" as rigorously distinguished from the purely academic discipline that generally conceals the marks that cast light on the figure's historical content. Although Kristeva privileges the avant-garde moment, the literary examples employed in our discussion will be drawn from different periods to demonstrate how semiotics is not only pertinent to late modernity. The logic of the semiotexte argues that *all art* effects a rupture with symbolic institutions and suggests how the political is in some sense reinscribed in textual production. Aesthetics is a space in which performances are elaborated in relation to the semiotic but in a manner that gives shape and form to sensory experience without fusing with symbolization. This elaboration does not involve the mere acceptance of repression "but instead constitutes a post-symbolic (and in this sense anti-symbolic) hallmarking of the material that remained intact during the first symbolization."[29] At the same time, for Kristeva, the rearrangement of the repressed content should not be confused with *Aufhebung* [negation/preservation] as generally conceived.

Kristeva argues in her early work that the Hegelian dialectic was "overturned" in two separate moments during the nineteenth century. First, Karl Marx overturned the dialectic when he aligned history with material existence, instead of summarizing a series of moments in the unfolding of philosophical reason. Kristeva also reminds us of how the category of production dominated Marx's understanding of history. According to this reading, the dialectic was overturned a second time when the subject was redefined in terms of a contradiction that played itself out on the level of language and practice. Hence, rather than understand history as the domain of production alone, Kristeva invites us to read literary texts as demonstrating how historical experience engages the subject as a contradictory being: "If history is made up of modes of production, the subject is a contradiction that brings about practice because practice is always both signifying and semiotic, a crest where meaning emerges only to disappear."[30]

However, we might interpret this dual process as less of a two-step movement than as a break with previous idealisms, testifying to *the power of the remainder* to interrupt history and literary experience alike. From this perspective, Marxist history yields to a noncontinuous history through which material life is no longer assimilable to the utopian drive to "complete" history. Marx in this new trajectory would prepare us for the possibility of acknowledging how historical openings are less "necessary" than the provisional result of newly emergent praxes. History in such an account would no longer unfold according to totalizing factors but in an indirect, and sometimes, inverted manner. On the other hand, because the second overturning also contests a unilinear conception of historical development, literature would retain an important role in the process of social transformation. If avant-garde texts introduce a new meaning to the dialectic, this is not primarily "in addition to" or "alongside of" what occurred in the sphere of production. In this second overturning, Kristeva assesses the role of language in reshaping the material sphere to indicate how social relations have a quasi-material basis that overrides the more tangible significance of physical production.

Moreover, Kristeva places language in an unstable matrix that is irreducible to the productive base that philosophical idealism simply viewed as marginal to the dialectic. This unstable matrix is identified with avant-garde literature, but the avant-garde can be placed in a semiotic process that is not "pure" but, on the contrary, rifted with experiences of rejection and negation. The power of literature to "produce" the imaginary was theorized by Freud so that psychoanalysis prevents us from framing the imaginary apart from systems of constraint. In acknowledging the crucial role of signifying practices in foregrounding and enacting change, we need to suggest how psychoanalysis provides insight into social and political processes. This excursus will entail an exploration of Rimbaud's prose poems, which functioned early in the twentieth century as seminal contributions to avant-garde poetics but also indicate how a semiotic dimension invalidates their literary reception as essentially formal performances.

RIMBAUD AND SEMIOSIS

The psychological implications of the new semiotic were already present in Kristeva's textual model for interpreting signifying practices, just as they anticipated a critical position that allowed her to affirm a belief in the sensible imagination in subsequent years. And yet, we might cite a single example of how this model can be used to read literature according to a semiotic principle that both calls attention to the role of rejection in constituting the world of the artist and opens the path of jouissance as an alternative to societal closure. Rimbaud's remarkable sequence of prose poems, *Les Illuminations* (1886), was largely written during the period when the writer participated in the Paris Commune of 1871 and is marked by a political crisis that impacted an entire society. It is impossible to separate the life history of the poet from a turbulent event that bears witness to an attempted transformation of social life, which was certainly aborted but persists as a lingering promise in the work of an author who endured and survived this violent upheaval.

This signal historical event was examined by Marx in *The Civil War in France*, where the notion of a break with an existing social system was foregrounded as a key to this moment's long-term significance.[31] On the one hand, what is perhaps most interesting about this historical analysis is not that it is "dialectical" in the sense of suggesting how a specific event can be interpreted teleologically but as a caesura in the scheme of time and as a kind of lost opportunity that announces possibilities that could not be realized historically. The essential modernity of Rimbaud's poetic sequence has been underscored by those who have tried to locate it in history no less than by those who read it in anticipation of an international modernism that evolved in its wake.[32] However, the Rimbaldian *text* is something other than the world of historical practices or the literary movement that developed out of its influence. Hence, we might consider that Rimbaud's politics emerges more strongly in his effort to enact a revolt on the level of *language* before it assumes a determinate position, particularly when the writer's actual position is difficult to identify with a concrete political stance.

In placing the psychoanalytic paradigm before the political one, we do not relinquish historical reflection or minimize its importance within the broader trajectory of ongoing social turmoil. Instead we delve into the conditions of life that would have been operative in the writer's own experience and would not be dissimilar to what can be found in society in general, conceived as an organism that resorts to sexual exclusion as among its founding practices. We learn from biographical accounts that Rimbaud experienced the maternal relation as profoundly ambiguous because remoteness and indifference were always an aspect of the maternal bond. His own poetry, therefore, foregrounds a conflict that produces recurrent images and highlights a lived experience that formed the basis for what he expressed in language. We might also say that in writing about this conflict, Rimbaud achieves "symbolic" (if temporary) resolution in poetic terms of something that was perhaps impossible for him to entirely master in life.

A thoughtful reading of Rimbaud's *Les Illuminations* reveals an ambiguous maternal figure whose appearance is beguiling and terrifying at once. Emerging as a vestigial memory in *"Après le Deluge,"* this figure surfaces in the poet's rejection of false heroism but also in his use of multiple perspectives, whereby the reader in invited to view the world as both sublime and artificial.[33] The maternal figure reappears in "Being Beauteous," a short prose poem that contrasts feminine beauty and the energy of the male poet but also provides an ironic view when the same figure emerges against the backdrop of winter. Here it is once again identified with cold purity but also with the beauty that miraculously springs like Venus from the sea.[34] Robert Cohn has discussed how "her beauty is pitted against a snow-scene in an extreme daemonic contrast" and refers back to the contrast between the dim fires and night forest that can be found in *"Après le Deluge."*[35] The dominant use of this figure is therefore forbidding and even painful, suggesting a psychological alienation that is only infrequently overcome in the narrative as a whole.

Two clues finally emerge to suggest how the narrator moves beyond the impasse of dejection, even when this movement may not allow him to escape from the circuit of isolation. First, the maternal figure makes a final appearance in the delicate piece, *"Aube,"* a morning song in which a figure of happiness and natural life enables the poet to embrace the summer dawn.[36] C. A. Hackett suggests that *"Aube"* ends in a symbolic rite in which ecstasy is not strongly achieved: "The dawn, evoked again in her veils, does not reveal her secret, and the child, although he embraces the goddess, only touches a fraction of her immense body."[37] In this transformation of the maternal figure from a malevolent being to one worthy of affection, Rimbaud invites us to work through a shift that is less of a movement toward wholeness (because the dawn of summer must pass as well) than a vision of how rejection can turn into love. Second, in *"Génie,"* the concluding prose poem in the series, the poet celebrates the male body in a manner that is jubilant and affirmative, suggesting an almost Nietzschean joy that evokes an unknown but hopeful future.[38]

In Rimbaud's poetic sequence, which is in many ways inaugural but remains largely unexplored as a semiotic resource, language functions as counter to classical and modern mimesis but also to the academic assimilation of the avant-garde to a limited set of technical objectives. If we follow Rimbaud's journey as a movement beyond individual consciousness, we see that the poet has transformed a sense of rejection into an expression of creative ambiguity and instinctual openness. The distracted moment that freezes life in a spirit of self-absorption yields to fascination and aesthetic freedom. What is being imitated in this case is a psychic process that frees the mind from previous constructions. Rimbaud is haunted by abjection to the degree that the maternal figure is sterile as well as abundant, associated with the coldness of death as well as the warmth of life, but the struggle that the poet reenacts goes on in the realm of language and is irreducible to what might be interpreted in narrowly psychoanalytic terms.

At the same time, Rimbaud's quest remains elusive from certain standpoints, particularly when we consider how the final emergence of the ego ideal (if this in indeed an insightful reading of the final prose poem) is mysterious when viewed from the standpoint of a recurrent dejection that rarely suggests how the maternal presence can provide a basis for a cumulative transformation. The process that enables Rimbaud to write a new kind of poetry could be investigated dialectically, apart from the political situation that the poet endured, in view of how this poetry inspired avant-garde writers to explore revisionary interpretations of his work, particularly in the twentieth century. At the same time, if this process is in any sense transformative, the role of awareness in the construction of figures needs to be viewed in a way that brings together semiotics and an approach to cultural formations that challenges the standard psychoanalytic view on how the ego enters the world through Oedipal constraints.

FIGURATION IN CONTEXT

Kristeva's consistent, if often heterodox, reading of Hegel is important for various reasons, and the attempt to rethink basic elements in Hegel's system along semiotic lines entails a new interpretation of dialectical thought. For the purposes of this study, we shall focus on four major areas that give the semiotic interpretation of Hegel its characteristic novelty. Some of Kristeva's criticisms of Hegel will be familiar to readers who are acquainted with the available commentaries, but they also extend semiotics beyond its original, Peircean formulations. The reading of Hegel that Kristeva proposes, particularly in statements that can be found throughout her early writings, can be related to the problem of figuration. Without arguing that figuration is reducible to the Hegelian figure because it functions as a link in the dialectic, we need to clarify the degree to which Hegel is able to contribute to a semiotic project that draws on dialectical themes and innovations.

First, Kristeva has shown us that Hegel's system is not a mere repetition of the idealistic thesis that places the ego at the center of a process through which the world becomes accessible. Hegel can be read as the last in a series of philosophers who posits the subject as the starting point for conscious reflection and who argues, in his mature work, that the subject ultimately becomes the all-consuming fulcrum of absolute knowledge. Kristeva chooses to read Hegel instead as a philosopher of disinvestment or uprooting (*Hinausgerissenwerden*) to emphasize aspects of dialectical experience that are inherently disturbing and that place the ego in a processual element that is inseparable from the movement toward greater comprehension.[39] She therefore rejects the tendency to align dialectical philosophy with Cartesian assumptions about the ego as a controlling agent that generates increasing levels of certainty, while also acknowledging that the role of consciousness in dialectics needs to be reconceived: "Although Hegel was the first to identify and put so much emphasis on this movement and its negativity, he subsumes it under *the presence of consciousness*, which Heidegger in turn over-emphasized, by reducing the essence of the dialectic to it."[40]

At the same time, without reinforcing the tendency of many critics to identify dialectics with ego-logy, Kristeva does not argue that Hegelian thought is able to integrate the semiotic *text* in its rigorous procedures. Particularly by introducing death into the signifying process, textual experience in the new semiotic disturbs the tendency of conceptual thought to privilege unity over heterogeneity. Kristeva's critique of structuralism employs semiotics by taking the side of the subject in a new manner, and this gesture evokes the possibility of truth to the degree that truth is a figural term, rather than the meaning of a proposition or the mere name of an unfolding totality. However, in contrasting the semiotic text to Hegelian knowledge, Kristeva suggests how the figural occupies a *space* that should not be confused with a science of the known.[41] Truth in this figural meaning would include aesthetics, and not as the immediate testimony to truth or even as a sphere of judgment that has been denied cognitive status, but as a mode of experience that is situated in a project that bears witness to both dispossession and the rekindling of sense that transforms abstract prospects into actual ones, "spiritual" motives into practical achievements.

Thus, Kristeva's view of art and culture also carries the aesthetic in a new direction that was indeed anticipated by Hegel, whose late work also goes beyond classical mimetic theory in arguing that modern art is inherently concerned with sensible contents that cannot be assimilated to conceptual schemata. This second modification of Hegelian themes allows us to interpret artistic production as figural, rather than as a mere succession of figures. Mimesis in Kristeva's early work is not the "mirror" of some more adequate reality but precisely what calls attention to a break that has been instituted, assuming that we are able to penetrate to the semiotic core of cultural production. In her later work, the maternal provides the site for a movement beyond mimesis through the experience of separation and bonding. Both nonclassical mimesis and maternal subjectivity reopen the aesthetic and not as the detached expression of autonomy but as a meeting place for what is in flux and only acquires significance in a specific cultural milieu. In Hegel and Kristeva alike, mimesis gives way to a nonmimetic background. This nonmimetic background prevents figuration from being assimilated to classical (whether Platonic or Aristotelean) poesis, thus aligning the aesthetic tradition with a new relation to the sensible. In this sense, both Hegel and Kristeva open up a figural, as opposed to a merely figurative, approach to artistic expression, which becomes in this new trajectory a sign of disjunction but also provides the space within which meaning can be improvised in cultural terms.

Moreover, Hegel as an aesthetician suggests that art has come to an end at the precise moment that it passes beyond the classical moment when substance and spirit were able to coincide.[42] And yet, what appears to be pessimism on Hegel's part can be reinterpreted as a response to an ongoing process that stretches into an unknown future, whereas Kristeva's apotheosis of the avant-garde provides us with a backward glance over a whole range of aesthetic phenomena that loses its appearance of stability once the semiotic dimension has been reintroduced into aesthetic interpretation. This brings us to the third way that Kristeva can assist us in rereading Hegel because the thesis that art is at an end becomes a mere prelude to unstable but also more "spiritual" modes of aesthetic production, once the avant-garde is taken to prefigure an art that is no longer bound by the principles of classical aesthetics. This rereading of Hegel (as preparatory to the semiotic turn) would allow us to relate art to a gradual *reduction* of presence, that is, to a narrative where truth is not only about the increasing distance between spirit and substance but where this process frees aesthetics from Greco-Roman hegemony.

The fourth and final area where Kristeva suggests rapprochement with Hegel's thought concerns the implicitly ethical stance that is woven into the "truth" of post-Kantian idealism. Hegel offers us a phenomenology whereby the subject dissolves as a monadic construct and stresses the processual nature of this movement, so that human persons are now formed in need, desire, and pain. Hegel also reorients ethical theory so that the welfare of persons becomes a matter of acknowledging social contexts and ceases to be defined (as in Kantian philosophy) as an adjustment to formal rules. Kristeva distances her approach to ethics from that of Hegel, who is read as ultimately identifying art with a "purifying" function that subordinates semiotics to philosophy.[43] At the same time, the "truth" of the subject in Kristeva and Hegel is no longer determined primarily in terms of an opposition between empirical constraints and noumenal principles but inheres in the movement of a narrative in which loss and recuperation alternate in the sphere of becoming.[44] "Hegel" would then be the name of a discourse that is able to reveal aspects of our historical condition through the signs and images that announce the cultural world itself. The literary chapters that follow are intended to clarify some of the crucial links in this cultural movement and to demonstrate how the space of figuration constitutes the setting of this complex process.

NOTES

1. Julia Kristeva, *Revolution in Poetic Language*, trans. Margaret Waller (New York: Columbia University Press, 1984), 111.
2. Ibid., 118–21.
3. Ibid., 121. Freud's short article, "Negation," enables Kristeva to move beyond a purely logical understanding of this crucial concept and to explore a psychological interpretation of negation as intrinsically related to the process of expulsion and exclusion. See Sigmund Freud, "Negation," in *The Standard Edition of the Complete Works of Sigmund Freud*, trans. James Strachey (London: Hogarth Press, 1925), 19:237–39. The possibility that psychological considerations are important to the development of conceptual thought, however, does not mean that the symbolic order is reducible to its genesis.
4. For a psychoanalytic approach to Hegelian phenomenology, see especially Paul Ricoeur, *Freud and Philosophy: An Essay on Interpretation*, trans. Denis Savage (Delhi, India: Motilal Banardidass Publishers, 2008), 422–30, 439–58, 459–72, 509. An interpretation of Freud that is implicitly teleological is contained on pages 472–93. Ricoeur distinguishes the role of archaic symbols in a psychoanalytic logic of repetition from the spiritual movement that undergirds Hegelian dialectics on pages 117–20.
5. Kristeva, *Revolution in Poetic Language*, 110.
6. Ibid., 158.
7. Ricoeur argues implicitly that the social sciences in their commitment to unmasking the deeper structures of motivation are compromised by an infinite regress so that any "hermeneutic of conflict" would be the product of a specific methodology. The three "masters of suspicion" (Marx, Nietzsche, and Freud) are thus identified with a kind of inverted foundationalism whereby appearances hide realities that are assessed as inessential by traditional metaphysics. See Ricoeur, *Freud and Philosophy*, 32–35. Kristeva in contrast takes up a more ontological version of this conflictual hermeneutic in stating that rejection is linked to the symbolic on a functional level but also continually disrupts symbolic processes. Conflict in the Kristevan model would not be methodological but inherent in the unceasing movement of thought between semiotic motility and symbolic structure.
8. Kristeva, *Revolution in Poetic Language*, 57.
9. Ibid., 57–59.
10. Separation from the mother is crucial to the movement beyond primary narcissism: "Dependence on the mother is severed and transformed into a symbolic relation to another; the constitution of the Other is indispensable for communicating with another." Kristeva, *Revolution in Poetic Language*, 48. However, the fuller implications of the role of the mother in this process are explored later in Julia Kristeva, *Tales of Love* (*Histoires d'amour*, 1983). In Kristeva's later, more developed view, the mother introduces a radical alterity that involves separation but sustains a bond, thus constituting a third sphere (different from both the narcissistic ego and the mother) in which the other can be encountered *as* other. Such an argument, which departs from Lacan's dualism, recalls the Hegelian argument of how A can be both A and not A at the same time. A lucid account can be found in Sarah Beardsworth, *Julia Kristeva: Psychoanalysis and Modernity* (Albany: State University of New York Press, 2004), 61–77.
11. Kristeva, *Revolution in Poetic Language*, 76–78.
12. Adorno's *Aesthetic Theory* integrates the insights of both Freud and Hegel in a revised conception of mimesis that probably has its origins in Walter Benjamin's early reflections on the origins of language. Adorno draws on the psychoanalytic paradigm of the unconscious and the survival of the past as a potential site of liberation, emphasizing how "[t]he primacy of the object is affirmed aesthetically only in the character of art as the unconscious writing of history, as anamnesis of the vanquished, of the oppressed, and perhaps of what is possible." See Adorno, *Aesthetic Theory*, trans. Hullot-Kentor (Minneapolis: University of Minnesota Press, 1997), 259. It is important to emphasize that neither Benjamin nor Adorno interpret mimesis in the classical mode of either Plato or Aristotle.
13. Adorno, *Aesthetic Theory*, 79.
14. Contrasting Mark Warren's approach to Nietzsche to that of Martin Heidegger, Sara Beardsworth mentions how Nietzsche can be read as demonstrating a crisis in legitimacy

(rather than merely of reason) when the critique of Platonism is deepened to embrace the social conditions that constituted philosophy in ancient times. Hence, the institution of slavery does not merely impact late antiquity and underlie the rise of Christianity but is more broadly coextensive with the spread of metaphysics. For details, see Beardsworth, *Julia Kristeva*, 7–10. From this standpoint, Nietzsche's conception of slave morality implies the critique of an institution as well as an interpretation of how classical metaphysics is inseparable from the conditions of life that dominated late antiquity.

15. Possible comparisons between Nietzsche and Bakhtin remain a topic for future research. Perhaps Nietzsche's lingering preoccupation with Kant is what has prevented such comparisons from being more fully explored. Significantly, in their interpretations of Greek texts, both thinkers contest classical unity as either Socratic or Platonic in origin, without attempting to salvage unity through "metaphysical" arguments. The notion of the "carnivalesque" (which constitutes an analog to the Dionysian) is most extensively deployed in M. M. Bakhtin, *Rabelais and His World*, trans. Hélène Iswolsky (Cambridge, MA: MIT Press, 1968).

16. For Bakhtin, the standard opposition between poetry and prose results in an assimilation of poetry to theology, which tends to promote a monological discourse that represses linguistic difference and obscures the important of sociolects. For a more complete exposition, see especially M. M. Bakhtin, "Discourses in the Novel," *The Dialogic Imagination*, ed. Michael Holquist, trans. Caryl Emerson (Austin: University of Texas Press, 1981), 259–422.

17. Without arguing that Kristeva provides a metanarrative of decline in which the symbolic and semiotic are severed, Beardsworth argues that Nietzsche's prognosis of nihilism is operative in much of Kristeva's later work. This argument is consistent with the contention that history becomes more of a site of constraint than a scene of liberation after Kristeva's early period came to an end, and it contends in principle that Kristeva's thought is a decisive confrontation with modernity itself, rather than a mere expression of the modern sprit. See Beardsworth, *Julia Kristeva*, 12–15.

18. Julia Kristeva, *Powers of Horror: An Essay on Abjection*, trans. Leon S. Roudiez (New York: Columbia University Press, 1982), 13.

19. Ibid., 10.
20. Ibid., 72–73.
21. Ibid., 73.
22. Ibid., 30.
23. Ibid., 88.
24. Kristeva, *Revolution in Poetic Language*, 79.
25. Ibid., 210.
26. Ibid., 180.
27. Ibid., 88.
28. Ibid., 181.
29. Ibid., 163.
30. Ibid., 215.

31. Marx provides an analysis of the Paris Commune before it could produce the new society that it obscurely prefigured. Marx argues, at least momentarily, that the commune is not to be denigrated when a society of producers is heralded in the emergence of a contending power: "The Communal *régime* once established in France and the secondary centres, the old centralized government would in the provinces, too, have to go to the self-government of the producers." See Karl Marx, *The Civil War in France* (New York: International Publishers, 1940), 58. Hannah Arendt, while citing a pertinent passage from the same text, argues on the contrary that Marx would later minimize the political significance of the Commune. Cf. Hannah Arendt, *On Revolution* (New York: Viking Press, 1975), 260–61, n64, 324.

32. Kristin Ross provides suggestive remarks on the literary significance of social history to the construction of Rimbaud's late poetry as distinctively nonsymbolist. Ross emphasizes the referential nature of Rimbaud's late poetry, especially in taking issue with the suppression of reference that is implied by Saussurean linguistics and its critical successors. In moving away from Ferdinand de Saussure, Ross enables us to appreciate Rimbaud as more than a poet of texts but as situated in a "space" that is historical and autobiographical at once. See Ross, *The*

Emergence of Social Space: Rimbaud and the Paris Commune (Basingstoke, Hampshire: Macmillan Press, 1988), 87–90.

33. Arthur Rimbaud, "Les Illuminations," in *Collected Poems*, trans. Martin Sorrell (Oxford: Oxford University Press, 2001), 256–57.

34. Ibid., 266–67.

35. Robert Cohn, *The Poetry of Rimbaud* (Princeton, NJ: Princeton University Press, 1973.

36. Ibid., 286–89.

37. C. A. Hackett, *Rimbaud: A Critical Examination* (New York: Cambridge University Press, 1981), 72.

38. Rimbaud, *Collected Poems*, 310–11.

39. Kristeva, *Revolution in Poetic Language*, 185.

40. Ibid., p. 184. Unlike Kristeva, Heidegger's identification of Hegel with an "egological determination of being" would place dialectical philosophy rather firmly in a metaphysical tradition that it would be incapable of exceeding. See Martin Heidegger, *Hegel's Phenomenology of Spirit*, trans. Parvis Emad and Kenneth Maly (Bloomington: Indiana University Press, 1988), 126. Heidegger's misreading of Hegel is revealing in suggesting how his own philosophy might be compared to Hegel's without being reducible to it. My later discussion of Maurice Blanchot is partly concerned with the phenomenon of reversal, which provides one venue for reading the two philosophers comparatively.

41. Kristeva, *Revolution in Poetic Language*, 187–88.

42. Hegel's widely cited "end-of-art" thesis relies on an implicit valorization of the classical era, when the artist was still able to master all knowledge for aesthetic purposes: "In all these respects art, considered in its highest vocation, is and remains for us a thing of the past." See G.

43. W. F. Hegel, *Aesthetics : Lectures on Fine Art*, trans. J. M. Knox (Oxford: Clarendon Press, 1975), I:11. Hegel also provides an unfolding cultural narrative in which "romantic" art, beginning in the medieval period and extending into late modernity, embraces many possibilities that are impossible to assimilate to a classical reading of his aesthetic theory.

44. Kristeva, *Revolution in Poetic Language*, 233–34.

45. Partial agreement with Hegel can be discerned in Kristeva's discussion of how negativity as "the fourth term of the dialectic" no longer supports a formalistic construction of normativity: "The *ethics* that develops in the process of negativity's unfolding is not the kind of ethics that develops as obedience to laws." In the same context, Kristeva also notes that Hegelian aesthetics enhances this negative role, drawing the subject into the community in a manner that is both discursive and free. Kristeva, *Revolution in Poetic Language*, 110.

Chapter Two

Spenser's Renaissance

Ideality and Discourse

Edmund Spenser's originality as a Renaissance poet has to do with his use of literary procedures that express but also complicate his relationship to Renaissance humanism. On the one hand, Spenser's grand epic, *The Faerie Queene* (*FQ*), is a contribution to world literature that cannot be read in isolation insofar as the author was both a transmitter of European tradition and a participant in the political affairs of his time. As an early partisan to empire-building, Spenser can be read as a problematic child of his age, whose poetry becomes a cautionary tale in the way that misguided policies shape and, perhaps, distort literary intentions. However, although Spenser's epic contains an allegory of military justice, it also concludes with a literary sequel that stems from motivations that are irreducible to the author's service as an overseas colonial soldier.[1] Based as it is on classical conceptions of virtue, Spenser's "Book of Courtesy" (*FQ* VI) carries us from the trial of one woman, deemed to be offensive, and the ritual seduction of another, who is no doubt innocent, only to enact a spiritual movement from the lowest level of temporal life to a vision of mythic perfection. This movement is phenomenological while it also engages issues of language that exceed the boundaries of Platonic thought. My discussion engages Renaissance mores, anthropology, and religious traditions but leads to remarks on how Spenser's epic culminates in a specific *discourse* that articulates a political ethos and, within the limits of Renaissance epistemology, helps us grasp the significance of his work in figural terms.[2]

SPENSER'S VIRTUE OF COURTESY

Spenser's celebration of courtesy as a virtue involves an appreciation of social values as well as a commitment to transcendent notions of the good. This peculiar combination cannot be understood apart from a philosophical appraisal of the poet's view of nature. On the one hand, Spenser identifies nature with the principle of fecundity and abundance. According to this view, which mainly derives from Aristotle, nature emerges as a productive force and a spectacular point of origin (*FQ* III.vi.42). On the other hand, Spenser also maintains that nature can function as the invisible source of moral virtue. The latter more strictly Platonic conception of nature informs his representation of major characters and influences his critical attitude toward pagan mythology.[3] The difference between these conceptions of nature can be understood in term of the tension that governs *The Faerie Queene* as a whole. The Aristotelian conception is more closely related to traditional conception of political authority. At the beginning of "The Book of Courtesy," for instance, courtesy as a virtue is associated with the reign of Queen Elizabeth (*FQ* VI proem 6, line 4). Thus, Spenser seems to associate courtesy as a virtue with the legitimate rule of a contemporary monarch. At the end of the same book, however, the idea of pastoral as a place of magic and innocence reinforces the Platonic conception of nature and suggests that Spenser does not wish to derive virtue from either a limited experience of nature or from political arrangements. I wish to argue, later, that this precarious tension is resolved in favor of a neo-Plotinian ontology that is intended to integrate the immanent force of nature with an ethical ascent toward divine insight.

The idea that virtue can be institutional as well as basic to human communities underlies Spenser's epic narrative as a recovery of place that happens *in* language and ultimately concerns the movement of the soul toward imaginative fulfilment. In the introductory stanzas of the epic, Spenser wishes to establish the connection between courtesy and everyday concerns. Although courtesy as a virtue belongs in the hall of princes, it is also said to be "the ground, / And root of ciuill conuersation" (*FQ* VI i.1, lines 1–6). Spenser indicates in this way that courtesy goes beyond specific political interests and penetrates the language of civilized life. Hence, we might argue that courtesy, even more clearly than the concept of nature, becomes for Spenser the basis not only for politics but also for an ontological movement that underlies the thrust of his epic poem, at least in its final stages. This possibility, however, needs to be explored in terms of the strongly Aristotelian definition of courtesy that the poet employs, which seems inadequate to the degree that a narrow understanding of virtue does not provide room for the emphasis on language that the poet is also intent on retaining.

The more overtly political meaning of virtue is implicit in the figure of Calidore, whose "gracious speech, did steale men's hearts away" (*FQ* VI.i.2, line 6). While functioning as a counter to pure nature and its attendant virtue, Calidore must discover a relationship between the wisdom of humanity and the demands of political life. Near the beginning of his adventures, we learn about the "innate gifts" of Calidore; his honesty and love of truth are commended (*FQ* VI.1.3, line 9). The philosophical basis for this combination of talents can be found in Castiglione's *Book of the Courtier*. Here Gasparo explains to Ottaviano that certain important virtues cannot be learned, and then contends, "I think that to those who have learned them they have been given by nature and by God."[4] However, Calidore's education takes the form of a "recollection" of virtue that allows him to partially overcome the difference between nature and politics. This difference is inscribed in the movement of the narrative as a whole, which testifies to the inadequacy of the court as a source of moral integrity and the need for divine guidance as an element in genuine order.

Unlike other heroes in Spenser's epic, Calidore does not dominate his own narrative or exert a direct influence on events that unfold primarily when he is absent. In the structure of Spenser's literary epic, he vanishes at the end of Canto ii and reappears prior to Canto ix. Although he takes part in the movement toward knowledge, Calidore is by no means the center of Courtesy for the precise reason that we do not observe him as performing a crucial role until late in the narrative. It would seem that Calepine in some way substitutes for him during his long period of absence. Less artful than Calidore, Calepine tries to assume to role of the traditional epic hero; however, his presence never ceases to remind us that Calidore is no longer the commanding figure at the heart of the narrative. Nevertheless, although he lacks the manifest qualities of the epic hero, Calidore's virtue is credible and unobtrusive. His role is related to the way that he embodies a political virtue that goes beyond the customary understanding of the (practical) art of politics and its reliance on a limited company of persons.

Calidore helps us understand that "courtesy" is probably the Spenserian form of Aristotle's "near-friendliness"; it, too, properly belongs to the man who is neither subservient nor disagreeable.[5] Occupying the mean between two extremes, courtesy thus defined is a kind of goodwill that enables us to relate to everyone in a like manner: "Eunoia or goodwill bears some resemblance to friendship, but it is not exactly friendship, for we may feel goodwill towards strangers and persons who are not aware of our feeling—a thing impossible between friends."[6] If understood in these terms, courtesy is not a specifically political virtue in its engagement with an alterity that exceeds what is generally assumed to constitute a community of like-minded friends. At the same time, while it draws strangers into its warm embrace, courtesy also might be a precondition for the emergence of more exalted forms of experience. Although it would be wrong to argue that courtesy is *necessarily* a precondition for the appearance of beauty or the experience of love, we might imagine cases in which courtesy foregrounds various delights of the mind and senses. In a manner that might be related in some way to the notion of courtesy, Aristotle argues further that eunoia might be viewed as the seed of friendship in the same way that the experience of beauty can nurture love, while also reminding us that the latter experience is hardly equivalent to love for a living person.

At the beginning of Book VI, we retreat as readers from the plains, mountains, and rocky coasts to enter the world of Faerie land. The scene of courtesy is a pastoral countryside. Violence and sadness pervade this world of archaic values: "There is an older tradition of 'gentilesse' derived from Provence and France, running through medieval Romance literature, which had its rules and casuistry too, but expressed itself chiefly in actual examples and a pervading chivalrous tone."[7] But the tradition of courtesy can involve the sudden appearance of various truths. Harry Berger suggests that the repetition of specific motifs structures Book VI as a whole: "The most frequently repeated motif is, significantly enough, that of a character surprised in a moment of deversion."[8] All such moments must be understood within a moral context. For instance, the motif of the interrupted couple appears twice. Each time, the discovery of love moves us closer to Mount Acidale, while many scenes of recognition precede the great unveiling that unfolds near the end of the "Book of Courtesy" (*FQ* VI.x.27–28).

COURTESY'S PHASES OF ASCENT

Spenser's "Book of Courtesy" contains three phases of ascent that are traditionally read as a neo-Plotinian allegory but might also be viewed phenomenologically, if the concept of phenomenology can be broadened to include the insights of G. W. F. Hegel as well as Edmund Husserl and Martin Heidegger. The role of negation in this tripartite scheme is initiatory to the slow ascent from a discourteous world. And yet, while the concept of negation performs a decisive role in this sequence, reminding us of how Hegel transformed the Platonic tradition into something uniquely modern, the theme of ascent is linked in this progression to the possibility of imaginative fulfilment, thus suggesting the pertinence of Husserl to the "spiritual" implications of Spenser's narrative. Moreover, this same movement could also be described as a poetic phenomenology that unfolds in a series of moments in which Being itself is partially disclosed as a lighting of space that needs to be understood hermeneutically. Thus, Spenser's final narrative is amendable to a Heideggerian reading as well because every moment in this unfolding also points back to the question of how this entire sequence is lit up, if indeed its deepest purpose is to clarify the meaning of courtesy as a virtue and theme.

Courtesy involves interrelated episodes that engage three different women, each of whom represents an important stage in the movement toward increasing perfection. Berger summarizes how the three figures communicate distinct possibilities: "Mirabella projects the germinal form of frustration, Serena and her cannibals the germinal form of desire, Pastorella and her swains the germinal form of poetic recreation, all of which are infolded by Colin's vision."[9] The extreme discourtesy of Mirabella results in an ecclesiastical court summons. The glorification of Serena among cannibals is the parody of a religious ceremony. Finally, the capture of Pastorella by Calidore is the prelude to the final version of love on Mount Acidale. When viewed phenomenologically, Mirabella can be identified with the moment of division when the world of the senses is negated to promote, in a single dialectical move, the truth of the spirit. However, Serena's abduction repeats this move, without submerging the dominant figure in a degrading ritual that would cancel out phenomenological appearance once and for all. Nevertheless, the role of Pastorella is both to restore nature and to transform it, while also constituting a political allegory in which a social hierarchy is naturalized and then given a quasi-religious meaning that casts light on the sequence.

The trial of Mirabella establishes a low point in the history of Courtesy, just as this initial episode dramatizes the pitfalls of immediate experience. Spenser refers early to "the trial of true curtesie" where an ecclesiastical court must pass sentence on a loveless Mirabella (*FQ* VI proem 5, lines 1–2). The illusions of the world are often mistaken for ideal beauty: "But virtues seat is deep within the mynd, / And not in outward shows, but inward thoughts defynd" (*FQ* VI proem 5, lines 8–9). Mirabella—which literally means, "the look of beauty"—is a woman who uses her beauty to obtain power over men, to enamor and ruin them. The jury that presides over her trial condemns her to do penance: tomorrow she must walk the earth and love as many men as she ruined (*FQ* vii.37). Mirabella's suitors are feudal retainers of Cupid and her plea of mercy is a religious petition. Both of these factors seem to indicate that Mirabella takes part in an ecclesiastical, rather than a civil, trial.[10] This interpretation supports the view that love is a central issue in Book VI and that to be loveless is the supreme discourtesy in Spenser's poetic phenomenology.

The abduction of Serena by cannibals, in contrast, leads to hermeneutical issues that are deeply woven into the fabric of Spenser's humanism. On the one hand, we condemn the behavior of the cannibals as abhorrent. The abduction of Serena is particularly shocking insofar as it places a brutal practice in a primitive religious perspective. The cannibals who adore Serena eventually raise her "divine" body on an altar of sacrifice (*FQ* VI.viii.42–45). We instinctively reject any analogy between a savage practice and humanly acceptable modes of worship. This response, however, should not prevent us from coming to terms with the full meaning of this event as an episode in

Renaissance anthropology. Before the festivities begin, the cannibals must be restrained by a superior guide; it seems that "religion held even theies in measure" (*FQ* VI.viii.43, line 9). Spenser's humanistic perspective allows him to imagine the rudiments of order in this aboriginal context. By directing his people to the altar, the religious guide seems to organize them into a social whole. Compared with this event, the love of Mirabella is regressive; her beauty does not "rise" but actually "descends" into a physical world: "Spenser's transition to the cannibal ring logically reduces the sophisticated evil to its confused origins again and, in effect, allows him to begin all over again."[11]

Spenser's anthropological imagination probably owes a great deal to Michel de Montaigne's famous essay on cannibals that the poet seems to have known. After discussing the habits of cannibals at some length, Montaigne integrates a moral perspective into his argument that works along with his willingness to contemplate the unthinkable: "I am not so anxious that we should note the horrible savagery of these acts as concerned that, whilst judging their faults correctly, we should so be so blind to our own."[12] Like Montaigne, Spenser attempts to link anthropological awareness to a potential enhancement of normative standards. We might even say that Spenser's anthropological awareness relativizes the opposition between primitive and civilized, even though he clearly does not argue that cannibalism is morally acceptable. The comparative perspective that Spenser adopts within the sphere of the cultural imaginary is not at odds with specific religious and ethical commitments but participates in the same principles that animate Renaissance humanism generally. Moreover, the hidden role of the religious ritual is to plunge the reader back into a world of practices that signifies a new level of engagement with worldly existence. Readers will learn in a short moment that this engagement prepares them for a version of pastoral that breaks with the savage past and marks the entry of religious consciousness into the sphere of the aesthetic.

Hence, the "raising up" of Pastorella both glorifies nature and prefigures its transformation (*FQ* VI.ix.8). The name constitutes the figure as socially credible but cannot be assigned a "pure" meaning precisely because it possesses an initiatory status, while idealization always invites a degree of confusion: "In naming her, the swains reduce her from an aristocrat to a shepherdess; in worshipping her, they exalt her from an aristocrat to a goddess, identifying the symbol with the reality to which it refers."[13] The ironic nature of this apotheosis only becomes evident later in the narrative when we discover that Pastorella, child of nature, is really a high-born daughter (*FQ* VI.xii.20). If the cannibal ring commemorates the lowest stage of human culture, then the pastoral ring represents the beginning of aesthetic experience. The poetic qualities of the ring prepare us for the reduced geometry of intellectual beauty and the less ambiguous use of symbolism that will predominate in the closing scenes of the poem.

The encounter between Calidore and Pastorella's protector, old Meliboe, further complicates the poet's evocation of nature, which as the poem progresses becomes increasingly difficult to disentangle from human affairs. After chasing the blatant beast from court to country, Calidore resumes his place in the narrative after his long absence and invites us to imagine him once again taking up a moral role. However, while visiting Meliboe's pleasant lodging, Calidore expresses envy for the life of rural simplicity (*FQ* VI.ix.9). An "entraunced" Calidore momentarily rejects his political vocation as he speaks to the wise recluse (*FQ* VI.ix.28–29). Meliboe responds to Calidore's patronage of bucolic life simply by reminding his listener that "[i]t is the mynd, that makest good or ill" (*FQ* VI.ix.30, line 1), thus undercutting the idea that nature is nobler than contemplation and reflection. And yet, Spenser presents Meliboe as only a relative contrast to Calidore: "Boethian stoicism was not Spenser's whole card; but neither was there any reason to doubt that he meant Meliboe's 'sensible word' (*FQ* VI.ix.26) as the expression of one facet of an acceptable attitude."[14]

POETRY IN THE PLACE OF NATURE

The figure of Calidore is traditionally associated with the name of Sir Philip Sidney. This identification forms the basis for our optimism with respect to Calidore's future. At the same time, his political role introduces a basic ambiguity that pertains to the difference between art and experience, particularly as it pervades the conclusion of Spenser's poem.[15] Calidore is the man of the world whose gifts raise him above common ambitions. As an exemplar of courtesy, he must mingle with others and advance the cause of virtue, but his idealism derives from an ideal court, rather than from a purely political one: "In Book VI diplomacy is less a technique than a symbol, and Spenser does not show Calidore's exquisite tact simply in order to make him more convincing as a Renaissance courtier."[16] The fulfillment of political service requires an inspired vision of the supernatural because nature itself is less resourceful than the most truthful of poets: "Her world is brazen, the poets deliver a golden."[17]

In Spenser's epic, the return to pastoral culminates in the attempted integration of nature into the world of language that is suggested by poetry. Our first glimpse of Venus is significant in this regard: her place in the poem excludes nature as a densely material entity (*FQ* VIx.7, lines 1–5). Within this context, Calidore envisions the hundred dancing maidens (*FQ* VI.x11, line 6–7). The Three Graces appear in the center of a ring and circle a solitary figure, who wears a rose garland. Because the beauty of the central figure surpasses that of all others, she is "that fair one / That in the midst was placed parauant" (*FQ* VI.x.15. lines 6–7). However, we learn from the narrator that this is Colin Clout's lost love: "Thy loue is there aduaunst to be another Grace" (*FQ* VI.x16, lines 8–9). This lone figure seems to be little more than the trace of someone who dwelled in the rural setting. But in a moment, the entire apparition suddenly vanishes. The disappearance of the single figure is the precondition for the emergence of an aesthetic perspective on the Three Graces, but this will require a separate elaboration.

The rough shepherd who has played his pipe in a fit of anger then proceeds to offer his intruder an interpretation of the vision as a whole. What we learn about the central figure gives us insight into the moment of transformation. At first glance, she is "but a country lasse, / Yet she all other country lasses farre did pass" (*FQ* VI.x.25, lines 89). Her preeminent beauty distinguishes her from all other women. From another standpoint, however, she seems to condense, or contain, the qualities of her companions (*FQ* VI.x.27, lines 1–3). No longer a country maiden, she finally becomes "Greta Gloriana, greatest maiesy" (*FQ* VI.x.28, line 3). From one standpoint, reconciled in spirit to the virtue of his Queen, Calidore can now return to his beloved Pastorella. The tension between ideal and real worlds is only momentarily abated when the figures of earthly and divine love are linked: "For a moment the beloved is poised alone in a visionary splendour; in the next moment she recedes to make room for Gloriana though, with the words, 'Sunne of the world,' the two Ideas make brief contact."[18]

This final trope can be interpreted in terms of two different kinds of phenomenology. From the perspective of classical Husserlian phenomenology, Spenser's conclusion sustains an extended opposition between ideality and nature. The ideal world that emerges toward the end of the poem is brought into being through a complex set of experiences that enable the knower to meditate on the status of consciousness. The "brief contact" that occurs in the final stages of this mediation is the achievement of imaginal fulfillment in which the ultimate, if sometimes hidden, intentions of the knower momentarily fuse with the object itself. And yet, this moment of fusion does not abolish the difference between natural and transcendental standpoints. For instance, in this case, Calidore remains a Renaissance courtier with political ambitions that tie him irrevocably to the empirical world and perhaps compromise his ability to rise above circumstances and dwell in the spiritual sphere, except in passing. The tension between Calidore and the ideal world, or politics and a transformed nature, may be too great to uphold the stated opposition in any strongly convincing way, thus suggesting the need to consider another phenomenological standpoint that would accommodate time and history.

Hence, this same conclusion might encourage us to rethink the opposition between the transcendental and the empirical in terms of a phenomenology that accepted this difference as a starting point for a different sort of reflection. The phenomenology of Hegel emerges as an early challenge to this oppositional framework, and not as the science of an all-embracing consciousness but as a staging of language in which the terms of this opposition are held in question. Thus, Hegelian phenomenology reconceives of the transcendental not as a standpoint on the object world but as a transformation that occurs within the linguistic sphere, which displaces the priority of nature without, however, arguing that nature only subsists in the sphere of the mind. I would like to suggest how Spenser's epic anticipates Hegel's phenomenology but also falls short of its most compelling insights insofar as it enables us to imagine variations in time—just as it attempts to harmonize the difference between nature and society according to classical models.

DISCOURSE AND THE ORDER OF TIME

The vision on Mount Acidale reveals Spenser's indebtedness to traditional iconography. Spenser works with the same principles that govern the composition of Sandro Botticelli's great painting, "Primavera." For instance, the painting shows Venus standing between two groups of maidens: one group produces an earthly Flora, but the other group contains a lovely Castitas, who turns toward a heavenly Mercury. Taken as a whole, this entire sequence (or action) reproduces the basic structure of Plotinian spirituality.[19] The separate moments of this sequence only become simultaneous within the sphere of the canvas. As a poet, Spenser presents us with a similar movement by means of language. In the uncertain identity of the central figure on Mount Acidale, we discern the flickering visage of an earthly maiden or a celestial queen. The rhythm of the poem intensifies from one stanza to the next: beauty haunts us as it turns into silence. Calidore's chivalrous mission may have led him to discover an actual Gloriana, but it also suggests that ideal beauty must transcend the limitations of the one who listens. Unlike Colin Clout, with whom the identity of the poet ceases to be confused, Calidore must live in the tension between ideals and their fulfillment. As he leaves his pastoral setting, Calidore prepares to perform his remaining duties.

When we return to how the iconographic constellation relates to Spenser's epic poem, we encounter problems of interpretation that complicate what might otherwise seem to be a literary translation of an iconographic theme. Humphrey Tonkins has traced the image of the Three Graces back to the figures of Action, Pleasure, and Contemplation as they emerged in the visual arts and were subsequently adapted to literary purposes.[20] Underlying this literary appropriation is the project of reconciling opposites, according to the Platonic model of a departure from everyday life and a subsequent return to origins, which we will learn is a deeper meaning of Calidore's engagement with the vision at hand. Within the more specific domain of literature, this project involves the attempt to rethink the basic division that besets chivalric romance (where love is perpetually at odds with honor), so that the image of the Three Graces gives us both a way to reflect on the division and the possible role of the epic poem in overcoming it.[21]

Nonetheless, although the Plotinian interpretation of the image is a dynamic one, the more strictly Platonic reading of the poem and the vision on Mount Acidale seems to be inevitable, adding a degree of stability, if not rigidity, to whatever significance can be derived from it. A Platonic reading would subordinate Action and Pleasure to Contemplation, uniting the three components of an ideal life under the authority of the intellect in a manner that would echo the tripartite division of the soul and allow courtesy to be coordinated with political civility.[22] But it is also clear that Spenser invites us to envision the sovereignty of Contemplation in active terms because Calidore actually *intrudes* on the dancers, and "thus pushing through to the Centre, he is given new strength and energy by being made witness to the mystery of courtesy itself."[23] The role of Pastorella in this whole process is perhaps ironic because, unlike Mirabella, she belongs to the court all along and, therefore, allows us to better understand why pastoral as a genre tends to reinforce social hierarchies, instead of putting them in question. The idea that we merely rediscover in pastoral the social structures that are already present is supported by Pastorella's prior insertion in the world of the court and by Calidore's love for her.[24]

Spenser's use of pastoral romance is part of a new direction in Renaissance literature that contrasts strongly to what can be found in heroic styles of writing. While Richard Boiardo, Ludovico Ariosto, and Torquato Tasso offer the reader "sinister fictions" in literary works where bucolic enticements function as obstacles to the heroic quest, Spenser compares to Sir Philip Sidney and Jorge de Montemayor in providing nature with a different role in a poetic adventure.[25] This brings us back to the mysterious aspect of Calidore's sudden disappearance in the middle of the narrative, which might be viewed as morally irresponsible from the vantage point of what we customarily expect of heroes. And yet, C. S. Lewis effectively argued long ago that it would be a serious mistake to interpret Calidore's stay in the countryside with "pastoral truancy" and an abrogation of Spenser's high sense of moral purpose: "The shepherd's country and Mount Acidale in the midst of it are the core of the book, and the key to Spenser's whole conception of courtesy."[26] We might go beyond this endorsement and say that the pedagogical role of the countryside in Calidore's itinerary ends up complementing his vision on Mount Acidale precisely because it occurs outside the narrative, forming the absent center that provides this phase of the epic with its subjective meaning.

The importance of Calidore's absence is underscored, rather than denied, in his role as witness to the dance of the Three Graces, which elevates him to the level of an *aesthetic observer*, to the degree that he can reflect on what the dance means. Surely in the wake of Kant, aesthetics is not to be confused with the Platonic theory of art that remains a structural feature of cognitive conceptions as propagated by Immanuel Kant's rationalist predecessors, Christian Wolff and Alexander G. Baumgarten. Nonetheless, we have noted how Calidore initially intrudes on the dancers, so that his outsider status complicates his aesthetic stance, even when we might like to justify his intrusion (in the manner of Kant) by referring to the disinterested nature of aesthetic inquiry.[27] A. C. Hamilton emphasizes how Calidore's singular intrusion constitutes his separation from knowledge rather than his unity with it: "We may see in Calidore's desire to know a repetition of the Fall, Adam's act of eating from the tree of knowledge through which he lost the vision of paradise."[28] In contrast, as the figure who serves as the model for understanding courtesy *as a discourse*, Calidore cannot be absolved of his role in an epic that requires him to act and certainly to resume his struggle against the blatant beast, who has merely passed from view but remains present in the world at large.

The end of Courtesy, therefore, leaves us with two different ways of viewing Calidore's role in the epic. On the one hand, Calidore introduces a sense of the aesthetic as a perspective on spiritual knowledge that is better suggested by the figure of Pastorella than by the male protagonist. Calidore is able to glimpse a meaning that remains separate from him, but it is Pastorella, rather than Calidore, who more perfectly mingles semiotic agility with spiritual insight as a sublime accomplishment. Perhaps in a contrary manner, Calidore stands for the refinement of a discourse that is practical and requires worldly engagement to achieve (temporary) realization. Of course, what might be called a contradiction could be avoided by arguing that aesthetics and discourse are merely opposed perspectives that operate in separate domains and do not need to be integrated into a unified adventure. Nonetheless, this reading would not only place Calidore outside the climax of the poem but would separate education (which is perhaps the major theme of the poem) from the final goal of the epic. Hence, the opposition between an aesthetic perspective that takes time into account but requires a timeless realm to be stabilized and a discursive virtue that is only meaningful if it is exercised in political space suggests that Spenser himself is struggling with an unresolved conflict—and one that needs to be considered within the context of sixteenth-century poetics and epistemology.

This conflict can be gauged in terms of both the status of the image in sixteenth-century Protestant hermeneutics and the function of nature in the literature of the same period. Linda Gregerson has contended that "[t]he semiotic lineage from Plato to Augustine is fraught with much internal division" but remains consistent in insisting that language and desire are structurally at one.[29] The Reformers took up the problem of the image to address the tropological features of a sacred text that was inherently unstable to the degree that it already allowed for a broad range of responses that largely derived from its sensuous appeal. The problem of idolatry, therefore, is not separable from scripture but emerges as a problem of reading that persists to the degree that the sign itself is not to be understood as a vehicle of transparency but is necessarily linked to *aesthesis* and must be brought into the sphere of the mimetic before it can be assimilated to dogmatics. However, the relationship between aesthetics and mimesis is by no means straightforward: the poet attempts to integrate the iconic aspects of language into a strategy of reading, so that the poem encourages "an idolatrous response from the reader—the 'enjoyment' of signs for their own sake," just as it attempts to reform this response in breaking a fascination with surfaces.[30] Although this reading of the poem seems to work better for the early books in Spenser's epic, the rift between enjoyment and iconoclasm is what impedes us from fully accepting the traditional view of nature as a principle of unity, that is to say, as the sphere into which all of the elements of the poem are drawn as the focus of a contemplative knowing, to be reconfigured as poetic in some new way.

What Spenser's poem shows us, in this reading, is the discrepancy between a poetics that encourages one sort of reading and a dogmatics that aligns a Platonic view of nature with a reformative approach to moral waywardness. The place of aesthetics in this process cannot be clarified precisely because it has not yet emerged as a distinct hermeneutical possibility. We have emphasized how the virtue of courtesy can be conceived as a discourse that Calidore develops in the course of his adventures, rather than as a static code of conduct that does not require social interaction or political sensitivity. Nonetheless, if Calidore is on the side of aesthetics as a response to experience and as a possibility of reading, his aesthetic function cannot be given historical significance but is ultimately aligned with the contemplative view of nature that presides at the end of the poem. The conflict between discourse and nature as a source of order and hierarchy remains implicit to the poem, but it does not permit language to acquire genuinely historical features. It may be somewhat paradoxical that the strictly Aristotelian definition of courtesy allows us to imagine a movement beyond the classical view of nature that otherwise would restrict Calidore's significance to a set component in an old-fashioned allegory. This definition has the advantage of implying an openness on the level of social practices that Platonic cosmology, especially when combined with orthodox theology, is unable to contain when the poem invites the reader to experience symbolic fulfillment.

If aesthetics is to be assigned a new meaning that does not exclude history but inscribes history in its construction, we need to move onto a new terrain that challenges the Platonic view of things, just as it prepares a discourse that would be inherently historical insofar as it would not be assumed to mirror an unchanging nature. The contribution of Romanticism to an understanding of these issues is considerable, not so much because it always provides clarity on aesthetics, discourse, or the opening onto history that needs to be deployed if we are to develop more flexible definitions, but because it stages the crisis that surrounds the emergence of these terms as disciplines or counterdisciplines in modernity. Spenser has demonstrated how the concept of nature, as articulated in Renaissance poetics, does not challenge the social or political norms that inform the world that he presents in figurative terms. We might assume that this challenge could be taken up successfully if the sign were no longer embedded in visual experience and nature were freed from its dependence on the word. The Enlightenment is often assumed to provide a flexible concept of nature as a guide to political and social reform; however, it just as clearly shows us how nature became the setting for the crisis that its "concept" was intended to confront and resolve.

Although Spenser's sixteenth-century imaginary foregrounds the role of resemblance in the relationship between language and the world, Michel Foucault has suggested how the quest for similarity leads to an infinite regress in which the "object" of inquiry cannot be brought to light: "A dark space appears which must be made progressively clearer. That space is where 'nature' resides, and it is what one must attempt to know. Everything would be manifest and immediately knowable if the hermeneutics of resemblance and the semiology of signatures coincided without the slightest parallax."[31] The gap between interpretation and the being of the world cannot be bridged in a ternary system that continues to produce a proximity to the same. Either the ternary system founders in uncertainly when the opposition between two principles is endlessly reproduced, creating an endless regress that permits no conclusion, or else one of the two principles achieves dominance and knowledge basically becomes a matter of representation.

The moment of representation is "classical" in providing a model for abolishing this distance and assigning discourse a univocal meaning when signs are placed on a table, allowing them to be compared. But if early modern thought presupposes the gap between language and the world as a precondition for representation, enabling language to be conceived as an object of knowledge, has the knower been displaced in a manner that renders him unknowable? The manner and degree of displacement might be not visible within a system of representation that simply passes over the absence, or never acknowledges it, due to its inability to recognize what it cannot contain. Hence, if the question of self-knowledge cannot be asked within an early modern framework, perhaps the moment when this framework ceased to be dependable was also the occasion when knowledge itself acquired an uncanny double, while the Age of Representation drew to a close.

NOTES

1. The author provided us with his own account of his service to Lord Grey in Edmund Spenser, *A View of the State of Ireland as it Was Written in the Reign of Queen Elizabeth* (Dublin: Printed for Lawrence Flin and Ann Watts, 1763). Spenser's "Book of Justice" (*FQ* V) provides a chronicle of this period of military ardor in the author's life that sharply contrasts with the tone and spirit that pervades the narrative of Courtesy.

2. As derived from my reading, or revisionary misreading, of Michel Foucault's text, *The Archaeology of Knowledge and the Discourse on Knowledge* (trans. A. M. Sheridan Smith [New York, NY: Pantheon Books, 1971]), the word "discourse" as employed in this study argues in favor of a new methodological awareness of how discontinuity and rupture cannot be expunged from our accounts of history. Despite occasional lapses into a regrettable structuralism, Foucault complicates his previous commitment to archeology in this work that decenters the unities that are normally assumed to be adequate to interpretation. Discourse in this sense is not as diffuse a term as "language," but it would operate in an open space that, in Spenser's poetry, would not be limited to a classical theory of virtue, even as it attempted to embrace it.

3. For instance, while *FQ* II.xii abounds in classical allusions, Spenser inverts a facile naturalism in his use of ancient sources, both literary and philosophical, in recapitulating Odysseus's journey to the Isle of Circe. Guyon resembles Odysseus in his voyage into the Bower of Bliss but also knows how the struggle against artifice—which here assumes the form of Acrasia's attempt to seduce and deceive—can have ethical import, just as it limits the power of images to thwart and corrupt the heroic questor. This instructive example demonstrates the possible alliance between Platonic conceptions of the good and Spenser's literary iconoclasm.

4. Baldesar Castiglione, *The Book of the Courtier* (New York: Anchor Books 1959), sec. 11:295.

5. In seeking a middle position between extremes, Aristotle describes two attitudes that run from excess to deficiency: "In the other sphere of the agreeable—the general business of life—the person who is agreeable, supposing him to have no ulterior object, is 'obsequious'; if he has such an object, he is a 'flatterer'. The man who is deficient in this quality and takes every opportunity of making himself disagreeable may be called 'peevish' or 'sulky' or surly'." The middle position is one that Aristotle does not name but might be identified with Spenserian courtesy. Cf. Aristotle, *The Ethics of Aristotle*, trans. J. A. K. Thomson (London: Penguin Books, 1971), IV.vi:70–71

6. Aristotle, *The Ethics of Aristotle*, IX.v:269.

7. Graham Hough, *A Preface to* The Faerie Queene (New York: Norton Library, 1963), 202.

8. Harry Berger, "A Secret Discipline: *The Faerie Queene*, Book VI," in *Form and Convention in the Poetry of Edmund Spenser*, ed. William Nelson (New York: Columbia University Press, 1961), 40.

9. Ibid., 51.

10. Cf. Arnold Williams, *Flower on a Lowly Stock: The Sixth Book of* The Faerie Queene (Ann Arbor: Michigan University Press, 1967), 108.

11. Berger, "A Secret Discipline," 58.

12. Michel de Montaigne, "On Cannibals," in *Essays*, trans. J. M. Cohen (New York: Penguin Books, 1976), I.31:113.

13. Berger, "A Secret Discipline," 61.

14. Alastair Fowler, *Spenser and the Numbers of Time* (London: Routledge and Kegan Paul, 1964), 224.

15. We might argue that Calidore's actions as a Renaissance courtier unfold in the political sphere and never leave behind the world of everyday experience. In the sphere of art, however, the reader ultimately confronts the difference between the natural, if sublime, Pastorella and the supernatural Gloriana, which expresses a basic ambiguity that lies of the heart of Spenser's pastoral romance. For these reasons, Pastorella, rather than Calidore, assumes symbolic value as the figure that in some sense bridges everyday life and the transcendent sphere that provides the poem with its system of support.

16. Donald Cheney, *Spenser's Image of Nature: Wild Man and Shepherd in the* Faerie Queene (New Haven, CT: Yale University Press, 1966), 185.
17. Sir Philip Sidney, *The Defense of Poesy* in *Sir Philip Sidney: Selected Prose and Poetry*, ed. Robert Kimbrough (Madison: University of Wisconsin, 1983), 108.
18. Berger, "A Secret Discipline," 72.
19. Cf. Edgar Wind, *Pagan Mysteries of the Renaissance* (New York: Norton Library, 1968), 105. The Plotinian reading is borne out by the visual arts tradition that the poem seems to sustain, even if Spenser was unaware of Botticelli's "Primavera." Its basic form is emanation—conversio—remeatio. The Zephyr's "decent" into Flora leads to the "conversion" in the Dance of Graces. "Re-ascent" occurs in the turning of Castitas toward Mercury. It would be interesting to compare this scheme to a dialectical reading, allowing us to "negate" nature in favor a speculative movement toward unity, especially in view of Hegel's willingness to read Plotinus as a kind of precursor.
20. Cf. Humphrey Tonkin, *Spenser's Courteous Pastoral: Book Six of* The Faerie Queene, (Oxford: Clarendon Press, 1972), 274–80.
21. Ibid., 277–88.
22. Ibid., 278. It would be a mistake, however, to interpret this moment too rigidly, even though Platonic (and Aristotelian) systems privilege contemplation over action and prevent us from accepting the internal perspective as more than a viewpoint on a larger whole that the protagonist cannot master. The problem is that an aesthetic, rather than a theological, perspective is not crucial in the classical economy of Renaissance cosmologies and the qualified iconoclasm of Reformation poetics.
23. Ibid., 289.
24. Ibid., 291–94.
25. Ibid., 296.
26. C. S. Lewis, *The Allegory of Love* (Oxford: Oxford University Press, 1932), 350. This point of view is perhaps best sustained in Ficino's reading of Plato, which brings together beauty and truth in a manner that allows them to be distinguished: "But what do I bid you love in the soul?—the beauty of the soul. The beauty of bodies is a visible light, the beauty of the soul is an invisible light: the light of the soul is truth." Marsilio Ficino, *Ficino's Commentary on Plato's* Symposium, trans. Sears Reynolds Jayne (Columbia: University of Missouri, 1944), 157.
27. Kant's emphasis of the role of disinterestedness has the advantage of bolstering the scientific claims of aesthetic judgment, but it also establishes distance from the object world and, therefore, has the disadvantage of sustaining a contemplative relationship to what is considered to be worthy of judgment. While sometimes opposed to that of the rationalists who were his precursors, Kant's aesthetic project is frequently expressed in a quasi-scientific manner that threatens to undermine its originality. See Immanuel Kant, *Critique of Judgment*, trans. J. H. Bernard (Amherst, NY: Prometheus Books, 2000), 2:46–48.
28. A. C. Hamilton, *The Structure of Allegory in* The Faerie Queene (Oxford: Clarendon Press, 1970), 202.
29. Linda Gregerson, *The Reformation of the Subject: Spenser, Milton and the English Protestant Epic* (Cambridge, UK: Cambridge University Press, 1995), 65–66.
30. Ibid., 145–46.
31. Michel Foucault, *The Order of Things: An Archaeology of the Human Sciences* (New York: Routledge, 1989), 33. The gap in knowledge that the ternary model cannot close prevents sixteenth-century epistemology from becoming a thematic of representation. It is significant in this regard that Spenser's resistance to modernity, as clearly suggested in his allegorical use of Tasso and Ariosto in *FQ* II.xii ("The Book of Temperance"), prolongs medieval tendencies, even when it can be read as a didactic expression of Renaissance humanism.

Chapter Three

Image in Wordsworth

Space/Time and Semiotics

The significance of William Wordsworth's poetry is difficult to consider apart from an autobiographical dimension that emerges in various works that were produced during different periods in his lifetime. And yet, a careful reading of the penultimate book of *The Prelude* (1805) suggests that the author placed strong emphasis on poetic moments that were far more than a sequence of unrelated experiences.[1] While acknowledging this emphasis, I argue in this chapter that Wordsworth's poetry is modern in its transformation of epic themes through its use of evocative images that enable aesthetics to be related to ethical concerns and to be viewed through the mind of the poet. This emphasis enables various moments to be presented on the basis of scenes that neither correspond to "inner" (or psychological) experience nor to external realities. Wordsworth enacts the question of literary tradition in terms of an approach to poetic time that is performative, thus suggesting the role of figurative space to both the ethics of writing and the interpretation of history as the site of rupture and community. My conclusion maintains that Wordsworth takes up the poetic image in a way that discloses the semiotic core of his literary project, just as it suggests how the human mind can transcend its aesthetic apotheosis.

WORDSWORTH AND AESTHETICS

Wordsworth's *Prelude* can be read a sequence of moments that culminate in a vision of undeniable grandeur and abiding humanity. However, the "method" (if this term can be applied to poetic works) that the poem employs in articulating this vision is only presented in the penultimate book of the poem. Here Wordsworth refers to "spots of time / Which with distinct pre-eminence retain / A vivifying Virtue," and thus suggests that his poem is inscribed with a vital design and possibly Aristotelian emphasis on the moral importance of poetic moments (*P* XI, lines 258–60). This declaration of intent testifies to the poet's long-term purpose. On the one hand, Wordsworth belatedly acknowledges the importance of memory to the design of his literary composition, which foregrounds "the growth of the poet's mind" in terms of vivid, personal experiences. At the same time, this admission suggests the question of how seemingly discrete experiences unify a literary narrative that relies on the life of the individual poet as its point of departure. Wordsworth's problem is one that will haunt all poets who attempt to compose extended compositions in the wake of the classical epic and its unified sense of narrative time. His attempt to solve an intractable problem will seem excessively "Romantic" to later generations of poets, but perhaps his actual attempt to stipulate the terms of this solution needs to be viewed in a broader hermeneutical context to be clearly assessed.

Wordsworth's declaration of poetic principles, occurring after he presented numerous examples of how isolated experiences can be raised to the level of singular insight, can be read as an early effort to confront radical subjectivity as a threat to meaning. Instead of viewing this declaration as instating a subjectivity that potentially undermines the possibility of connected experience, we might instead read it as an affirmation of narrative on aesthetic grounds. The key to this move is indeed the poet's resistance to any form of subjectivism that would undo the possibility of an ethically tinged narrative. For Wordsworth, this resistance is sometimes called "nature" and bears many of the burdens that this word necessarily carries along with it. Hence, arises the illusion of Wordsworth's conservatism, which appears to link his work to the neoclassical systems of the eighteenth century rather than to the unstable world of Romanticism.[2] However, Wordsworth's affinities to the poetics of the previous century is more apparent than actual because the nature that he celebrates is perpetually in motion and difficult to disentangle from the task of defining poetry as an opening onto what is ontologically other, rather than objectively self-contained.

Wordsworth's poetry can be read as confronting two intractable problems. The first problem is distinctively modern and concerns the status of representation as a frame for experience. Without rejecting this frame entirely, Wordsworth indicates in his poetic theory how this same frame is subject to an endless dispute because it is threatened with the possibility of disintegration as the site of variable intensity that has no distinct location. The expression "spots of time" is in fact an invitation to merge both space and time in a single designate that is neither one nor the other but somehow carries the meaning of both. Once again, this same designate begs the question of how experience can be represented as space when it arrives as time without being distorted in its representation. Thus, we need to ask ourselves how a "vivifying Virtue" can be discerned for the purpose of poetic exposition if experience provides the basis for determining what values or rules provide criteria for guiding human conduct. Surely this second problem is related to the first in pointing back to the issue of grounds, which needs to be rethought if norms are imminent, rather external, to human experience. The link between the "images" of experience that are named "spots of time" and the interpretation to be assigned to them returns us to the role of subjectivity in assessing the ethical significance of individual moments.

Aesthetics is often assumed to be opposed to poetics, marking a break in our ability to recognize art as a human activity, that is, according to criteria that were in place from Greco-Roman antiquity until the end of the eighteenth century. This new discipline adopts a subjective stance toward the world and is also one that accepts the standpoint of experience, not the experience of solitary individuals but experience as a matrix that establishes connections *between* subjects, as agents for whom communication becomes possible on the basis of language and cannot be reduced to a closed system. The transition from rationalist conceptions to a more socially based conception of the aesthetic can be seen in Immanuel Kant's attempt to link the universality of aesthetic judgments to the possibility of the *sensus communis*, which, at least in principle, attempts to harmonize the claims of the sensibility and human nature.[3] Aesthetics in this way emerges as the heir to classical poetics, which prioritizes idea or act as the locus of cultural modeling. With the aesthetic revolution, however, poetics is eventually transformed into a discipline that poses questions concerning how the relationship between subject and object can be negotiated so that experience provides the medium *through which* normative questions can be related to the temporal condition of the spectator. Hence, from this standpoint, Kant's conception of experience would only be preparatory to a more radical conception of how life itself can provide the setting for complex reflections on how norms are to be negotiated.

Of course, this description can be made to seem circular insofar as experience might be said to validate norms if it possesses "value" in advance, in which case its role is predetermined. However, in Wordsworth's poetry, value is not simply derived from experience but needs to assume the form of a performative before it can be exhibited. To speak of performatives in this case is not only to evoke the possibility of (re)enactment but also to evoke a narrative discourse that is "mythic" to the precise degree that it tells a story that *repeats* the stories of the past, perhaps not in the style of the great classical narratives but nonetheless in a diegetic idiom that does not merely copy the external world. Classical literature might come to mind, but just as the fusion of cognition and norm is more apparent than real in Wordsworth's poetry, we soon discover that his use of myth is only superficially aligned to what occurs in the traditional epic. Hence we might say that, unlike what is discoverable in classical poetics, Wordsworth's poetry is a performance that reminds us of how values are more "formal" than real, testifying to the radical uncertainty that underlies all performances of value, just as it indicates how the myths of modern times are no longer the sign of sacred origins but have evolved into fictions that break with ancient cosmologies and could not have found a place in classical (theocentric) narratives.

At the same time, Wordsworth can be read in relation to the aesthetic turn that provides a coherent alternative to classical poetics that it varies, while also introducing a new instability to both the composition of the poem and in the reader's reception of literary content. Wordsworth's poetry is inseparable from the emergence of a special kind of textual indeterminacy, which is misunderstood whenever psychological motives are imputed to the narrator. At the same time, textual indeterminacy does not undermine the possibility of assigning normative significance to what emerges on the level of figural enactment as meaningful experience. The problem then becomes one of determining how the poem can be read as a narrative in which virtue is enacted *through* experience, which becomes the setting for an "enlivening" that is irreducible to the subjective disposition of the one who narrates or the person who reads. In the examples cited, we will learn that Wordsworth reconfigures the potential of myth to reconstitute the elements of narrative in a loosely defined synthesis in which the parameters of the poet's authority are radically redrawn and recomposed.

LITERATURE AS PERFORMANCE

Wordsworth adopts the counterintuitive claim that poetic authority is sustained by experience when experience seems to be incapable of guaranteeing the integrity of literary form. By reducing the distance between life and literature, Wordsworth challenges the view that literary creativity is a self-conscious activity that is easily separated from the poet's contact with the world. In proceeding in this manner, however, he also invites us to consider how experience informs (conscious) thought, just as consciousness become more than the condition for the possibility of our knowledge of objects. In a manner that profoundly modifies Kant's transcendental standpoint, Wordsworth shows us how poetry is a performance that is not merely *present to* experience but acquires its shape *as* and *through experience* in a way that redraws the boundaries of classical poetics to constitute a new notion of canonicity that departs from the traditional understanding of nationhood and problematizes the theological underpinnings that are used to legitimize poetry as the expression of a stable and religiously inflected self.

The challenge of defining the subject matter of modern poetry is implicit early in the poem when Wordsworth ruminates on how he might "settle on some British theme, some old / Romantic tale, by Milton left untold" (*P* I, lines 179–80). The names of Odin, Mithradates, and Sertorius are taken up as to signify ancient heroes who opposed tyranny as recorded in the annals of Plutarch and Gibbon (*P* I, pp. 185–201). The names of Dominque de Gourges, Gustavus I, and Wallace are more strongly associated with either religious freedom or national liberty in the modern context (*P* I, lines 201–19). And yet, without denying the force of these examples, Wordsworth speaks of how he has begun to "yearn towards some philosophic song / Of Truth that cherishes our daily life," while just as quickly remarking that he is too immature to accept this seemingly unexceptional task (*P* I, lines, 228–38). What this sequence suggests is that the poet is aware that his task requires a new justification, even though he might have been entirely justified simply in imitating the political motives of heroic men. The point is not that classical mimesis is completely unjustifiable as a means for rendering ancient or modern subject matter, but that another subject matter demands a response that is more appropriate to the new poetry.

Wordsworth's vivid account of how his own "personal" canon was formed through early reading is therefore far more than an affirmation of national sympathies but instead provides a literary context for the poet's development that becomes significant as much for what it omits as for what it includes. If "Residence at Cambridge" does not provide a memorable setting for purely academic endeavors, this unconventional narrative of student life replaces the standard eighteenth-century curriculum when it replaces the classical learning with a reminiscence of Geoffrey Chaucer, Edmund Spenser, and John Milton (*P* III, lines 276–93). Chaucer is mentioned as a storyteller who incites laughter among the hawthorn trees, whereas Spenser and Milton, although identified with the affairs of state, are associated either with the moon (Spenser) or youthful purity (Milton). But what is peculiar about this colloquy of poets is the nonappearance of William Shakespeare, whose absence may be attributed too quickly to the bard's devotion to the genre of drama, rather than to poetry in the strict sense. A more plausible interpretation hinges on the role of performativity in Wordsworthian poetics, which becomes the immediate theme of the dramatic scene that follows the poet's naming of precursors. At the same time, before moving on to describe this scene, we must reflect for a moment on how narrative seems to be uppermost in the poet's mind because the three poets named are preeminently chroniclers of spiritual aspiration, either of stages along the way to perfection, virtue, or human destiny.

With this narratological thematic in mind, we can assess the following scene in which the poet's youthful confrontation with Milton needs to be read—not only as a failure to appropriate a major precursor's influence but also as a recognition that the great poet's aims were different from his own (*P* III, lines 299–328). Again, this scene of Dionysian exuberance might be cited to assert Milton's inimitable authority, just as it is presented as a source of shame for the jejune student of poetry. The pseudo-religious quality of this scene (which is also a scene of humiliation) unmistakably marks it as a rite of initiation that refers to chapel, surplice, and organ pealing in the presence of onlookers. However, the burghers who observe this scene of drunkenness are also the prosaic citizens who lack the enthusiasm of the uncontrollable devotee. The gap between the onlookers and the ritual of the rebellious student, no doubt intoxicated by the *language of* Milton as much as by the thought of taking up his poetic mantle, if only in a symbolic way, is too great to produce a convincing spectacle of how poetic experience can serve a meaningful role in constituting a *work* that could be shared by a community of readers.

Nonetheless, we might also view this rather sudden introduction of psychological and poetic instability in terms of a sphere that has begun to be constituted in a marginal capacity, even if it does not emerge in a manner that permits complete or even partial articulation. On the one hand, and in a fairly positive capacity, Wordsworth's (re)staging of youthful drunkenness through his "reading" of Milton calls attention to the performative status of poetry itself, not in a reductive sense (for instance, in arguing implicitly that poetry is basically no more than a public performance) but as a linguistic insight that does not rest on the simple opposition between the performative and the constative but on a "position" that indicates how this contrast has been contaminated:

> My Surplice gloried in and yet despised,
> I clove in pride through the inferior throng,
> Of the plain Burghers, who in audience stood
> On the last skirts of their permitted ground,
> Beneath the pealing organ! (*P* III, lines 318–22)

Although we might want to argue that a sort of vestigial self-sameness enables Wordsworth to "return" to his previous state of mind as the sober reader of literary classics, we are perhaps more strongly persuaded that the moment of radical destabilization, as enacted in this poetic moment, is also a sign of how he is not merely telling a life story or narrating an experience of uncertain meaning but suggesting the need for tradition just as he is providing a moving "image" in its actual impossibility.[4]

Moreover, the space in which the youthful protagonist finds himself is not simply that of a failed community but also looks forward to a community that is relatively new to poetry. The spirit of instability that would not be at home in a work that was defined by the rules of classical poetics begins to acquire a provisional significance in a situation where onlookers struggle in vain for a common perspective on the immature literary performance. What needs to be emphasized in this case is the aesthetic potential of this loose assortment of spectators and their object of concern. Clearly, the reader senses how the sheer *weight* of the burghers, embodying the virtues of the town against the artificial traditions of the sequestered college, prevents them from imagining the young student in comic disarray as anything more than a failed performer. However, we only need to envision a more accomplished protagonist constituting the occasion for aesthetic reflection and, thus, the "world" of the poet as a preeminently *free world* among all of the worlds that might be created by the arts.[5]

However, this moment has not yet been reached and lies in the future of a poem that is being assembled in an empty space. Nonetheless, the empty space of performance proves crucial to the development of a poem that narrates a process of becoming, instead of merely providing the outlines of a self that can be separated from time. Whatever can be said about the self that emerges in the course of the poem requires an unceasing attempt to clarify the context in which the protagonist acts and where displays of Virtue cannot be grasped apart from the occasions of their appearance. In such a situation, the self is no longer a unified entity, existing in an ideal or even virtual state, separate from the world, but a function that is defined by gaps and interstices that constitute the space in which various issues are negotiated and engage the reader in a quest for productive repetition. In such an ill-defined context, while the protagonist confronts separate situations that require different responses, the poem is threatened with a fluid subjectivity that prompts the reader to ask questions about the unity of the narrative and to wonder how these evocative moments are to be linked to the development of the poet-narrator. The danger of subjectivity emerges as a cautionary tale that is fraught with meanings that are not restricted to the reading of literature. The question of how Wordsworth confronts this danger needs to be explored as one that engages the problem of time on a literary basis

TIME PAST, TIME FUTURE

Wordsworth's major poem, *The Prelude*, is customarily identified with the rise of psychological modes of reading that place the reader or literary protagonist in the center of literary interpretation. Certainly Friedrich Schleiermacher, as a member of the early Romantic circle of philosopher-critics, advocated a psychologically oriented hermeneutic that would later acquire a more systematic expression in the work of Wilhelm Dilthey. Key to Schleiermacher's hermeneutic was an emphasis on "divination" as a loosely defined method that enabled the reader to penetrate subjective meaning, which was coupled with a belief in the possibility of retrieving the original intentions of the author whose text was taken to be the object of inquiry. Such an approach to the interpretation of texts would be refined in Dilthey's complex appropriation of Schleiermacher, which late in the nineteenth century was vastly extended to include a historical subject matter that was kept separate from hermeneutics during the previous period.[6] Even if they were largely unaware of this long and enduring intellectual tradition, readers of Wordsworth pay homage to its power and influence when they adopt the standpoint of lived experience, together with the subjectivity of the author, as the nucleus for whatever can be achieved in the elucidation of literary texts. This predisposition, however, is precisely what prevents Wordsworth's poetry from being read as a rare instance in which the psychological and historical not only become indistinguishable but break down as separate categories, thus promoting a new moment in the history of reading, even if that moment is difficult to assign a name.

If nineteenth-century hermeneutics increasingly became the domain of both psychology and history, Wordsworth demonstrates how this domain can just as easily assume the site of a hermeneutical conflict as it becomes the space in which the difference between these two disciplines is either mediated or at least partially overcome. The figure of the discharged solider, returning from tropical lands, appears in Wordsworth's poem at the precise juncture that the reader least expects an interruption in a brief passage from Kendal to Hawkshead that follows the survey of student life at Cambridge (*P* IV, lines 400–504). The veteran's ghostly appearance is so startling that we are likely to miss its possible significance, if we draw the conclusion that this figure is either a sign of the narrator's physical exhaustion or an intruder who simply does not belong to the terrain of a pleasant woodland journey. The ambiguous significance of the veteran's appearance gives rise to two equally plausible interpretations of his significance.

On the one hand, the psychological reading would link the figure of the veteran with internal conflicts in the mind of the poet, which are merely externalized in the ghostly form that can be related to the poet's own past, perhaps as an incompletely repressed trauma, or if viewed more philosophically, as an immemorial alterity that cannot be assimilated to an ongoing present. Psychoanalysis might be applied to this brief narrative, arguing that it dramatizes in advance the crisis in feeling that the poet would experience later in life, so that the soldier's initially stiff demeanor and inability to express what he has experienced indicate an anxiety in the poet himself, who already worries that his powers may not be adequate to the task. Wordsworth's lucid report describes an uncanny disruption on two different levels:

> There was a strange half-absence, and a tone
> Of weakness and indifference, as of one
> Remembering the importance of his theme
> But feeling it no longer. (*P* IV, lines 475–78)

The speaker's relationship to the veteran is disrupted in the "strange half-absence" that prevents the one who bears memories of the past from being clearly recognized. Moreover, the memories themselves are perhaps retained *in some mechanical way* but remain disconnected to the degree that they are no longer felt by the speaker who is able to communicate them. This condition of double estrangement suggests a recurrent repetition in which what happens the second time prevents the "original" trauma from being thematized as a separate event, that is, as an event that could be separated from the veteran's (unspoken) narrative.[7] From a different but analogous perspective, we might even add that this moment of nonrecognition has ethical significance, marking the eruption of an irretrievable past that is the token of an alterity through which time erupts in opposition to any assertion of self-identity.

Somewhat surprisingly, the ethical twist that can be given to the veteran's appearance can be enlarged on to embrace a more external narrative that emerges at this juncture, not as the self-conscious and admittedly imperial project of the veteran's masters, but as an oblique entry, a seemingly marginal intrusion that provides the poem with an unmistakably historicist edge. In this regard, postcolonial criticism offers one basis for a hermeneutic that testifies to the power of social and political forces to structure a landscape that otherwise might dissolve into the psychic peculiarities of the poet himself. However, as much as this broader history might be invoked as a sort of guardrail against excessively psychological readings, we might also argue that the discharged soldier does little more than suggest the workings of history on the most abstract level, instead of providing a convincing discourse that instates its importance. Nonetheless, the poem does contain references that can be directly linked to this episode so that the historical background of the poem can be used to deepen more fully what this specific image, if taken on its own, seems to leave out.

Mary Jacobus has argued that Wordsworth basically evades history in presenting us with the visage of the discharged soldier as returning from the West Indies, an obvious setting for the Atlantic slave trade, while hesitating to fully explore the importance of slavery to the writing of *The Prelude*. However, Jacobus also provides details to argue that the narrative of John Newton, the slave trader turned Evangelist whose name ironically evokes that of the Isaac Newton, can be coupled with that of the veteran and the world of maps and diagrams that were tools of empire designed by scientific minds (*P* VI, lines 160–74).[8] This coupling already seems to refute the claim that Wordsworth evades history. The argument is taken much further, however, when the tale of Druidic sacrifices on the Salisbury Plain is said to depend on a Miltonic conjuration of darkness, implying a blindness to violence and repression (*P* VII, lines 327–36).[9] My criticism here is that Wordsworth's use of Miltonic rhetoric need not be taken so literally; hence, blindness may be more of a horrible upsurge of the unspeakable, rather than a coating of poetic language in traditional sanctity.

Before disappearing, the discharged soldier simply utters familiar platitudes about God's oversight, as if to resolve both his own and his listener's anxieties through recourse to a hackneyed allusion to divine wisdom (*P* IV, 494–95). These remarks almost undo the ascription of religious motives to the poet's early and rather oblique encounter with history. Nonetheless, historical contextualization becomes inconclusive when it depends on a narrative that the veteran does not provide and when related details are scattered in the poem, leaving only residual traces of what might have been confronted in a more direct manner. The poem's "external" reference seems to be incapable of grounding the reading in a definitive manner and fails to combine with the psychological reading to produce a hermeneutically unified perspective on a single moment in the poem.

Nonetheless, both perspectives—the psychological and the historical—retain validity to the degree that the narrator assumes a diegetic role that is indeed similar to what can be found in classical literature, even when Wordsworth's use of this device is highly original. The narrator does not simply offer us pictures but tales that pertain to the nature of poetry as conceived by an author who has already positioned himself in a literary tradition that remains incomplete. To reduce this position to a matter of intrapsychic conflict or imperial history would be to miss the duality of a narrative yielding different meanings that can be held together, if not perfectly unified. Moreover, this duality is communicated in an "image" that is dialectical in the sense that Walter Benjamin specifies in attempting to suggest how time can be brought to an *apparent* standstill, without becoming a frozen pattern of arrested movements.[10] This image is irreducible to a representation of empirical life but articulated through language by a poet who compares in some respects to the narrator who draws on myths to shape the moral and political priorities of the classical epic. Like the mythic narratives, Wordsworth's image is a space-time assemblage that is not merely the concretization of a temporal moment but concerns a "spacing" that problematizes the simple "before" and "after" that is conventionally employed in grounding historical and literary chronologies. And yet, this image also *fades* and, therefore, cannot be assimilated to any poetics designed to stabilize narrative content under the eye of an eternal present.

We can envision more clearly the duality of this image, as well as its fading quality, as Wordsworth tentatively elaborates on an aesthetics of reading that is always haunted by the possible dissolution of literary form.[11] In the succeeding book of the poem, the narrator evokes two models of reading that beg the question to how space and time might be thought together, in a single image, rather than in opposition to one another. The poet-narrator begins by relating the story of a friend, who journeyed to a cave by the sea only to read Miguel de Cervantes's *Don Quixote* and contemplate two disciplines on an allegorical basis (P.V, lines 49–139). We learn of how a mounted knight arose mysteriously in the desert, offering the speaker two objects, a stone and a shell, as if to suggest the contrast between Euclidean geometry (space) and prophetic literature (time). The teller of this tale clearly states that the shell is the more valuable object, expressing a preference of poetry over geometry (*P* V, lines 89–90). The shell itself is a duality, containing an ambiguous meaning; it allows the speaker to listen to "[a] loud prophetic blast of harmony," but it also foretells the destruction of the world (*P* V, lines 93–99). Nonetheless, the shell is not simply a harbinger of doom; it compares to many gods who "[h]ad voices more than all the winds, / And was a joy, a consolation and a hope" (*P* V, lines 108–9). Upon disappearing, the traveler bearing the two objects becomes both the knight errant of Cervantes and a "Phantom Arab" who somehow combines reason and madness through unstable images that fragment and unify, dissolving the present and foretelling a time to come.[12]

A DISCOVERY OF HISTORY

Wordsworth's discovery of history in "Cambridge and the Alps" is certainly a high point of *The Prelude*, but it is also coupled with a sense of radical finitude together with an awareness that the human imagination can function in contrast to historical determination to signal what a purely symbolic grasp of time cannot raise to the level of philosophical reflection. On the one hand, Wordsworth as poet-narrator seems to be saying, at least in this context, that history exceeds the scope of his narrative, either because our relation to it is imperfectly mediated, or because it cannot be communicated in its power and density through the vehicle of poetic discourse. In a different manner, Wordsworth may also be saying that history is indeed knowable insofar as it leaves the traces of its passing in the words of both participants and witnesses, whose testimonies are reliable to the degree that they offer the basis for an affective response to what is in the process of occurring, those momentous events that no doubt continue to occur, even if at a considerable remove from the space of the poet. In discussing Wordsworth's own position on this issue, the second interpretation will be shown to be closer to the truth, and yet the purpose of mentioning both interpretations is to suggest how the first one is almost always in play, indicating why the evidence of the senses—now understood, not in a narrowly empirical fashion, but as the only secure starting point for serious reflection—must be heeded whenever we offer historical judgments of any kind.

Wordsworth provides a firsthand account of how the French Revolution immediately impacted the lives of ordinary people when describing his land-ing in Calais on July 14, 1790, which would be commemorated as Federal Day and intensely remembered among all who shared in the new spirit of liberty (*P* VI, lines 355–82). The young poet also participated in this jubilant mood and then passed with fellow Englishmen into a pleasant monastery where food was served, before the same troupe entered the Convent of Chartreuse only to continue on their journey to Switzerland (*P* VI, lines 408–525). This entire sequence is presented as continuous, rather than as involving discrete spheres of existence; in other words, the opposition between a strictly secular event (the storming of the Bastille) and the openness of the community of brethren is not presented as a rupture but as a variation along the same register, thus suggesting how historical experience can be said to pervade political and religious life equally.[13]

However, as the young traveler proceeds on his journey, the metaphor of "crossing" is destabilized to the degree of generating a chiasmus that inscribes the *difference* between imagination and the events of history no less than it reinforces the power of change to alter the speaker's world in its entirety. The poet-narrator then relates how, on proceeding on their journey through the Alps, his own group temporarily separated from companions only to learn from a local mountain guide that they had *overshot their mark* and needed to backtrack to meet up with them (*P* VI, lines 501–19). Nonetheless, the task of reuniting with the group presupposes a physical gap to be surmounted as well as a metaphorical one, unless that same space can be articulated as either abyssal or cataleptic. Indeed, any sure footing that is recovered calls up an answer that "[t]ranslated by the feelings which we had/ Ends in this: we had crossed the Alps" (*P* VI, lines 523–24). The statement of the guide, an ordinary peasant who no doubt communicates the news of the crossing in French, is perhaps occluded by the difficulty of translating feelings into words; and yet, the same statement conveys two meanings of the word *crossing*: On the one hand, the poet-traveler has crossed the Alps in a physical sense; at the same time, the narrator has entered a new and largely unknown world that offers complex challenges to the poetic mind.

This challenge becomes abundantly clear when the narrator moves from what might have generated a historical digression to an enthusiastic tribute to the human imagination in the long passage that pertains to the Simplon Pass (*P* VI, lines 525–48). This lyrical celebration unfolds "in such strength/ Of usurpation, in such visitings / Of awful promise," as if to convey the sense of radical instability that the imagination can induce, just as it intimates a spirit of transhistorical "[g]reatness" in calling attention to the infinite space that surpasses temporal conditions as an opening to both space and time (*P* VI, lines 532–42). Wordsworth evokes the imagination as both a force and a spirit at this decisive juncture, which means that the deviations of any specific historical project become insubstantial when considered from the standpoint of our highest possibilities. Nonetheless, this same evocation can be read as an attempt to both acknowledge the work of history and to prevent the reader from misidentifying the mutations of any historical moment with the full range of what is possible from the perspective of the imagination.

Hence, we should not be surprised to discover that Wordsworth's sense of history is both hopeful and apprehensive, forward looking, and alarming in turns. Geoffrey Hartman has suggested how the space of the imagination can involve a departure from the pressures of history, freeing the mind from the limitations that poetry is able to surmount as a matter of principle. Arguing that in 1804, the imagination rather than nature became the poet's guide, Hartman compares this turn to what occurred when Beatrice became the guide to Dante through the assistance of Virgil: "It is not nature as such but nature indistinguishably blended with imagination that compels the poet along his negative way."[14] More recently, Paul Fry has drawn attention to the importance of Samuel Taylor Coleridge to the notion of the (aesthetic) imagination that emerges in passages that concern the Simplon Pass. Wordsworth is said to register the productive discrepancy between a more strictly Kantian view of the imagination, as ultimately subordinate to the ideas of reason, and a stubborn insistence on the empirical conditions that enable us to relate the imagination to some sort of sensuous background.[15] In Fry's reading, this emphasis need not imply a sharp disjunction between the human imagination and history, unless history itself is assumed to exceed the scope of what can be imagined.

Paul de Man, in contrast, has explored this disjunction in a style of criticism that rejects the imposition of any historical teleology on the narrator's quest. To support this reading, de Man encourages us to envision the poet-narrator's return to the vicinity of the Convent of Chartreuse, now revisited in the wake of the revolutionary upheaval that has transformed the surrounding landscape itself into a place of gloom and foreboding (P VI, lines 549–56). A scene of autumnal decay, presented in some detail, is followed by a spectacle that conflates "[t]umult and peace, the darkness and the light" that are "all like the workings of one mind, the features / Of the same face, blossoms upon one tree, / Characters of the great Apocalypse," so that the difference between image and emblem becomes all but indiscernible (P VI, lines 256–72).[16] For de Man, Wordsworth's later pessimism is already fully evident in this totalizing movement, which contaminates the earlier paean to the imagination that precedes the backward glance over the ruined ecclesiastical hermitage: "The future is present in history only as the remembering of a failed project that has become a menace."[17]

And yet, de Man's conclusion is inadequate, even if strongly articulated, for two reasons that need to be developed separately. First, Wordsworth's identification of the French Revolution with historical calamity implies a reference to the Terror, which is not specifically evoked but certainly constitutes the background to the sense of ruin that overwhelms the poet-narrator as he compares the convent before and after the great upheaval that initiated a strictly secular order in which religion no longer had a secure place. The violence that characterized the revolution may not have been apparent to the youthful narrator as he first arrived in Calais and welcomed the parading celebrants; however, the image of the convent retains a meaning that goes beyond the moment of heightened excitement. It becomes *aesthetic* in the precise sense of pointing to the transience of time, which can engulf all objects but also serve to commemorate what can be remembered. Of course, in using the word aesthetic in this sense, we depart from the aesthetics of Kant and his insistence that the judgment of the beautiful must be disinterested and that the experience of the sublime generally overwhelms the observing subject who is in need of ethical guidance. Indeed, this use of the word is more in harmony with what is prescribed by G. W. F. Hegel and the possibility of gathering and reflectively preserving what has been experienced historically. Moreover, in carrying the social orientation of Hegelian aesthetics perhaps beyond what Hegel himself specified, we might also say that the scene of arrival that the poet commemorates suggests how the communal setting prepares us for a new sense of openness that no longer operates on the difference between time and eternity. Thus, on a deeper level, this same image also points to the power of the imagination to enliven thoughts and feelings in a manner through which the future announces itself in a moment of hospitality that interrupts any attempt to foreclose the historical space in which the poet has been able to dwell.

SEMIOTIC THRESHOLDS

What has been discussed as Wordsworth's discovery of history raises the question of how the poet-narrator experiences the events of his own period in a manner that is both open to novelty and informed by a dynamic that is convincing. Although the poem might be discussed in terms of various "spots of time" that exceed the scope of all but the most comprehensive analyses, Wordsworth's narrative includes an account of his rather disappointing stay in London and later excursions into nature, just as his extended residence in Paris enables him to highlight the revolution as both a philosophical ideal and spectacle of unrestrained violence. However, all of these moments remain scattered and perhaps even fragmentary to the degree that they evade the possibility of narrative agency, which needs to be related to the poet-narrator before it can be ascribed a motivational significance. Nonetheless, Wordsworth's placing of the discourse on time is no accident but occurs *after* the poet-narrator has offered reflections on the events in France; moreover, it is communicated in a language that opens up the question of the will as a faculty that has been placed *under critique* by a rigorous use of gender categories, thus conveying a departure from standard forms of historical representation. It should be noted, for instance, that although the mind remains "lord and master" over the spots themselves, that same mind is said to exercise a feminine influence over outer experience, which functions as the "obedient master of her will" (*P* XI, lines 269–73).[18] By the same token, the autobiographical tone of the poem reemerges strongly when the poet-narrator identifies his younger sister and closest friend as companions whose proximity enabled him to bring his journey to a tentative conclusion. Although both figures lend themselves to "idealistic" reconstructions of the poem's end, we might also consider them as posing semiotic challenges to any reading that would place the narrative in a framework of hermeneutical closure.

The vision on Mount Snowdon that Wordsworth presents in the stunning conclusion unfolds so quickly that, dazzled by its energy and brilliance, we are likely to believe that the entire poem culminates in this single moment of solitary consciousness. But this impression is not so easily maintained when we consider, for instance, the primitive rites of sacrifice that are remembered to have occurred on the Plain of Sarum in Druidic times (*P* XII, lines 312–36). These rites remain a disturbing antecedent to the final vision but nonetheless compare to the abduction of Serena that occurs in Spenser's Renaissance epic, where the subsequent raising up of Pastorella constitutes a neo-Platonic allegory of transfigured nature. Thus, while Mount Acidale might be compared to Snowdon, Spenser's culminating vision pertains to artistic perfection, whereas Wordsworth's poet-narrator suggests "metaphysical" problems that are difficult to resolve in a traditional framework. The basic question in this regard concerns how, without evoking some form of divine intervention, Wordsworth can move from unjustifiable acts of violence to a single moment that mitigates, without necessarily absolving, previous wrongs.

We should not be surprised to learn that in addressing this question, Wordsworth returns to the question of the self, not primarily as a problem of agency but as an ontological concern that has been basic to the poem from the outset. What might seem surprising is the way that this concern is inseparable from an awareness of how the self is originally divided as "[t]wo consciousnesses" instead of one, so that it is both "conscious of itself / And of some other Being" (*P* II, lines 32–33). For Wordsworth, this "split" in consciousness is precisely what modernity conceals when he compares the self to a rock that has been fissured only to be replaced by a new meeting room, no doubt serving a pedagogical function that obstructs genuine self-consciousness (*P* II, lines 33–41). I would like to suggest, however, that this fissure is not to be understood in Cartesian terms, as the simple opposition of subject and object, but as an acknowledgment of a primordial division (*Urteilung*) in life itself, even when life is conceived as self-consciousness, as perhaps most clearly articulated in the writings of Graf Yorck, who forms a possible bridge between Hegel and a later phenomenology.[19]

This rift is ultimately transposed in the setting of Mount Snowdon, where the ocean opens up a chasm that enables the poet-narrator to name the human imagination as the faculty that somehow comprehends the whole of nature, ultimately subsuming it as an independent entity that cannot be thought as alien to the mind. But this movement does not occur at all once. Moreover, the split in consciousness that can be identified early in Wordsworth's poem is reproduced in a process of doubling that occurs between the narrator and the setting in which he finds himself. Thus, after the initial departure on a warm, summer night, the poet-narrator proceeds through mist and clouds to the base of the mountain, where the slow ascent begins, leading to a circle of light that is cast by the full moon, glowing more brightly overhead as the traveler moves forward (*P* XIII, lines 36–42). We have the distinct impression that the narrator's vision concerns the consciousness of the speaker, especially when the sudden influx of light and risen moon shine on the promontories and tempestuous sea below (*P* XIII, lines 42–53). We learn in that later context that "the Moon looked down upon this shew / In single glory," but the mist itself is said to be "fractured" rather than whole, so that the doubling that occurs between the narrator and nature also mirrors what occurred previously in the poem in the sphere of consciousness. While this scene is forbidding, the poet-narrator testifies to the possibility of equilibrium between the imagination and forces of nature, suggesting that the poem can be grounded through an analogy between them. At the same time, this analogy is radically unstable and cannot be sustained, precisely because the process of mirroring produces an infinite regress, instead of a coherent image of unity.

It is at this point that the narrative suggests how a psychoanalytical reading might be useful for navigating out of the impasse to which the poem also refers in attempting to check the power of nature to dominate poetic consciousness (*P* XIII, lines 60–65).[20] If narcissism is primarily pre-Oedipal in remaining locked in Lacan's *stade du miroir*, the way out of this doubling process is not to be found in the mechanisms of desire, which would assume a purely metonymic form in closed subject positions, but would imply what Julia Kristeva has called metaphor, now redefined as "a journey towards the visible" that (in the psychoanalytic session) allows for idealizing identification.[21] Now this identification would require an opening or "space" that combines emptiness and narcissism, which constitute "the zero degree of imagination" in a general economy of drives.[22] Indeed, rather than identify this move with the achievement of post-Oedipal adulthood, Kristeva returns to Sigmund Freud's own formulation of a "father of individual prehistory" to underscore the neutral condition in which identification can occur in a discourse that is (relatively) restrained, thus instituting the psychic space "that sets up love, the sign and repetition at the heart of the psyche."[23] This space is therefore an ethical one, not in the sense of providing specific rules to be followed in concrete situations but in enabling the individual to escape the overwhelming power of the drives so that the positing of goals, rather than the issuing of commands, can assume the form of freely chosen tasks.

How can this process be said to operate in Wordsworth's poem? When the poet-narrator suggests that the imagination conveys the image of a divine mind, transcending the individual and expressing perfection, he also refers to how this same image is raised by a certain "underpresence" that allows the mind to shape its contents out of what would otherwise remain external (*P* XIII, lines 66–84). Both the moon and the landscape of Snowdon are said to merely *resemble* what occurs in the imagination itself and that becomes "a genuine counterpart / and Brother of the glorious faculty / Which higher minds bear with them as their own" (*P* XIII, lines 84–90). In psychoanalytic terms, we might say that the imagination opens up a "space" in which the Logos can function—initially through the presence of the poet's sister, but also through his friendship with Coleridge—as a more fully "subjective" grounding, not by analogy but through the "usurpation" of nature, to end the mirroring process that arguments by analogy necessarily evoke. In the arrest of the mirroring process, the significance of the poetic image is transformed from a basically reflective mode to a speculative one, allowing the reader to bring together aesthetics and semiotics, to the degree that such a conjuncture is possible.

This enlarged conception of the imagination remains abstract, but just as Kant's categorical imperative is ethical only to the degree that it unfolds in a space this is empty of content, we might say that this figural space (lacking figures) provides the precondition for the acts of virtue that Wordsworth sometimes contends are the bequest of nature itself.[24] Nonetheless, once this phase of the poem has been attained, the role of time allows us to invoke the Hegelian appearance of the absolute idea where spirit attains presence through the memory of its many phases, just as it begins to more fully assess its journey through time. Nevertheless, we would not be able to think this moment unless the poem itself somehow embraced a dialogical component that invalidated the centrality of the solitary consciousness to this complete movement. A reading of the poem that appealed to Hegel at this juncture would need to step beyond a transcendental view of an ego that does not engage the world empirically. On the contrary, if the imagination "were reason in her most exalted mood," instead of a faculty that ceased to be important to the highest reaches of consciousness, then the "moving soul / Of our long labour" would acquire a different meaning altogether (*P* XIII, lines 159–65).

Wordsworth's belief in the value of the imagination is couched in terms that cannot be construed as an exaltation of an individual consciousness that surveys the past in a vacuum of time and history. The poet-narrator who speaks of reason as transformed imagination reminds us that the goal of his journey is inseparable from this same faculty and needs to be distinguished from the metaphysical notion of a disembodied observer who surveys life in a detached manner. Particularly when the poet's sister is evoked toward the end of the poem, we cannot assume that the question of gender is tangential to the poem as a whole (P XIII, line 204–39). Her appearance argues against a reading that would identify the poet-narrator with a mode of self-consciousness that failed to acknowledge the existence of others and suggests a transformation of the *moral* reason of Kant, elevating desire from the limited significance that it possessed in critical thought to the meaning that it acquires for Hegel. Her appearance cannot be subsumed under abstract categories but introduces a *semiotic* dimension in a poem that only seems to follow a one-sided narrative from the somewhat adolescent yearning of the young male poet to the "heroic" propensities of the adult witness to historical upheaval. This dimension is integral to the poem and requires that the reader put out of mind the lingering suspicion that the author has merely revised the "classical" project of assuming an updated role as epic historian.

Moreover, we feel that it is no accident when the poet-narrator, who is Wordsworth himself, once again introduces his listener and companion poet, Coleridge, whose name becomes a motive for celebrating the value of poetry itself (P XIII, lines 339–61). Referring at last to the early literary narratives that Coleridge produced in the effort to communicate a common purpose to their first audience, Wordsworth reminds us that his own purpose has been to render "the history of a Poet's mind" in a manner that his friend would find acceptable (P XIII, lines 383–403). This history presupposes a listener who was unlike the poet who composed the poem that can be read from beginning to end. The "dialogical" aspect of Wordsworth's telling is not only evident in the conversation that the poet evokes in this brief tribute to a literary colleague, but also in different stages of the poem itself, which show the reader how various modes of consciousness often exist side by side, and sometimes in conflict with one another. The narrative that comes to an end would not have been what is was if it only unfolded subjectively without also telling a story that drew together the many strands of a life in which growth and travel, life and transformation, were inextricably woven into a plausible account of what came to pass in one time for a powerful and irreplaceable poet.

NOTES

1. William Wordsworth, *The Prelude, or Growth of a Poet's Mind*, ed. Ernest de Selincourt (Oxford: Oxford University Press, 1970). All citations refer to this text.
2. Wordsworth can be read through an "older rhetoric" that engaged the English poets who are central to eighteenth-century neoclassicism (James Thompson, Thomas Gray, William Collins, and others). Lindenberger suggests that this reading is based on the opposition between

pathos and ethos, with the latter evoking the poet's interest in concrete life. See Herbert Lindenberger, *On Wordworth's Prelude* (Princeton, NJ: Princeton University Press, 1963), 20–39. Although my own approach does not follow this traditional path, I feel that this opposition rather clearly frames Wordsworth's problem as a poet, without allowing us to come to terms with how it was invalidated through his response to the temporality of moral experience.

3. Kant's thesis of a *sensus communis* is crucial to his argument that the aesthetic has public significance in enabling subjects to share judgments and, in this way, express a common humanity. It can be seen that Kant was indebted to the Enlightenment belief that human nature may even form the basis for shared governance in his aesthetic theory, which paradoxically can be viewed as political, even when it was not intended to be read that way. For details, see Kant, *Critique of Judgment*, sections 20–22, 40, 92–95, 169–73.

4. This entire episode in Book III supports Harold Bloom's thesis that the poet works under an "anxiety of influence," and it argues just as strongly that Wordsworth was uncomfortable with Milton because his own poetry was, in some respects, non-Miltonic. Taking his cue from Søren Kierkegaard and Martin Heidegger, Bloom suggests that poetry is no longer a predominantly representational medium and that the poet's reading is a misreading insofar as repetition is never a mere "reproduction" of a previous poem but always a creative variation. See Harold Bloom, *The Anxiety of Influence: A Theory of Poetry* (Oxford: Oxford University Press, 1997).

5. Kant places poetry over all the other arts in a manner that anticipates the elevation of poetry that occurs in Hegel, and perhaps in a similar spirit, he presents poetry as an art that enhances human freedom. It should be noted that in bringing together poetry and freedom, Kant emphasizes the *inadequacy* of language to what it suggests in the mode of the aesthetic: "It expands the mind by setting the Imagination at liberty; and by offering within the limits of a given concept amid the unbounded variety of possible forms accordant therewith, that which unites the presentment of this concept with a wealth of thought, to which no verbal expression is completely adequate; and so rising aesthetically to Ideas."

See Kant, *Critique of Judgment*, section 53, p. 215. Kant also distinguishes poetry from rhetoric and refers to the latter as a purely dialectical art, which in this case would mean that it was calculated to please the listener in the style of the orator as opposed to that of the genuine poet. We might apply this definition to what Wordsworth has to say about the imagination, while mentioning that his youthful intoxication with Milton can be read as a "staging" of the great poet along rhetorical, rather than poetic, lines.

6. Gadamer offers a history of hermeneutics that begins with Schleiermacher and culminates in Dilthey, who elevated the role of "lived experience" (*Erlebnis*) as a fundamental datum for the interpretation of life, literature, and history. In his critique of early hermeneutics, Gadamer argues that Dilthey was encumbered by a Cartesian methodology that posited disconnected experiences as discrete units, thus precipitating his move toward historicism and the crisis in "values" that followed in its wake. For details, see especially Hans-Georg Gadamer, *Truth and Method*, trans. Joel Weinsheimer and Donald G. Marshall (New York: Crossroad Publishing, 1991), 173–97, 218–42.

7. When viewed in this way, the theory of repetition first emerges in Sigmund Freud, *Beyond the Pleasure Principle*, which subverts classical psychoanalytic theory because it prevents repetition from being subordinated to the development of the adult ego. (A more detailed discussion of how repetition can be related to the traumas of modern life can be found in my discussion of Benjamin and Freud, particularly in the conclusion to this book). Bloom's notion of repetition is comparatively hopeful insofar as it emphasizes the possibility of divergence from instinctual patterns that otherwise would block the creative process. From the latter standpoint, Wordsworth's use of the Discharged Soldier's repeated tale would not inscribe the "fate" of the poet but only warns of a poetic failure that is by no means inevitable.

8. For details, see Mary Jacobus, *Romanticism, Writing and Sexual Difference: Essays on The Prelude* (New York Oxford University Press, 1989), 69–83. Wordsworth's evocation of John Newton indicates how the stranded voyager would "draw his diagrams with the long stick upon the sand, and thus / Did oft beguile his sorrow, and almost / Forget his feeling"—while conjuring a Blakean image of Urizenic repression that can be related to the blank gaze of the Discharged Soldier. Admittedly, Wordsworth swerves away from this implicit condemnation,

but he momentarily implicates both the former slave trader and the soldier in this forceful image.

9. Ibid., 83–93.

10. Benjamin's description of Paul Klee's painting, *Angelus Novus*, allows him to argue that progress is an evasion of the forces that enable time to "stand still" in heightened moments of insight. The implied suggestion is also that such moments constitute images through which aesthetics assumes an emancipatory role. See Walter Benjamin, "Theses on the Philosophy of History," in *Illuminations* (New York: Schocken Books, 1968), 257–58.

11. This possible dissolution of form often assumes the guise of writing, which is not to be confused with what the poet attempts to embrace in an ongoing struggle with tradition but is instead a force that disrupts all symbolic satisfaction, endangering the possibility of self-reflection and the consciousness peculiar to it: "It not so much the burden of the past that inhabits him as this insubstantiality inherent in all writing—in autobiography as well as epic." See Jacobus, *Romanticism, Writing and Sexual Difference*, 158.

12. Fry notes that the narrator in *Don Quixote* is said to have derived his tale from an Arab storyteller, probably Cide Hamete Benengeli, who is not believed to be dependable, thus contributing to the dreamlike quality of this episode, which might also evoke the *malin génie* of Descartes as well as the condition of Samuel Taylor Coleridge, whose life by then had become a waking dream. The upshot of these conjunctures is especially disturbing: "What this madman tells the dreamer is that the stone and the shell, the always reliable basis of Wordsworth's ontology, are not a stone and a shell but books." See Paul H. Fry, *Wordsworth and the Poetry of What We Are* (New Haven, CT: Yale University Press, 2008), 236. It is no accident that this discussion of books follows the appearance of the Discharged Soldier, who not only "introduces those painful feelings that one can experience on behalf of all humanity" but also foregrounds perishability and the failure of garments to adequately name what they cover. Ibid, 134–35.

13. Hartman emphasizes how, in depicting the Convent of Chartreuse, Wordsworth is more concerned with nature than with a specifically religious institution. This concern, however, does not express a belief in nature that derives from materialistic premises: "The conquest of nature is here aided by an impulse from nature herself. The monastery's sublime natural setting *bodies forth* the ghostliness of things." Geffrey Hartmann, *Wordsworth's Poetry 1789 – 1814* (New Haven, CT: Yale University Press, 1964), 58.

14. Ibid., 48.

15. Aesthetics in passages involving the Simplon Pass would seem to be more Kantian than Hegelian insofar as the imagination is difficult to assimilate either to the order of reason or to an empirical sphere from which it might be said to derive. Fry argues that in such passages, Wordsworth is again writing with Coleridge in mind, and ultimately tends toward the transcendental option, which Fry interprets psychologically to offset the pull of nature that otherwise would undermine aesthetic transcendence. For details, see Fry, *Wordsworth and the Poetry of What We Are*, 123–25. Although sympathetic to Fry, I feel that we need to move cautiously and integrate a temporal dimension into the poem that Paul de Man acknowledges and then seeks to discredit.

16. The opposition between image and emblem underlies Paul de Man's analysis of how W. B. Yeats allegedly broke with Romantic naturalism, especially in his early book, *The Wind in the Reeds*, where he abandoned a poetics based on sense experience to embrace a style of writing that conceived of nature itself as sign rather than substance. For de Man, Romanticism and French Symbolism never departed from a belief that the poet discovered the word in objects, whereas Yeats's "emblematical" poetry suggests that the object-world is language in origin. For details, see Paul de Man, "Image and Emblem in Yeats," in *The Rhetoric of Romanticism* (New York: Columbia University Press, 1984), 162–72. Jacobus indeed argues that "[t]his entire passage, with its simile of the cave as book, unmasks the hidden terror of the Vale of Condo" just as it "compensates for the threat to the self [that is] inherent in writing, offering, as a privileged instance of writing, *apocalyptic* writing." See Jacobus, *Romanticism, Writing and Sexual Difference*, 14.

17. Paul de Man, "Wordsworth and Hölderlin," in *The Rhetoric of Romanticism* (New York: Columbia University Press, 1984), 58–59. De Man's sensitivity to textuality is not in itself a

liability, but it does short-circuit the possibility of connecting Wordsworth's poem to the public events that de Man, in the same essay, begins to name in situating the journey through the Alps in historical time: "The poetry partakes of the interiority as well as the reflection; it is an act of the mind that allows it to turn from one to the other." Ibid., 59. Evoking Romantic ideology at its most sophisticated, de Man's use of the word "reflection" in this statement clearly evokes the "philosophy of reflection" from which Hegel sought to extricate himself in his diatribes against Kant, Johann Gottlieb Fichte, Friedrich Heinrich Jacobi, and Friedrich Wilhelm Schelling.

18. See William H. Galperin, *Revision and Authority in Wordsworth: The Interpretation of a Career* (Philadelphia: University of Pennsylvania Press, 1989), 184. Galperin argues that "the inarticulate freedom to be inferred from the spots" needs to be contrasted with "the represented, idealized freedoms of enfranchisement and revolution," allowing the political legacy of a masculine mind (and will) to be placed in question. In his conclusion, however, Galperin argues that Wordsworth's project can be read as a kind of "self-fathering," whereas my own conclusion attempts to navigate between solipsism and semiotic nondifferentiation as twin dangers. Galperin's position, in contrast to my own, implies that the (poetic) self is unified through a paternal metaphor as the poem comes to an end. Ibid., 189–91.

19. Gadamer acknowledges that Count Graf York's writings on the topic of life are suggestive as well as inconclusive but nonetheless begin to bring together Hegel and Husserl. For details, see Gadamer, *Truth and Method*, 251–54.

20. Jacobus also explores a psychoanalytic reading of the poem and uses Kristeva as a guide to this purpose. See Jacobus, *Romanticism, Writing and Sexual Difference*, 271–73. However, the notion of figural space that emerges in my subsequent interpretation of the poem formalizes the qualitative leap from Kant's theory of the imagination to Hegel's reason, while also employing Freud's "individual father of prehistory" as an ethical trope. Without merging Hegel and Freud, I attempt to use their systems of thought as complementary.

21. Julia Kristeva, "Freud and Love: Treatment and Its Discontents," in *The Kristeva Reader*, edited by Moril Moi (New York: Columbia University Press, 1986), 247–48.

22. Ibid., 242.

23. Ibid., 243–44.

24. Citing Kant's *Critique of Judgment* as a key text in this reading, Jacobus maintains that the Snowdon incident "becomes a sign of imminent usurpation, or the workings of an imagination paradoxically driven to exceed the confines of the nature on which it depends." See Jacobus, *Romanticism, Writing and Sexual Difference*, 291. Although Kant's aesthetic theory is pertinent to a rigorous reading of the Snowdon passages, I suggest that "imminent usurpation" oversteps Kant and anticipates Hegel, whose (ethical) reason preserves aspects of the Kantian legacy but needs to be considered as an alternative model.

Chapter Four

Shelley's Double Vision

Figural Counterworlds

Percy Bysshe Shelley's final and unfinished poem, *The Triumph of Life* (1822), has elicited critical responses that are not only inconsistent but complicate the author's position in the Romantic canon.[1] This chapter explores how the figure of Jean-Jacques Rousseau performs a special role in *The Triumph of Life*, a poem that also contains a disturbing vision of Enlightenment history. I begin with a discussion of Harold Bloom's reading of the poem to focus on how crucial tropes structure the literary work as a whole. This part of the discussion entails close reading but also enables me to explain how the poem offers a critique of Romantic naturalism while having ethical implications, even when ethics tends to curtail the interpretive possibilities that the poem contains. The poem is then examined through Paul de Man's deconstructive criticism, which foregrounds the linguistic dimension in the poem, just as it suggests how autobiographical aspects underlie a poem that can be read as a scene of tropological conflict in which figures dissolve in a never-ending series of rhetorical shifts. However, in my subsequent analyses, I attempt to renovate a (re)figurative reading to ultimately adopt Hegelian aesthetics as the basis for placing the poem in a context that remains open to the some of the most powerful and, potentially, disturbing insights of psychoanalysis.

NATURE AS ADVERSARY

A reading of *The Triumph of Life* that explored the poem in its complete unfolding would have to examine how language assumes different registers in the work as a whole. In an early study, Bloom diverges from aesthetic approaches on one level in arguing that Shelley's final poem can be read through the practice of mythmaking that enabled the poet to compose his entire oeuvre. At the same time, Bloom also argues that this poem should be considered on its own, rather than as continuous with the previous works when he provides a close reading that is uninfluenced by other poems to which it might be compared. Indeed, he focuses on some of the most disturbing aspects of this literary work, while indicating the likely sources that Shelley drew on in writing the poem. The result is an overview that is quite different from a linguistic approach, not only in its details but also, more importantly, in its philosophical implications. In brief, Bloom's analysis allows us to identify the figure of Rousseau (as distinguished from the Rousseau who lived in time) with naturalistic reductionism, which assumes a theoretical guise whenever abstract cognition reifies our sense of life, substituting the experience of life with intellectualized representations of it. However, the possibility of going beyond naturalistic reductionism only emerges once Bloom begins to explore the figure of the brightly lit chariot, one of the two figures that lie at the heart of the poem as a structured performance.

Near the beginning of his analysis, Bloom warns against the pervasive critical tendency to interpret various figures in terms of conventional associations and to freeze meaning before the poem unfolds. A. C. Bradley's manner of reading Shelley through Plato and Dante thus prevents the figure of the sun from merging in its various modalities, which need to be investigated contextually before they can be delimited.[2] Countering Bradley's suggestion that the figure of the sun, as it initially emerges in the poem, determines the entire course of the narrative, Bloom notes that the narrator falls asleep and enters a dream state that opposes the movement of nature (lines 21–30). For Bloom, the figure of the sun provides a potential contrast to the inner life of the poet: "As all things rise, in answer to the summons of the sun, the poet does the reverse; he makes day into night, night into his day," and, in this manner, poetry separates itself from the processes of nature (lines 26–27).[3] The fate of the sun in this poem is complicated but needs to be related to the development of the poem as it progresses: "In the vision of Rousseau, which takes place within the poet-protagonist's vision, the ultimately obscuring sun will figure again."[4]

From this perspective, the appearance of the Chariot of Life can be interpreted as an inversion of life, rather than as its fulfillment. Bloom argues that the chariot itself and the dancers who gather around it add up to a vision of natural man that can be linked to a certain reading of Blake (lines 41–175). Significantly, the light that surrounds the chariot is said to be too cold for the sun and stars that glow behind it (lines 77–79). Drawing on the work of Northrop Frye, Bloom traces the origin of this figure back to Ezekiel, whose vision previously influenced William Blake, but also to John Milton and

Dante; however, he also emphasizes that the chariot *cannot* be viewed as either divine or beneficent because it harbors a deformed Shape who turns the traditional allusion into a dark parody (lines 86–95).[5] The narrator compares the throngs that dance near the chariot to a trunk that has lost its vitality and has entered its final winter (lines 120–27). The Chariot of Life is therefore an inversion of the lifeworld as a place of phenomenological unity. The fate of the dancers who move ahead of the chariot only heightens the ferocity of their dance (lines 138–60).

Shelley's final poem not only includes the poet-narrator but its literary structure also includes Rousseau's discourse, which involves a conversation and crucial intertext. Bloom acknowledges that the poem alludes to Dante's "Purgatorio," cantos xxviii and xxix, where the protagonist's encounter with Matilda is echoed in the narrator's inquiry concerning the identity of Rousseau (lines 176–78).[6] The irony of the addressee's response is compounded once we learn that Rousseau no longer has eyes and simply cannot see (lines 187–88). In arguing against Bradley, Bloom then emphasizes how the parallel to Dante must break down once we admit that Rousseau cannot guide Shelley as Virgil guided the medieval Christian poet and observed him with hope.[7] From another standpoint, however, we might consider how Rousseau is not only a suitable guide for a poet like Shelley but also emerges as a witness when he recounts aspects of his own past that become instructive, even though they have assumed an unalterable form, because of the afterlife to which he has been condemned.

While Virgil serves as a detached guide in Dante's quest, Rousseau remembers what he accomplished in a world where he once suffered and has come to endure (lines 200–7). Paul Dawson has argued that Shelley's Rousseau, in contrast to Dante's Virgil, assumes a dual function that compounds his significance.[8] The fallen Rousseau is seriously constrained in his movements, but he combines the notion of witnessing with a verbal reenactment of his life on earth, which he invites the poet-narrator to consider in the scheme of its unfolding. This is not exactly guidance in the positive sense; moreover, the sensibility that is brought to view in his words cannot discover itself in any one object or find its home in finite experience. Dawson also suggests that his words constitute a discourse that is not always trustworthy: "The only testimony that Rousseau has to impart is his own account of his career, and this evidence is not necessarily to be interpreted in the way that Rousseau would choose."[9] For this reason, Rousseau's unreliability as narrator qualifies not only his credibility as a representative figure but also raises questions as to whether his place in the poem is less about history than about the way that history is sometimes narrated.

Indeed, after this testimony is revealed to us in both its failings and impact on history, we might recall that Shelley's own view of Rousseau was profoundly ambiguous and irreducible to any easy judgment. Edward Duffy has shown how Shelley would have been susceptible to the popular understanding of Rousseau as a sign of the sensibility and also as a harbinger of the French Revolution.[10] Timothy Clark, however, has argued that Shelley's picture of Rousseau after 1815 began to include a more strongly biographical interest that probably derives from his reading of the *Confessions*.[11] The idea of placing Rousseau both inside and outside the European Enlightenment is suggested in the poem, which positions him as succumbing to weariness, rather than as chained to the chariot in a vast procession that includes Greek philosophers, a prominent Renaissance scientist, and the compromised intellectuals of modern times (lines 208–73). Rousseau clearly views himself as among the moderns, especially when he contrasts the impersonal virtues of the classical poets and the passions that his own words expressed and then instilled among those who heeded them (lines 274–80). This same self-image, however, does not have to be viewed in positive terms once the reader notices that Rousseau is apparently exhausted, rather than vigorous and enthusiastic.

Rousseau's dream of passage also suggests a movement from youth to adulthood and the fading of divine light into quotidian reality (lines 308–42). Bloom refers to Wordsworth's Immortality Ode as both an influence on Shelley and also as a source of confusion for later commentators.[12] But his most serious criticism is reserved for Bradley's broadly Platonic reading of the "Shape all light," the figure of the woman who appears in Rousseau's dream from the depths of a cavern as rainbow, song, and harbinger of forgetfulness (lines 352–81). In sharp opposition to Bradley, Bloom extends his previous reading of the poem to include this later and crucial figure. The scene from Dante's "Purgatorio" that was mentioned before again provides the basis for Shelley's unique inversion: "The Shape is a diabolic parody is the Witch of Atlas or Dante's Matilda; that is part of the meaning of the 'Triumph'."[13] This reading seems to be supported in full when we learn of how the Shape suddenly reduces the thoughts of the dreaming Rousseau to dying embers, putting out "the lamps of light" that shone before him and turning the daylight into darkness (lines 382–93). Moreover, the Luciferian aspect of this event is communicated in the description of the Chariot of Life that finally overtakes the dreamer (lines 412–38). The theme of triumph is suggested ironically when "a moving arch of victory" is thrown into the air by the *second* appearance of Iris, who now deeply problematizes her earlier role (lines 439–45). For Bloom, this entire sequence is a composite of moments that acquire a sinister and perhaps violent meaning only as the shape of light emerges and Rousseau responds to its appearance.

Bloom admits that the shape of light is perceived from different standpoints before its hidden qualities become manifest, but this admission does not alter his manner of interpreting the shape as essentially demonic. Dawson argues, however, that Bloom's thesis is just as misleading as the thesis that it was designed to criticize. In other words, our reading of the poem gains as little from Bloom's Gnosticism as it does from Bradley's Platonism. We need to raise the level of the debate so that the meaning of the shape is no longer based on a specific moral assumption: "It is the assumption that Rousseau makes, and it consists in seeing the individual's salvation or damnation as originating outside himself."[14] This perceptive criticism indicates the possibility of investigating Rousseau's discourse, not as an irrefutable source of truth but as the vehicle through which we can learn about Rousseau, especially as the poet-narrator comes to understand him. Something that the poem demonstrates is that Rousseau either seeks a perfect embodiment of the ideal in the world of experience or supposes that the ideal only exists beyond it. From such a standpoint, Rousseau views life "only as the absence of value, as all that is opposed to the ideal Shape and has displaced it."[15]

AUTOBIOGRAPHY AS LANGUAGE

While often brilliant and insightful, Paul de Man's reading of *The Triumph of Life* in his essay, "Shelley Disfigured," is haunted by the belief that the poem is autobiographical in some unclear sense. Early in this essay, de Man remarks on how the final version of the poem offers us the spectacle of the poet as in "close proximity to Rousseau" in contrast to what is suggested in previous versions, so that the poet's own fate becomes hard to disentangle from that of Rousseau.[16] De Man argues later in this same discussion that the narrative of Rousseau as enacted in the poem enables various questions to be asked but never answered. When the figure of Rousseau enquires into the origin, place, and purpose of the first Shape who visits him, the answer produced turns out to be the spectacle that prompted the question (lines 177–88). De Man comments: "This movement of effacing and of forgetting becomes prominent in the text and dispels any illusion of dialectical progress or regress."[17] It would seem that this movement cancels out the possibility of understanding just as it recurs in a structured process that only seems to subsume it.

De Man goes on to underscore the allegedly mechanical nature of the operation that becomes ascendant in Rousseau's encounter with this mysterious entity.[18] We are hardly surprised, then, when de Man comes to identify the figure of Rousseau with the event of defacement, which is conceived in violent terms and invariably merge his own literary testimony with the movement of history itself.[19] After explaining what he means by defacement, de Man returns to Shelley's own words to emphasize how unconscious elements indeed structure the dream of Rousseau that lies at the heart of the poem. In this context, de Man (perhaps echoing Bloom) mentions how Wordsworth's Immortality Ode allowed readers to interpret Shelley in Platonic terms, whereas the play between presence and absence is more complicated than the metaphor of birth suggests.[20] The uncontrollable nature of this play informs de Man's description of whatever light overwhelms both the narrator and Rousseau, early and late in the poem.

These crucial points already indicate how de Man tends to focus on matters of language rather than on specific passages that allow us to read the poem as a play of tropes. In de Man's account of Rousseau's dream, water is linked to synesthesia and the reference to Iris performs a traditional role in a local economy of signs (lines 335–57).[21] Disfigurement, which is closely related to defacement, is basically the process through which water erodes whatever has been marked, thus constituting a metaphor for an interpretative scheme in which differences are blurred and faces can no longer be perceived as discrete. And yet, the "Shape all light" that appears later in this developing and rapidly shifting narrative is not explored in the context of its initial appearance. Shelley's use of light imagery is instead placed in opposition to the more severe demands of cognition. De Man notes that Shelley's poem engages the theme of music in a manner that foregrounds "the literal and figural aspects of language."[22] Music in this case, however, is not an ally of representation but instead constitutes the figure as an illusion of meaning.[23] In other words, the figure of light is conceived nonaesthetically as a site of disarticulation, rather than as an aesthetic vision in its own right or as a discourse with a delimited significance: "We now understand the shape of the figure to be the figure for the figurality of all signification.[24]

The outcome of de Man's analysis requires that we read *The Triumph of Life* as a poem that erases all of Shelley's previous work because figuration is the perpetual (re)enactment of a violent forgetting. This would imply that Shelley's final poem was always already inscribed in the movement of a literary journey that was in some sense over even before it began. From this standpoint, Shelley's own death could be viewed not simply as the culmination of a series of actions that may have literary significance but as equivalent to the death of Rousseau himself. Moreover, Shelley's poem becomes autobiographical when we cannot separate the disfigurement of Rousseau from the death of Shelley, whose demise ceases to be an unrelated occurrence but constitutes the origin of the poem. Finally, this same analysis seems to argue that the poem *prevents* reading when it foregrounds a movement toward blockage that cannot be surmounted because it enshrines disfiguration is its movement and, thus, compromises reading itself.

And yet, could Shelley's poem allow the moment of blockage to be envisioned in terms of a more dynamic (but nonetheless non-totalizing) relationship to the possibility of meaning?[25] Such an approach would allow us to envision how tropes not only repeat themselves but also interlock in poetic narratives that remain perpetually open to their own performativity. The openness of poetic narrative in this case would not coincide with unreadability but with possibilities of reading that were perhaps interminable but also allow the reader to grasp how identities acquire provisional and comparative meaning in textual arrangements. In developing this approach, we first need to return to the poem and clarify how figuration performs a positive role in the poem, without necessarily arguing that it can ground the reading in a manner that escapes the pressures of time and history. But such a view of figuration would alter the usual meaning assigned to the word "aesthetic," particularly because it has come to be associated with Immanuel Kant's attempt to limit its significance.

FIGURAL CONJUNCTIONS

Bloom and de Man acknowledge that the Chariot of Life implicitly inverts the values of life, but neither critic is prepared to read Shelley's poem in aesthetic terms or at least not in a manner that argues on behalf of aesthetics as crucial to a sustained appreciation of the poem. De Man's stronger resistance to aesthetics is significant in this regard because it derives from a linguistic disjunction that has been formalized as a theory of figuration. But if de Man seems to depart from a focus on appearances, Bloom falls short of allowing the literary text to reveal itself as an aesthetic unfolding to the degree that his approach to Shelley's poem correlates reader response to a moral conception of the figure. Without denying that figures can have moral implications, we require a different approach to the figure if the poem is to be appreciated in aesthetic terms. For instance, the process through which the figure might be apprehended as *changing* in the mind of the dreamer—in this case, Rousseau as a literary construct—might constitute a line of interpretation that illuminates different attitudes that cannot be reduced to a single meaning.

An interpretive problem then emerges, not in the aesthetics of reading but in the questionable assumption that aesthetics is primarily concerned with our *immediate* experience of either the world or cultural objects. By reducing the scope of aesthetics to this focus on immediacy, we damage our ability to respond to what is nonpresent in what appears to us. To return again to Shelley's poem, we should be able to consider the possibility that Rousseau's dream is not simply a negative journey into darkness and error but a journey that acquires poignancy from loss and division. The cold light of the chariot and the wild music that accompanies the throngs who gather beneath it do not possess aesthetic meaning, but the world to which they belong is one that provides insight into what has been inverted. The demonic element cannot supply the poem with its basic directives, but the poem is more than a moral typology; it engages the reader unpredictably on the level of both thought and sense experience. Shelley employs aesthetics in this manner when providing evidence of how various changes are registered in the structure of a given discourse, namely, the discourse of the fallen Rousseau, whose impressions of the "Shape all light" are relatively distinct from whatever the poet-narrator perceives as he listens to the account that the dreamer gives of the dream itself.

Clark has discussed how the "Shape all light" introduces two kinds of imagery that perform different roles in Rousseau's dream.[26] On the other hand, the shape first emerges through light on water that enters the dreamer's mind and only becomes disturbing in time, destroying his thoughts and extinguishing their power as he gazes on her. But in a different manner, the sounds associated with the shape pass from harmonious combinations to increasingly monotonous ones, culminating in the jarring rhythms of the final dance. Clark describes this entire movement as a "remorseless process" that invalidates any attempt to blame Rousseau for his ultimate plight. Shelley's poem instead provides a description of what Rousseau undergoes in a dream that reflects the dreamer's undoing. It also offers his "most succinct account of the active power's *inherent* waning and abandonment whose destructive effects had already been analyzed in the series of figures from *Alastor* onwards."[27]

Shelley's poem also combines belief and skepticism in a way that invigorates aesthetic response as an alternative to the death-in-life that the poem inscribes. Ronald Tetreault has remarked that the tendency toward skepticism that is prominent in Shelley's final poem is recurrent in his work, and that this skepticism does not acquire the virtue of necessity because of the poet's accidental drowning.[28] The prevalence of water imagery can be related to doubt and uncertainty but just as often serves as the prelude to what Paul Ricoeur has called "refiguration," a phenomenological term that describes how the reader can achieve new meaning on a narrative basis and reverse the process of defiguration that de Man assumes to be central to the poem.[29] In short, the aesthetic play that engages the literary reader allows for a reflective assimilation of complete passages that should not be confused with the externalization of abstract traits. Although the process of defiguration is undeniable, we also need to relate both the figure of Rousseau and the "Shape all light" as aspects of an aesthetic whole that allows for success and insight, even if the moment of illumination cannot be sustained outside the experience of consciousness.

Aesthetic play reaches its denouement before the poem concludes. As the Chariot of Life prepares its final ascent, the spirit of Rousseau remembers Dante as if to provide a nonappearing witness to impending doom but also to invoke a sphere of light and music that can dispel the darkness of the inverted world (lines 469–80). It was Dante who returned to the world from his journey through the afterlife to tell "the wondrous story / How all things are transformed, except Love," thus providing a name for what cannot be seen but informs the memory of the poet, just as it functions as the perpetual source of change without being overwhelmed by change itself. Love, in this brief memorial, is no longer a figure of seduction but becomes the name of a movement toward refiguration that allows us to imagine what connects us to possibilities that remain unrealized.[30]

Shelley's final poem pays tribute to life, even when it calls attention to how life values have been inverted. The poem as it stands ends on a question—"What is Life?"—to which the narrator does not offer a response (line 544). But this question evokes a response, if not a definition, in a short essay that enables Shelley to evoke more fully what his poem describes as in frantic disarray: "Life, and the world, or whatever we call that which we are and feel, is an astounding thing. The mist of familiarity obscures from us the world of our being. We are struck with admiration at some of its transparent modifications, but it is itself the great miracle."[31] We cannot help but read this evocation as a kind of commentary on *The Triumph of Life*, which remained to be composed when these words were written. What this tribute irrefutably indicates is that Shelley's poem is informed by an awareness of an unfamiliar world that does not have to lie "behind the scenes" or negate everyday life experience. Clarity concerning our true being is what enables life to emerge as "the great miracle" within a movement that is discontinuous, unstable and divided.

In arguing that Enlightenment science severed the connection between life and values, Alfred North Whitehead remarks that both Wordsworth and Shelley responded to an ensuing intellectual and cultural crisis by asking a series of questions that concern the issue of what is enduring in nature.[32] The "factical" dimension that the poets affirmed is in some sense irrefutable, but the "events" that emerge in their poetry are both transient and actual, forming sites of "value" that are aspects of concrete experience.[33] Values are not judgments but coherent interpretations that inform worlds of meaning. If actuality exists for us in this sense, we are close to interpreting it as an *aesthetic* phenomenon, which transcends the existence of particular things but does not allow us to dismiss questions of value.[34] Whitehead insists that although our sense of value is inseparable from facts that are shaped through limitation, things are not self-sufficient but endure as aesthetic for brief periods of time: "The endurance of an entity represents the attainment of limited aesthetic success, though if we look beyond it to its external effects it may represent an aesthetic failure. The conflict is the presage of disruption."[35] Whitehead's reflections on aesthetic attainment are easy to apply to Shelley's final poem, where the shape that presents itself to the fallen Rousseau points back to the moment of birth as the process of individuation and carries within it the moment of disruption, surmounting the limitations of natural consciousness itself.

Chapter 4
SPECTERS OF CHANGE

"The Triumph of Life" suggests Romanticism's proximity to the European Enlightenment but also registers Rousseau's distance from the intellectual milieu to which he owed troubled allegiance. We see this proximity and distance when a certain strain of Romanticism enters the aesthetic tradition that began with Kant and continues early during the nineteenth century in the work of both Friedrich Schiller and G. W. F. Hegel. What Kant in the early period of Romanticism would characterize as aesthetic is also inseparable from a crisis that erupted in the sphere of society and politics, giving the name of Rousseau a currency that may have been unfair to his legacy but is difficult to disentangle from the reception of his works and the legend of his character. Rousseau's ambiguous relation to the Enlightenment is part and parcel of his inability to wrest free from the system of thought that remained intact until the aesthetic revolution challenged it on a philosophical level. Nonetheless, Rousseau's modernity emerges most intensely in his passionate diatribes against a society that was indeed "unnatural" in the sense of separating essence from existence, while enshrining this opposition in systems that had no use for his poetic reveries.

On one level, we might say that Shelley is correct in placing Rousseau among the great figures of the Enlightenment who bring about an apotheosis of representation. The opening of Rousseau's own autobiography is telling in this regard, insofar as the author insists on unprecedented originality and, at the same stroke, invites readers to observe his total personhood through a presentation of the self.[36] The contradictory aspects of this initiatory gesture are not always evident, but they are easy to discern once we reflect on the historical limitations of a writer who is unable to represent without rendering the "origin" of representation unattainable.[37] That system was fully intact when Rousseau began to mingle lyric passages of singular intensity with political reflections that evoke civic perfection in the guise of natural order. However, Rousseau does not overturn nature as representation in paving the way for aesthetic reflection any more than he clears a path to history that others believe that they can explore by following him. He lives and thinks on a fault line that breaks open at a future date but remains only an imperceptible infraction for the duration of his time in the world, which neither contains nor fully rejects him.

And yet, on another level, if the age of representation is nourished by Rousseau during its final years, we might also say that Shelley is nonetheless correct to assimilate him to a sort of whirlwind that embraces the major figures of the Enlightenment in addition to its historical precursor, and to suggest that the final member of this series is the culmination of a catastrophe. This same catastrophe, however, is perhaps more strongly anticipated in Rousseau's own disordered imagination than through acts of defiance that evoke a sense of nature that he cannot represent. Here is Rousseau's description of his own process of composition:

> N'avez-vous point du quelquefois l'opéra en Italie? Dans le changement de scène, il règne sur ces grands théâtres un désordre désagréable et qui dure assez longtemps; toutes les décorations sont entremêlées on voit de touts parts un tiraillement qui faites peine, on croit que tout va renverser; cependant peu à peu tout arrange, rein ne manque, et l'on est tout surpris de voir succéder à ce long tumulte un spectacle ravissant. Cette manoeuvre est à peu près celle qui se fair dans mon cerveau quand je veux écrit. Si j'avais su premièrement attendre, et puis rendre leur beauté les choses qui s'y sont ainsi peintes, peu d'auteurs m'auraient surpassé.
> [Have you ever been to the opera in Italy? During changes in scenery, unpleasant disorder reigns for a long time in the great theatres; all of the furniture is intertwined; we sense on all sides a pressure that hurts and believe that everything is upside down: then, little by little, everything falls into place, nothing is missing, and we are surprised to see a delightful spectacle following this long tumult. That is somewhat like the process that goes on in my brain when I want to write. If I had known in the past how first to wait and then render in their beauty all of the things that were painted in my imagination, few authors would have surpassed me.][38]

This description is significant for various reasons. First, the tone is not that of a discordant revolutionary but that of an eighteenth-century man of letters who is at pains to describe the spontaneous character of intellectual labor. Rousseau uses a casual metaphor that derives from opera, a genre of music that is not always assumed to be highly serious. Moreover, the comparison of the human mind to a stage set seems deliberately anti-Platonic because it admits of the arbitrary and capricious, frankly evoking the power of semiotics over the certainties of semantics, instead of subordinating its own mental activity to preestablished order. In the end, Rousseau tells us that only a lack of patience prevented him from basing his thoughts on what might have been more fully visualized: "If I had known in the past how first to wait and then render in their beauty all of the things that were painted in my imagination, few authors would have surpassed me."

What Rousseau does not allow us to do is position himself as the founder of aesthetics in the formal sense, however much his style of expression might suggest that he deserves to be recognized as a forerunner of this new discipline. This honor of course goes to Kant, whose *Critique of Judgment* is neither a direct response to a historical upheaval or an "autonomous" construction that is unrelated to what occurred in the political sphere. Kant's tentative support for the French Revolution that "finds in the hearts of all spectators (who are not engaged in this game themselves) a wishful participation that borders closely on enthusiasm" and is said to originate in human nature.[39] Moreover, the significance of Rousseau to Kant's aesthetic theory can be aligned to both its social milieu and its emancipatory potential.[40] However, what optimistic readings of Kant do not always acknowledge is the turbulence that underlies his own aesthetic project, which is threatened by an inherent opposition between the beautiful and the sublime as modes of experience that are too dissimilar to be contained easily in the same propaedeutic.

Although the judgment of the beautiful clearly falls under the aegis of the aesthetic, Kant theorizes the sublime as a border condition that lies somewhere between the properly aesthetic and the rule of the ethical, thus destabilizing the entire sphere of aesthetic judgment. If the two figures that lie at the heart of "The Triumph of Life" can be read to suggest a movement from increasing turbulence to enhanced stability, we might consider Shelley's poem to be an exemplary exercise in Kantian aesthetics that reverses the order in which the philosopher presents the beautiful and the sublime. However, this reading would interpret the two figures as basically separate, rather than as comparable experiences that may have common features. It would also marginalize what is inherently disruptive in the poem, which is hardly reassuring in its melancholy conclusion.

At just this juncture, a Hegelian reading of Shelley's poem begins to acquire credibility, not as a means of reconciling two figures in a manner to suggest hermeneutical continuity but as a basis for bringing together opposing terms of a severe contrast through an underlying negation, or trauma, that sustains both of them.[41] And yet, in this case, negation is not to be understood as a solitary positioning that might be performed by a reader who merely denies the authority of one figure to affirm that of a succeeding figure, nor does it entail the simple process of substitution whereby one figure is dissolved on behalf of a more credible alternative. Instead, Shelley's poem suggests that both figures are aspects of an extended negation to the degree that they "participate" in the mutual disruption within which nature ceases to be an abstract concern but loses its remoteness in the upsurge of aesthetic experience. Such a reading would not be a purely formal one, insofar as it specifies how this same disruption would be analogous to the event of the French Revolution as both the culmination and practical negation of the Enlightenment as an organized attempt to master nature through science and politics. However, rather than merely assert the occurrence of this disruption, this same reading shows how this disruption is carried into the poem in the mode of the aesthetic, which is now reshaped to engage the historical rather than to exclude it on a disciplinary basis.

The attentive reader may object to the blurring of distinctions that occurs in both Shelley's poem and in the Hegelian account of the French Revolution. In Shelley's poem, the fate of Rousseau seems to carry the history of European Enlightenment (including its precursors) along with it, undermining the possibility of sustaining the basic difference between scientific reason and Rousseau's wild fantasies, implying fanaticism and mental derangement.

Hegel as well seems to be willing to identify aspects of the Enlightenment with the excesses of the Reign of Terror, thus complicating any attempt to "save" a certain use of reason from historical aberrations.[42] And yet, what might be read as a leveling of all differences in Shelley's poem is presented as Rousseau's perspective on history, not that of the narrator or the author as such. This process casts light on what we might call the Rousseauian moment, particularly as it underwent extreme politicization during the revolutionary insurgency. By the same token, Hegel's implicit strictures against Maximilien Robespierre could be read as only one application of Rousseau's contract theory to the body politic, not as the final word on what Rousseau composed as passionate thinker or man of letters.

The blurring of the distinction between Rousseau and his intellectual milieu requires a critical rethinking of how the Enlightenment might be assessed as a complex phenomenon that also contains dangers that cannot be explained away as accidental aberrations. Shelley's treatment of this theme does not rest on a strict chronology in which Rousseau's demise comes at the end of an epoch that begins in the classical past. Rousseau is the focus of a crisis that requires a revision of how the past can be viewed and therefore becomes a sign of discontinuity, not as the caesura in a continuum, but as a break that brings a new—hitherto undisclosed—past into growing prominence. Hegel's criticisms of the French Revolution do not constitute an unequivocal rejection of it but provide a trenchant analysis of the metaphysical pretentions of the revolutionary extremists, who took nature to heart only to turn it against the possibility of an enlarged polis. And in both cases, the encoding of history does not abolish other narrative options that might have produced different results because the Enlightenment (which for Hegel is a relatively distinct phenomenon) remains "true" in a way that is not *reducible* to the fate of the revolution as it succumbed to abstract violence.[43] In Shelley's figuring of Rousseau, as in Hegel's treatment of French history, the past is either presented as an unsustainable burden or as a movement indicating the inadequacies of abstract thought, constituting the "metaphysics" that a dialectical approach to history was intended to surpass.

Moreover, the inclusion of this traumatic component in both the figuring of Rousseau and the unfolding of the French Revolution acquires long-range significance in Shelley's poem. Through the agency of disruption, aesthetics itself is reconfigured in a new "distribution of the sensible" (Jacques Rancière) that bears the impact of history at the moment that it departs from classical representation. In viewing the figures of both Rousseau and Dante as aspects of a singular experience that can be raised to the level of thought, if not perfectly unified, we begin to apprehend how aesthetics can be concerned with temporality and even how temporal disruption can be transformed into a "textual" possibility through the narrative of the medieval poet, who provides a way of reckoning with the spreading chaos and disorder that finally submerges the language of the narrator. Hence the word of Love, rather than the image of Dante, is what raises the poem to the sublime heights of momentary perfection, which never ceases to be an aesthetic accomplishment when it enacts the appearance of its undoing.

Shelley's final poem can be read as a performance that points back to the enabling preconditions of conscious thought itself, which provide the "being" in which the figure appears—through both irony and the language of spiritual awareness—as an emissary of what cannot be cast asunder. However, Shelley's poem is not dialectical in the sense of enabling him to master, even on a symbolic level, what has occurred and continues to occur as a cultural narrative. The poem depends on enabling conditions that are not to be grasped on the level of history alone. These conditions include an awareness of what was living and now appears only as nonliving, thus instituting the trauma whereby a certain political project has faltered only to survive through its aesthetic transfiguration. Nevertheless, because the figure of life that triumphs is not detachable from this failure or from the trauma that it presupposes, the movement of the poem as a whole is not a journey beyond time but rather a traversal within time that never coincides with either ideal perfection or the attainment of static repose.

The poetry of both Wordsworth and Shelley can be described as aesthetic but in a sense that acknowledges how time and history need to be experienced as forces of disruption in our reception of literature, instead of implying inaction and withdrawal from vital concerns. The role of narrative in each case is crucial to the retrieval of the aesthetic on new grounds; however, Wordsworth does not employ narrative in a manner that classical (or neoclassical) poetry strongly anticipates, and when Shelley offers an allegorical specter of Enlightened reason, he does not in this way affirm religious authority, even as a poet whose appreciation of Dante enables him to celebrate the word Love in an exalted form. Our task then becomes one of reconceiving narrative along the lines of both Wordsworth and Shelley, not necessarily on the basis of poetry as a genre but in a manner that nonetheless is able to recognize how narrative sequences are inscribed with nonclassical elements, that is to say, with disturbing and destabilizing invitations to read against the grain of critical orthodoxy. An aesthetic position that excludes a concern for narrative on principle may have scientific justification but it is also one that is hard to relate to literary works that are intrinsically diegetic and hard to integrate into a canon of taste. The following study was therefore conceived as a demonstration of how Kant's position, which ultimately separates transcendence from everyday life, is inadequate within the framework of literary history; moreover, it was also developed as a further clarification of how literature contains features that would have been inassimilable to classical or even Kantian aesthetics but acquire a novel significance when viewed in post-Kantian terms.

NOTES

1. See Percy Bysshe Shelley, *The Triumph of Life* in *Percy Bysshe Shelley: The Major Works* ed. Zachary Leader and Michael O'Neill (Oxford: Oxford University Press, 2003), 604–21.
2. Compare Harold Bloom, *Shelley's Mythmaking* (Ithaca, NY: Cornell University Press, 1959), 224, and A. C. Bradley, "Notes on Shelley's 'Triumph of Life'," *Modern Language Review* 9 (1914): 444.
3. Bloom, *Shelley's Mythmaking*, 225.
4. Bloom, *Shelley's Mythmaking*, 226.
5. Bloom, *Shelley's Mythmaking*, 231–42, and Northrop Frye, *Fearful Symmetry* (Princeton, NJ: Princeton University Press, 1947), 272–73.
6. Bloom, *Shelley's Mythmaking*, 254–55, and Dante, *Purgatorio*, xxvii–xxix, *The Divine Comedy*, trans. Allen Mandelbaum (New York: Alfred A. Knopf, 1995), 512–21.
7. Compare Bloom, *Shelley's Mythmaking*, 255, and Bradley, "Notes on Shelley's 'Triumph of Life'," 443.
8. P. M. S. Dawson, *The Unacknowledged Legislator: Shelley and Politics* (Oxford: Clarendon Press, 1980), 261.
9. Ibid., p. 263.
10. See Edward Duffy, *Rousseau in England: The Context for Shelley's Critique of the Enlightenment* (Berkeley: University of California Press, 1979). For the importance of Rousseau to Shelley's *The Triumph of Life*, see pages 232–39 and 241–56.
11. Timothy Clark, *Embodying Revolution: The Figure of the Poet in Shelley* (Oxford: Oxford University Press, 1980), 205.
12. Bloom, *Shelley's Mythmaking*, 263–65.
13. Ibid., 267. Bloom's statement counters the argument that the "Shape all light" is a manifestation of the ideal, an insistence that can be found in Bradley, "Notes on Shelley's 'Triumph of Life'," 455. However, although Bradley's reading of this figure may be incorrect, we are not necessarily in the position of having to read the poem as a whole apart from "ideal" considerations.
14. Dawson, *The Unacknowledged Legislator*, 273.
15. Ibid., p. 280.
16. Paul de Man, "Shelley Disfigured," in *The Rhetoric of Romanticism* (New York: Columbia University Press, 1984), 94.
17. Ibid., 98.
18. Ibid., 99–100.
19. Ibid., 101–3.
20. Ibid., 104–5.
21. Ibid., 107–8.
22. Ibid., 113.
23. Ibid., 114–15.
24. Ibid., 116.
25. In discussing *The Triumph of Life*, Jacques Derrida suggests that the paradox of reading emerges in the translation of any text, which depends on what lies between transparency and opacity: "Totally translatable, and it disappears as text, as writing, as a body of language [langue]. Totally untranslatable, even within what is believed to be one language, and it dies immediately." From this standpoint, the text becomes a "living on" or species of writing that is always already the repetition (of a trauma, for instance), even before it can be read as an original instance. See Jacques Derrida, "Living On: Border Lines," in *Deconstruction and Criticism*, trans. James Hulbert, ed. Harold Bloom (New York: Continuum, 1999), 102–3.
26. Clark, *Embodying Revolution*, 147.
27. Ibid., 247.
28. Ronald Tetreault, "Shelley: Style and Substance" in *The New Shelley: Later Twentieth-Century Views*, ed. G. Kim Blank (New York: St. Martin's Press, 1991), 22.
29. Ibid., p. 24. Paul Ricoeur's concept of "refiguration" is pertinent in this regard, implying as it does the effort on the part of the reader to carry the literary work beyond the stage of the

written and into the life of the responsive reader. For Ricoeur, refiguration demonstrates that the work of narrative is not simply about plot but involves modes of reception that can engage the reader on multiple levels. For a definition of this term as a contribution to phenomenology, see Paul Ricoeur, *Time and Narrative*, trans. Kathleen McLaughlin and David Pellaver (Chicago: University of Chicago Press, 1985), 2:160.

30. Tetreault, "Shelley: Style and Substance," 30.

31. Percy Bysshe Shelley, "On Life" in *Percy Bysshe Shelley: The Major Works*, ed. Zachary Leader and Michael O'Neill (Oxford: Oxford University Press, 2003), 633.

32. Alfred North Whitehead, "The Romantic Reaction," *Science in the Modern World* (New York: Free Press, 1967), 92.

33. Ibid, p. 93.

34. Friedrich Nietzsche famously argues in *The Birth of Tragedy* that "it is only as an *aesthetic phenomenon* that existence and the world are eternally *justified*," thus anticipating the phenomenological interpretation of world. See Friedrich Nietzsche, *The Birth of Tragedy and the Case of Wagner*, trans. Walter Kaufmann (New York: Vintage Books, 1967), 53. Nietzsche also assumes, perhaps as a mere thought experiment, the existence of a spectator and author of the world who contemplates what he has created, thereby limiting the artist's knowledge to a mere portion of a greater whole.

35. Whitehead, "The Romantic Reaction," 94.

36. Jean-Jacques Rousseau contends in the opening of his autobiography that his enterprise has no precedent and that it will have no successor. He claims that his goal is to render an image of himself that is true to nature, even though no likeness can be found in all of creation. Given to self-dramatization, he also contends that in breaking the mold that formed him, Nature left no basis for reconstructing what only his own account can bring to light. See Jean-Jacques Rousseau, *The Confessions* (New York: Penguin Books, 1953), 17. The author's short preamble argues that only his own writing can provide some sense of the life lived, a claim that becomes highly ironic once his own tendencies for dissimulation are openly acknowledged.

37. The discordant nature of Rousseau's appeal to the reader is emphasized in Jean Starobinski, *Jean-Jacques Rousseau: Transparency and Obstruction*, trans. Arthur Goldhammer (Chicago: University of Chicago Press, 1988). Starobinski argues that Rousseau, as autobiographer, frequently engages the reader as an onlooker, but that this effort is undermined when the author claims to be inaccessible. His reading maintains that publicity and the recession of origins form irreconcilable strands in Rousseau's literary project. This discrepancy, which is expressed rhetorically in Rousseau's *Confessions*, is a major sign that marks the fault line between two eras.

38. Jean-Jacques Rousseau, *Les Confessions de J.-J. Rousseau*, ed. George Sand (Paris: Charpentier, 1811), 116–17.

39. Immanuel Kant, *The Conflict of Faculties* (New York: Abaris Books, 1992), 153.

40. Hannah Arendt has developed the thesis that Kant's political philosophy remained undeveloped but is nonetheless implicit in the *Critique of Judgment*, which can be linked to his interpretation of the French Revolution. Cf. Hannah Arendt, *Lectures on Kant's Political Philosophy* (Chicago: University of Chicago Press, 1992). Adorno has specifically identified Rousseau as enabling Kant in his aesthetic project to preserve the revolutionary heritage of the early bourgeois epoch. Cf. Adorno, *Aesthetic Theory*, 63–64.

41. Rebecca Comay argues that Hegel's interpretation of the French Revolution reveals a sort of trauma, not only in the sphere of history but also as a defining feature of philosophical texts, beginning with those of Kant as analyzed by Hegel himself. While hardly spared the wounds of this trauma, Hegel anticipates psychoanalysis in his reading of Kant, his critique of Kantian morality and the aesthetic ideology that flows from it. See especially, Rebecca Comay, *Mourning Sickness: Hegel and the French Revolution* (Stanford: Stanford University Press, 2011), 96–109.

42. Compare G. W. F. Hegel, *Phänomenologie des Geistes* (Frankfurt am Main: Suhrkamp Verlag, 1976), 431–41; *The Phenomenology of Spirit*, trans. A. V. Miller (Oxford: Oxford University Press, 1977), 355–63.

43. Hegel, *The Phenomenology of Spirit*, 349–55.

Chapter Five

Proust and Aesthetics

A Narrative Sensibility

The simple realization that art is related to life, even when it is irreducible to narratives of actual occurrences, animates the philosophical approach to aesthetic experience that emerges in many, if not all, of its post-Kantian versions. For Jacques Rancière, this realization prepares us for the emergence of an aesthetic unconscious that demonstrates how the opposition between everyday life and its partial transcendence can be negotiated in literary terms. In this chapter, Rancière's reading of Marcel Proust's masterwork, *In Search of Lost Time* (*À la Recherche du temps perdu*), is examined in terms of how language performs a unique role in the fictional text, eventually allowing life and literature to be reconciled in nineteenth-century literary history. The reading of Proust becomes more complicated, however, when the critical tradition is shown to have taken up various uses of language as a problem of narrative, particularly in the wake of modern linguistics. This aspect of my discussion will enable me to explore a more specifically Hegelian approach to Proust, but also one that argues for a revised approach to modern aesthetics. My concluding remarks suggest how Julia Kristeva, particularly in the wake of psychoanalytic criticism, developed an approach to time and the imagination that provides insights into Proustian aesthetics and the narrative sensibility that his work exemplifies.

AESTHETICS AND THE UNCONSCIOUS

Before the difference between everyday life and transcendence becomes paradigmatic for artistic production during the nineteenth century, the category of the aesthetic was articulated in a manner that already presupposed the possibility of a rudimentary conception of the unconscious. For Rancière, Freudian thought only became possible through what we might call the aesthetic revolution, which enabled the regime of the aesthetic to replace the classical reign of poetics.[1] However, to grasp how aesthetics served as the precondition for the psychoanalytic hypotheses of the unconscious, we need to take a closer look at the construction of the aesthetic in both its Kantian and post-Kantian modalities. Kristeva indicated in her early work how aesthetics, emerging in the wake of a new approach to language, was no longer dependent on Kant's theory of judgment. Rancière has suggested how Kant's aesthetics was always already more than a theory of judgment, particularly when it is viewed from the broader perspective of its transformation throughout the nineteenth century.

Kant's decisive role in aesthetics is thus misconstrued if it is translated into formalization, pure and simple. Indeed, Kant's unique advance is inseparable from the conjunction of thought and nonthought that emerges within the aesthetic sphere itself. This conjunction is not only alien to classical systems but requires that we rethink how the subject is unified in Kant's propaedeutic so that the strictures of morality do not deform the aesthetic possibilities that somehow sustain them. At the same time, this conjunction also indicates a rupture with rationalism that has far-reaching consequences in the history of aesthetics, particularly when it indicates the limits of cognition as a faculty that seeks to integrate opposition into a unity. If the subject no longer operates entirely as ancillary to universal criteria, then it must perpetually rediscover a discordance between thought and what cannot be assimilated to conceptual understanding. Discordance might be in play whenever the subject consults the sensibility to judge the object in aesthetic terms, a maneuver that invokes a tension between faculties. Kant's theoretical advance therefore occurs at a risk that only becomes evident in the work of his successors. Rancière charts two aesthetic approaches that diverge in Kant's wake, both of which bear the initial division between intellect and sensibility within their opposed trajectories.[2]

First, G. W. F. Hegel rearticulates this division as an attempt to discover the immanence of the Logos in the pathos of life itself. This project places the prior opposition between thought and nonthought in a dialectical context that provides an expanded role for reason, rather than a continuation of the division between life and Logos. Hegel, like Immanuel Kant, develops an aesthetic theory that testifies to a rift in its own sphere concerning what cannot be assimilated to classical models. Nonetheless, more strongly than Kant, Hegel enables us to grasp, on a figural level, various contradictions that might be called "objective"—insofar as objectivity as a term can be used to describe psychic models. For instance, Hegel provides reflections on the narrative of Oedipus as a tale of transgression whereby the tragic protagonist effectively challenges the authority of the Sphinx in solving a riddle that ironically reveals his own fate. This same action, while marking the difference between man and beast, also indicates a relationship between the human and the nonhuman, just as it suggests a mode of descent that dialectics reveals in the mode of the aesthetic.[3]

Second, the Kantian advance is also given expression in the aesthetics of Arthur Schopenhauer and Friedrich Nietzsche. If Hegel sought the Logos in its other, Kant's successors were equally motivated by the possibility of discovering pathos in places where reason is generally assumed to be the undisputed master. Schopenhauer's will is not only a metaphysical category that subverts received interpretations of Kant's noumenon but also provides a gateway to an aesthetic of self-denial, as opposed to blind self-interest, in affirming the most questionable aspects of human existence. The will that exceeds representation is also the will that can turn against itself, insofar as its origin cannot be subjected to conscious control. By the same token, in his early work on Greek drama, Nietzsche proposes the myth of Dionysus as a unifying ground but never ceases to emphasize how primordial oneness is inseparable from an experience of ecstasy that divides as much as it unifies.[4] Although the aesthetic implications of translating the Logos into a mode of pathos are in some respects the opposite of what Hegel accomplishes, Schopenhauer and Nietzsche also sustain the difference between thought and nonthought, which underlies the movement of dialectics as well.

When applied to the reading of literature, the emergence of nonthought in the aesthetic binary can be related to the discovery of a more savage Greek world that was perhaps discovered by Friedrich Hölderlin, even before it was celebrated by Nietzsche. Rancière discusses how Pierre Corneille and Voltaire were unable to integrate the agonies of Oedipus into their work as dramatists for reasons of decorum but more importantly because the sufferings of the protagonist could not be effectively represented on stage.[5] The key to their resistance is no doubt representation, which constitutes the limit of the aesthetic in an era that has no vocabulary for presenting nonthought in dramatic terms. Corneille responds to this problem by rewriting the original Oedipus narrative to redistribute the possibility of guilt in three different characters. Voltaire in turn responds to the challenge of Oedipus in claiming that the subject is so defective that he simply could not have committed the crimes that are attributed to him. Corneille and Voltaire are united in excluding the trace of nonthought from their respective dramas, that is to say, they exclude the horrible excess that Oedipus personified in his haste and fury because of the problem that these passions would produce in a regime of representation.

This regime must be clearly distinguished from the regime of aesthetics but continues to impact the work of cognition, soon after its moment in the cultural sphere has passed. Perhaps for this reason, we might have difficulty in assigning a meaningful date to the birth of psychoanalysis insofar as it participates in two moments that are essentially different. The signs of its birth are present in the moment of aesthetics, but its historical emergence occurs later. Aesthetics is a formal discipline that allows for a new distribution of the sensible and also provides a basis for identifying art as art in terms that are no longer amenable to the order of representation. Psychoanalysis recognizes the power of nonthought to form, or at least preform, thought itself. Like aesthetics, psychoanalysis views the subject as both active and passive but as somehow combining oppositions in a process that implicitly decenters thinking in a manner that deprives thought of the capacity to coincide with its contents. Psychoanalysis also acknowledges that the conscious mind cannot escape the operation of the unconscious, just as it liberates a repressed content from what otherwise might violate the principles of aesthetic legitimacy. However, the possibility of rapprochement breaks down once we begin to examine how the problem of representation performs a different role in each discipline.

For Rancière, psychoanalysis contrasts methodologically to aesthetics when it organizes psychic events as temporal occurrences and provides explanations for their significance. First, in attempting to define psychoanalysis as a science, Sigmund Freud tends to maintain the value of placing psychic events in a temporal sequence. The practice of segmenting mental occurrences violates the noncausal basis for philosophical aesthetics, which does not necessarily pit explanation against description but focuses on the upsurge of sensible experience as an originary phenomenon. We might say that for this reason, aesthetics is an ontology in the precise sense of presupposing the elements within which art can be identified, apart from which the (modern) work would be unavailable to criticism. But in contrast to this minimal ontology, psychoanalysis in general operates as a system of explanations and in this way serves the purpose of furthering a therapeutic goal. Rancière argues that Freud chose the hieroglyph as the form of "mute speech" that offers the "labor of interpretation and the hope of healing" in contrast to the inarticulate power of the voiceless, thus restoring the classical sense of recognition that aesthetics had banished.[6] In adopting this model, Freud also abandons cultural texts at crucial junctures and speculates on how agents would have acted if they had been living individuals whose deeds could be anticipated by psychoanalysis.

As a reader of literary texts, however, Rancière is willing to carry a well-defined aesthetic approach as far as it can go, without suspending whatever psychoanalytic claims might be contained within a critical analysis. Nevertheless, if the notion of an aesthetic unconscious is to have any critical validity, we need to situate cultural production within a particular opposition that the philosophical exponents of aesthetics sought to address in offering an attempted resolution. For Rancière, the aesthetics of Kant and Friedrich

Schiller provide the parameters for reading literary texts that display various terms of this opposition, but this same opposition does not begin to display a coherent pattern until one century draws to a close and a new century offers a textual basis for a symbolic resolution that somehow integrates many of the partial insights of the preceding period. The notion of the aesthetic unconscious, rather than a purely psychoanalytic one, informs Rancière's analysis, and sustains his reading of Proust as well as his interpretation of recent French literary history.

PROUST'S DOUBLE NARRATIVE

Rancière has argued that Proust's work as a novelist shows us how modern literature articulates and attempts to resolve a historical crisis that most clearly emerges in the aesthetic theories of Kant and Schiller. According to this reading model, Proust indicates how the dominant conflict in nineteenth-century French literature was carried beyond a mere opposition and given a new aesthetic significance in the modern novel. His work demonstrates that aesthetics is a historical discourse that attempts to negotiate the opposition between transcendence and everyday life in fictional terms. More specifically, Rancière argues that metaphor in Proust's work has the capacity to transform a sense of doubleness into a new understanding of experience; it therefore functions as the sign of this difference and as the motive for bringing this opposition into the boundaries of art. Metaphor, in this argument, allows Proust to distance us from the everyday, that it to say, to produce fictive language, and then to employ form in a manner that introduces a new sense of the world through literature.

The boundaries between art and life are unstable, thus allowing literature to assume a vitality that refutes the strong opposition between the fictive and the real. In her own work on Proust, Kristeva has identified the doubleness of Proust's art with a cojoining of sensibility and intellect that challenges the classical (linguistic) opposition between sign and signified: "It is important to realize that the smallest unit in Proust's writings is not the word-sign but a *doublet*: sense *and* image, a represented perception or an embodied image."[7] This inherent flexibility allows us to imagine how specific texts engage the reader on a sensory level and also invite a reenvisioning of lived experience. For Rancière, Proust is exemplary in showing us how aesthetic experience provides the key to the relationship between art and life that fiction presupposes and transforms. Proust's originality in this argument can be traced back to a breakthrough that is not unrelated to the author's reading of *Arabian Nights*. Hence, if *impression* is the talisman that opens the cave of material, "architecture" is the word that allows the writer to produce literary works that are formally unified.[8] But the literary work of art is not constricted in a domain that simply dispenses with the sensibility. The impression derives from a singularity that is nonreferential; it does not communicate a message but bespeaks the unthinkable coalescence of a peculiar shock and the duality of metaphor. This shock both points back to life experience and marks the site where a new duality emerges through the vehicle of the literary work, which becomes the vehicle through which the redistribution of the sensible achieves singular meaning.

The Proustian impression is both a sudden and unpredictable response to lived experience and enables the reader to work out a transformative response to the literary text. In emphasizing the doubleness at the level of the impression, Rancière shows us that Proust's relationship to the past recalls both heterogeneity and the possibility of form that allows the literary work to acquire intelligibility through reading and interpretation:

> The material of the book can only be essential if it is necessary. It is necessary only if we are not free to choose it, that is, if it is imposed on us. But for Proust this impression takes on some obligatory characteristics: The impression is obligatory material insofar as it is a sign; it is already writing. The impression is double not only because it is felt in two temporalities at once; it is double because it is both the shock that disorients, breaks the boundaries of the world, and brings forth primordial chaos, creates meaning, establishes correspondences, and determines vocations. Dionysos's realm is that of Apollo and Hermes.[9]

When conceived in this manner, doubleness in Proust does not exclude shock but nonetheless must be distinguished from what Charles Baudelaire experienced and, according to Walter Benjamin, enabled him to write a new kind of poetry. Benjamin had contended previously that the two authors are in fact quite different, noting that Proust refashioned Bergsonian memory for artistic ends: "Proust immediately confronts this involuntary memory with a voluntary memory, one that is in the service of the intellect."[10] For Baudelaire, in contrast, the shock experience was not only primary but was also intended to be read historically, thus introducing a mode of time that Proust does not strongly evoke.[11]

Rancière describes how Proust combines sensation and language in a metaphorical leap into aesthetic plurality in contrast to the historical distance that Baudelaire's poetry so often encodes. This metaphorical leap is not metaphysical in the old sense because it involves primordial contact with sensations that suddenly decenter us when we come closest to what is near.[12] It does not sustain an opposition between a true world and an apparent world as the starting point for either the construction or the appreciation of art objects. Instead, metaphor is what springs into being when the shock experience disrupts the patterns of everyday life:

> It is metaphor alone that unfolds and makes manifest the *one* of pure sensation that punctuates the concatenations of habits and beliefs. Metaphor, as a power of both order and disorder, is charged with a twofold labor. It brings together distant objects and makes their coming-together speak. But metaphor also undoes the laws of representation. It is metaphor that inverts the earth and sun in Elstir's canvas, in conformity with the truth of vision that is also the truth of its allusion.[13]

Metaphor suggests how Proust attempts to undo the initial shock that temporarily destroys the narrator's relation to objects and to resist the tendency to stabilize the literary work through verbal representation. However, unlike what classical rhetoric codifies as adequate to its own canon, metaphor in modern literature suggests that life and art communicate—but only through their difference.[14]

This reconfiguration of the relationship between art and life is not to be observed within the framework of the literary work alone. Rancière also helps us envision this configuration through Proust's contribution to literary history, which can be read as a successful effort to resolve an aesthetic conflict. Proust is able to produce a literature that moves beyond the twofold impasse that emerges in "the Flaubertian frivolity of subject that drags form down to its insignificance and the Mallarméan essentiality that leads to the paralysis of writing."[15] Gustave Flaubert's contribution to the prose tradition shows us how the goal of verbal transparency culminates in an irrevocable plunge into material life. For Rancière, this plunge can be related to the project of abolishing art in time, which ought to coincide with the productive transposition of art into life and the abandonment of aesthetics through its fulfillment. However, instead of achieving this goal, Rancière suggests that Flaubert fails to move beyond a mere negation of aesthetics, while he abandons life to an immersion in material content. This failure is demonstrated in both *Sentimental Education* (*L'Éducation sentimental*) and *Madame Bovary*, two novels in which major characters demonstrate how blind ambition prevents aesthetic distance from fusing personal experience with self-understanding. Stéphane Mallarmé produces tightly structured poems, such as the early "*Hérodiade*" and "*L'après-midi d'un faune*" as well as the magisterial "*Plusiers sonnets*," inaugurating a style of formal writing that forsakes mundane experience, while alluding to a realm of pure essences that cannot be retrieved.[16] And yet, while envisioning poetry as a dramatic spectacle through which the body politic acquires utopian features, Mallarmé also fails to indicate how art can be translated into a redemption of everyday life.

While the avant-gardes have typically sought to fulfill the promise of aesthetics by closing the gap between art and life, Proust's masterwork can be shown to narrate the difference between art and life and to stage their possible reunion. Rancière argues that Proust balances this unstable opposition through form and content, thus producing an image of the aesthetic that testifies to the singularity of a writer who captured the significance of time in a redistribution of the sensible. In approaching this contradiction, Proust is exemplary in demonstrating how the oscillation between opposed principles lends coherence to the work of literature that invites us to read in view of a dual task. The two "ways" that are identified in the first and concluding books of Proust's great narrative encode opposed aesthetic options that remain operative throughout this text and indicate how life as lived is not incompatible with the transcendental thrust of the literary imagination.

Hence, in *Swann's Way* (*Du Côté de chez Swann*), if "Méséglise way" leads to a flat plain where the possibility of love is intermingled with the signs of natural growth, "Guermantes way" evokes a medieval past through water lilies and the steeple of Saint-Hilaire.[17] But this opposition is not contrived; it expresses two desires at the same time: First, it shows how quotidian reality is always already shot through with a sense of what surpasses and comes to us in material form; second, it shows how this same spiritual intimation introduces a tension with everyday life in various forms that escape the present. Proust in these passages echoes his early study of John Ruskin, but the perspectives of Marcel differ from those of Proust in the same way that a memoir differs from a unified work of art. At the same time, we would misread Proust if the opposition between narrator and author were assigned a strongly Platonic meaning.[18] Proust evokes a circularity that can be read as a meditation on the aesthetic tradition and also performs a formal role in bringing together discursive strands that are shown to be related, even if they are not inseparable. This is why in *Time Regained* (*Le Temps retrouvé*), the reader is ultimately encouraged to link back to Combray on learning that both the social poseur, Madame Verdurin, and Swann's daughter, Gilberte, have married into the Guermantes's family.[19] The interpenetration of aesthetics and a world that is in touch with sensory experience is crucial to the construction of the Proustian text, just as it is basic to how key documents in the aesthetic tradition invite us to break with rigid dichotomies. The result is a resolution of oppositions that were initially declared in Schiller's aesthetics and that has shaped subsequent cultural history. For Rancière, the double hermeneutic animating Proust's work provides a moving image of a discourse that has not been exhausted any more than it has been fully understood.

METONYMY AND METAPHOR

Rancière's interpretation of Proust draws on a revitalized conception of metaphor as an aesthetic experience that allegedly demonstrates how an initial sense of disorientation becomes the precondition for a more adequate understanding of the Proustian text. Rancière distinguishes the element of shock that is at work in Proust's use of metaphor from what can be found in Baudelaire, thus enabling the reader to maintain the capacity to move beyond spatial proximity in matters of language use and to facilitate transformations of the text on an imaginal basis. However, the earlier history of Proust criticism indicates a variety of approaches concerning how the reader integrates verbal tropes in a global response to an ongoing narrative. Stephen Ullmann's *Style in the French Novel* is no doubt a breakthrough study on how Proust used metonymic language to enable metaphor to achieve singular effects. His argument, however, is not only important in its linguistic implications but opened up a line of inquiry that is narratological in the broadest sense, thus allowing a series of important questions to be asked concerning how the author's work is composed.

Gerard Genette's structuralist appropriation of Ullmann's discoveries is to be found in "*Metonymie chez* Proust," which argues that the privileging of metonym over metaphor erodes a tendency toward essentialism that is evident in the words of Marcel and arguably has mislead readers into believing that the author himself was a sort of theologian manqué.[20] Moreover, in an argument that further develops Roman Jakobson's well-known article on the role of both metonymy and metaphor in linguistic pathologies, Genette also raises the question of how these two rhetorical devices operate together in forming literary narratives.[21] Although Jakobson clearly identifies metonymy with combination and metaphor with substitution, Genette argues that both devices operate together in narratives that require metonymic transfers; however, while metonymy has the more crucial role in guaranteeing motility, metaphor provides the narrator with the mnemonic anchor that allows transfers to unfold in terms of a past that is forever in need of recuperation. Thus, contiguity basically provides Genette with his model for understanding how tropes produce movement in narrative literature, but metaphor somehow provides a degree of stability, enabling metonymy to work productively toward realizing delimited ends. Indeed, Genette argues that narrative (*récit*) begins *within* metonymy and could not acquire its shape and form if contiguity did not somehow allow movement to occur through combination and displacement.[22] What Genette does not so clearly explain, however, is the internal process whereby metonymy and metaphor somehow interweave to produce coherent narratives.

This controversy becomes more complex once the insights of Ullmann and Genette are transposed into a reading of Proust that is not only informed by linguistics but places the tropological dimension in the text ahead of a concern for narrative in the strong sense. Paul de Man's reading of Proust centers around the figure of reading itself, but it also engages the question of narrative in warning the reader against any attempt to stabilize meaning in a progressive teleology. De Man's "Reading (Proust)" begins with a short discussion of the phenomenological tradition represented by Georges Poulet that focused on the reader's movement between memory and expectation before mentioning that Proust's novel is perhaps more concerned with reading than with this wandering viewpoint.[23] After providing a number of details on what leads up to the scene of reading, de Man notes that Marcel's decision to go to bed with a book almost coincides with the kitchen maid's act of serving coffee, whose comportment contrasts to that of Françoise, a more formidable source of household help: "The kitchen maid is only a pale reflection of Françoise; in substituting for truth, error degrades and outwears it, causing a sequence of lapses that threatens to contaminate the entire section."[24]

In examining the tropological background underlying Marcel's immersion in reading, de Man is at pains to argue against interpreting the Proustian text in static terms, even when linguistic oppositions are in play in the construction of spatial relations. Although inside is identified with a dark, cool place, the outside world is bright and warm, but these oppositions are deliberately merged, perhaps confused, when Marcel invites us to imagine the inside as possessing the qualities of the outside: "These initially static polarities are put in circulation by means of a more or less hidden system of relays which allows the properties to enter into substitutions, exchanges, and crossings that appear to reconcile the incompatibilities of the inner with the outer world."[25] In a long note, de Man cites another passage involving a painting by Giotto that Marcel encountered on one of his trips to Venice to support a radically non-naturalistic reading of how these polarities are effectively juggled. De Man in this way disputes "Genette's model of a reconciled system of metaphor and metonymy" and provides an argument against the closed nature of tropological systems that "depend on the necessary link between the existence and knowledge of entities," but the result is also a kind of hermeneutical impasse in which the figure itself becomes virtually unreadable.[26]

De Man's description of Genette's model as involving "totalization" is significant because it denies the possibility that the relationship between metonymy and metaphor might hold a key to an understanding of narrative, apart from the issue of whether this model requires the "necessary link" between existence and knowledge. It is of course not difficult to imagine how figural language might allow us to better understand narrative sequences without requiring existing entities because fictional narratives generally employ linguistic oppositions as conventions or faming devices, while the construction of narratives, with the aid of tropes, could be *dialectical* precisely because it was carried out in an aesthetic sphere that deemed external existence inessential. But to describe narrative in this way is to evoke dialectics more in the spirit of Hegel than of Karl Marx, even if we do not absolutely rule out the possibility that language possesses a material aspect that is disallowed by Sausurrean structuralism. De Manian allegory, we will discover, relies on a notion of materiality that derives from the disjunction between meaning and grammar that can be posited as an aspect of normal linguistic functioning; nonetheless, materiality in this sense announces the end of dialectics, rather than its beginning, unless dialectical thought can raise disjunction to a level that prevented its own recollection from coinciding with historical closure. What de Man seems to be saying, however, is that Genette's system operates on the assumption that binary oppositions derive from the world, and that lacking this assumption, his method of reading would not be able to achieve (totalizing) results.

De Man maintains that the trope of truth/error, introducing the scene of reading, already enables metaphor to be given priority over metonymy, and that the "naturalization" of language that metaphor implies is sustained in a peculiar use of synesthesia, which actually further confuses inner and outer worlds but allows substitution to serve a metaphorical purpose.[27] However, this momentary state of confusion is perhaps inadequate for establishing *a secure basis* for the metaphorical structure of the reading project; thus, Marcel is soon impelled to justify reading in more familiar terms: "The mental process of reading extends the function of consciousness beyond that of mere passive perception; it must acquire a wider dimension and become an action."[28] For de Man, this means that only a rhetorical justification can effectively argue that reading is more than an abandonment of the "real" world. This justification is largely motivated by the need to resolve the "ethical conflict" between imagination and action, which is heightened by a pleasure in reading that is not unrelated to the author's own pleasure in writing.[29]

De Man's subsequent analysis shows how Marcel's tranquility in reading is able to sustain, "*pareil au repos d'une main immobile au milieu d'une eau courante, le choc et l'animation d'un torrent d'activité*" ["as the repose of a hand, in a stream of running water, the shock and movement of a torrent of activity"], and thus extends his previous insight into how linguistic binaries (such as cool repose and heated activity) are often used together but without regard to external conditions, while also preventing metaphor from being elevated once and for all over metonymy, especially when proximity is a better explanation for the movement between qualities than is discrete opposition.[30] This deceptive use of tropes will seem to be metaphorical only to the inattentive reader. De Man openly objects to the naïve reading that would permit this elevation to occur: "The relationship between the literal and the figural series is always, in a sense, metonymic, though motivated but a constitutive tendency to pretend the opposite."[31] This avowal reinforces Genette's position, but it also sustains the recognition that Marcel, rather than Proust, subscribes to a seamless mapping of word and reference, a recognition that also seems to give metaphorical language its alleged stability.

De Man comes to this conclusion after examining the image of the fountain that occurs in the scene of reading, which is only misconstrued as metaphor when instead it merely demonstrates the permanent disjunction between aesthetic and rhetorical approaches to the text. What *appears* to be complementary in Proust's use of the fountain as a rhetorical figure for both the temporal layering and stasis that reading itself exemplifies, implying as well the underlying unity of inside and outside, is rather for de Man the sign of an impossible synthesis.[32] Hence, instead of maintaining that the fountain succeeds as a figure in guiding us toward a unified reading, de Man argues that it evokes two dissimilar readings, perhaps equally plausible but incompatible insofar as aesthetics and rhetoric imply different approaches to texts. Although de Man seems to focus more strongly on the tendency toward totalization that is inherent in aesthetic approaches, the danger of synthesis would be present in any attempt to elevate one type of reading over the other one. *Metaphor* from this standpoint would be the word that summarizes the danger, whether it occurs in the sphere of the visual imagination or in the realm of verbal expression. However, although aesthetics and rhetoric are no doubt *different*, the thesis that they are radically *incompatible* may depend on a relatively uncomplicated conception of aesthetics that is "classical" in its reliance on a visual continuum that would invariably operate in reading in contrast to a more sophisticated use of linguistic tropes. Is de Man's argument for radical incompatibility predicated on an adequate conception of how the aesthetic response to literary texts can make reading challenging? Before addressing this question, we need to return to how de Man applies his method of reading in concluding his study of Proust's masterwork.

While offering a strong challenge to the classical conception of allegory, de Man focuses on Proust's depiction of the lowly kitchen maid, who is not only named Charity but contributes to a narrative that modifies our perception of benevolence so that its "proper" meaning is no longer easy to ascertain. De Man notes that, in this depiction, Proust does not begin with the kitchen maid, or with a direct comparison to Giotto's Charity, but with Ruskin's own words concerning Giotto's paintings on the Virtues and Vices in Padua to call attention to semantic discrepancies. *Reading*, rather than direct depiction, motivates Proust the writer as he describes the kitchen maid, who is shown (in a way that recalls the charitable gesture of Giotto's Charity) to offer her heart to God "*comme une cuisinière passe un tire-bouchon par le soupirail de son sous-sol à quelqu'un qui de lui demande à la fenêtre du rez-de-chaussée*" ["as a cook would hand a corkscrew through a basement window to someone who asks for it at street-level"].[33] This small detail both calls attention to the kitchen maid's humble status and reminds us of another cook with whom she is easily associated: "The kitchen maid resembles Giotto's Charity, but it appears that the latter's gesture also makes her resemble Françoise."[34] Once again, we seem to be in the space of continuity, rather than metaphor, but de Man is intent on disrupting the usual meaning of contiguity in reminding us that Françoise has been the kitchen maid's cruel tormentor, a role that hardly qualifies her as charitable. Moreover, de Man also argues that neither Giotto's Charity nor Proust's kitchen maid can "read" the literal details that set them slightly apart from the symbolic meanings that their names inscribe. Giotto's Charity has a brisk manner that is unbecoming of her name, and Proust's kitchen maid bears a heavy burden—the sign of pregnancy—that conflicts with the institutional role to which she has been assigned, and even more so when her condition figures in the institution of art, a formidably permanent one.

Although de Man identifies this mutual blindness, or inability to read, with the crossing of two readings, the aesthetic and rhetorical, just as he attributes to Marcel a certain literary skill that Swann more evidently lacks, we might consider on the contrary how this skill is more typically limited in almost invariably requiring visual details to be actualized. Joshua Landy has coined the term "metonyphors" to describe the construction of hybrid figures that combine metonymy and metaphor, suggesting that Marcel uses them extensively because his mind basically operates in spatial terms.[35] Marcel's immersion in worlds, therefore, does not always endow what is perceived with authentic value; on the contrary, his perception of variety generally does not go along with crucial leaps of the intelligence, leading to concept formation. However, the difference between Proust and Marcel is not to be couched as primarily cognitive but can be related to the matter of creativity itself: "What is fascinating is that Marcel, far from adopting stories of his own, in fact dismisses fabrication as entirely irrelevant to artistic production."[36] In short, Marcel lacks a sense of how the imagination is essential to creativity, either to art or to the project of forming a self, even one that only exists provisionally. Thus, returning to the thematic of metonymy and metaphor, we might say that the more "metaphysical" side of this polarity is precisely what Marcel is unable to grasp and deploy in his own account of temporal experience.

Nevertheless, what I propose as an alternative to metonymic reductionism is not a robust defense of metaphor but a rather different inquiry into how metaphor and metonymy work together. This defense would have to embrace the unconscious as the background in relation to which, or against which, the self emerges *through narration* as both divided and whole, fragmented and unified. De Man has suggested how a residual materiality remains on the margins of Charity and Envy in Giotto's naming of his own allegorical depictions.[37] This residue can be found as well in the difference between the kitchen maid and Françoise, both of whom fail to reproduce the virtue that is named in different ways. But materiality in all of these cases is only discoverable through narration, either through Giotto's act of naming or through the misalliance between two cooks and the allegorical figure of Charity whose institutional meaning overlooks the difference between words and images. What de Man calls reading is the impossibility of articulating these differences, but it might just as well be linked to the possibility of an aesthetic unconscious, which would then form the background to any reading that unfolded in narrative time as the inassimilable horizon within which figural language can be recognized as at least partially intelligible. And yet, if the aesthetic unconscious performs a role in reading, it must be able to demonstrate as well how narrative provides the possibility of its own deployment as a *discourse* in which figures can be interpreted as neither the embodiment of pure forms (classical Platonism) nor as subordinate to universal truth (modern rationalism). Such a conception of the aesthetic unconscious, however, should also be able to indicate how the aesthetic was originally constructed as the "space" of figural interpretation itself.

DIALECTICAL AESTHETICS

Rancière cogently argues that the novels of Proust uniquely express the aesthetic contradiction that Schiller first discussed in his seminal text, *On the Aesthetic Education of Humankind* (*Über die ästhetische Erziehung des Menchen*, 1795). Schiller identifies this contradiction in terms of two drives, namely, the sensuous drive and the drive for form, which call attention to the difference between material existence and moral reason.[38] In the *Critique of Judgment*, Kant had proposed only five years previously that aesthetics performs the role of bridge between nature and freedom.[39] The disciplinary meaning of this opposition, however, derives from the dissimilar spheres of science and ethics and requires a mediatory sphere to mitigate an undue harshness and to prevent the sensibility from becoming superfluous. Schiller defines aesthetics as the sphere of freedom, which does not require a grounding in politics, although it may have political significance. At the same time, Schiller requires a third term, namely, the play impulse, to negotiate the conflict between heteronomy and formal rigor.[40] This third drive produces a sphere of activity that enables aesthetics to constitute human nature and to contribute, if only indirectly, to man's political future.

The elaboration of what this entails is fundamental and prevents us from identifying Schiller—who is correctly read as developing the legacy of Kant—as a mere epigone when in truth his originality largely consists in restoring political content to aesthetic theory. In short, Schiller provides a dimension to a philosophical debate that was arguably political in its longer history, if Kant's predecessors are read as continuing the classical conception of art that descends from Plato and is revitalized by Anthony Ashley Cooper, Third Earl of Shaftesbury and Edmund Burke.[41] Schiller extends the possibility of critique to include the political as it functions in a world that sustains the contradiction between nature and freedom. In such a situation, any possible redistribution of the sensible would assume an aesthetic meaning, just as it entails a critical relationship to political institutions.

We might pause for a moment and place Schiller's aesthetic project in the historical context to which it responds as a theoretical challenge. Kant argues that the judgment of the beautiful is disinterested because the subject's relation to the aesthetic object is not based on "the power of form over matter, or intelligence over sensibility."[42] In the wake of the French Revolution, Schiller formalizes the meaning of disinterested play as a freedom from domination that prefigures a new sort of community. For Rancière, Schiller's appropriation of "free play" presupposes a suspension of interests that normally oppose active engagement to passive reception. Rancière uses the example of the *Juno Ludovisi* as evoked in Schiller's aesthetic treatise to mark the difference between the regime of representation and the regime of art:

> The statue is a "free appearance." It stands thus in a twofold contrast to its representative status: it is not an appearance drawn from reality that would serve as its model. Nor is it an active form imposed on matter. As a sensory form, it is heterogeneous to the ordinary forms of sensory experience that these dualities inform. It is given in a specific experience, which suspends the ordinary connections not only between appearance and reality, but also between form and matter, activity and passivity, understanding and sensibility.[43]

The will of the sculptor in this example is suspended in the contemplation of the goddess whose perfection is inseparable from nonappearance. And yet, conscious inactivity is not primarily a refusal of politics but a style announcing a way of life that is no longer founded on an earlier antagonism. The earlier antagonism between the rule of nature and the rule of law, which expressed itself in representation or in the willful imposition of form, has been superseded.

The regime of the aesthetic requires an abandonment of the naïve approach to everyday life that is enshrined in representation as well as the more ideological defense of inequality that identifies nature with what is culturally constructed. What is generally called "dialectics" no doubt received an initial impetus from Schiller's description of aesthetic play, which implies both negation and preservation (*Aufhebung*) in the formation of a higher unity.[44] This description has the advantage of allowing us to better understand how aesthetics transforms the relationship of art to life through an active process, rather than through a mere withdrawal from practice. The object world that is negated through play is not abolished but held in suspension and preserved, not as representation, but as the space within which engagement unfolds. This process, which does not depend on the opposition between form and matter, is also not one in which a world is only given shape through the subjective will of the artist; on the contrary, the nonappearing object of aesthetic contemplation is the result of a practice but it testifies to a departure from the self-interested concerns that primarily define the object world in terms of use values.

Rancière's approach to Proust explicitly acknowledges the importance of the aesthetic tradition to reading a body of work that is not only crucial to the development of modern literature but can be situated in an unfolding opposition that remains instrumental to the way that art is currently institutionalized. Rancière argues that Proust was informed by an aesthetic problematic, even if the French author's reading of aesthetic sources and knowledge of the aesthetic tradition remains conjectural. But this reading of Proust through aesthetics tends to focus on Kant and Schiller as key figures in a revolution that undergoes considerable modification during the course of a century that arguably begins with Hegel and ends with Nietzsche. In offering us his own version of how this revolution entailed a transition from a regime of representation to the regime of aesthetics, Rancière claims that Schiller was able to seize on the critical possibilities that were inherent in the French Revolution when the negative aspects of this event could be transformed into a motive for exploring the sensibility's freedom from external coercion. Hence, while presenting Schiller as post-Kantian, Rancière also implies that Kant might be challenged as in some sense inadequate, to the degree that Schiller's aesthetics is hard to separate from political considerations that remain rather free-floating when restricted to formal categories.

We might also revisit the aesthetic tradition as it developed after and perhaps even in opposition to Kant to situate the Proustian narrative in different versions of the "aesthetic unconscious" that are perhaps better elucidated in relation to those came after the period of critical idealism, rather than in terms of Kant and Schiller specifically. Rancière mentions Hegel, Nietzsche, and Schopenhauer as thinkers who differently reconfigured the relation between Logos and pathos in their respective reflections on the aesthetic. In his own analysis of Proust's metaphorical approach to experience, Rancière engages Nietzsche's thought of the Dionysian as a nonconceptual principle that disallows an evanescent thing-in-itself from being posited as distinct from a cognized object. However, Nietzsche's advance over traditional metaphysics goes beyond a mere "recovery" of everyday objects as things in their own right. This advance also affirms the value of time in arguing that Western metaphysics is almost invariably a residual Platonism that resists the historical as a source of mutability and change. In this framework, Nietzsche's doctrine of the eternal return of the same, although controversial, can be read as a radical revision of all classical conceptions of repetition as the mimetic reproduction of founding identities.

While Hegel in most canonical readings would be difficult to place in this revisionary tradition, we might return briefly to the conclusion of the *Phenomenology of Spirit* where the oppositions between memory and forgetting, variation and repetition, and even identity and difference are renegotiated in terms of the problem of history. A careful analysis of "Absolute Knowing," the final chapter of this philosophical work, at least suggests that Hegel made a considerable effort to integrate the aesthetic imaginary into his overview of how Recollection (*Erinnerung*) retrieves the moments of the past in synthetic unity only *after* the work of forgetting has opened up a sort of blank space in which the new can emerge freely. While anticipating Vaihinger's "as if" in the style of what might be mistaken to be a Kantian thought experiment, Hegel more strongly enacts the passage of self-consciousness through the night of nonbeing only to include and distance himself from the aesthetic possibilities that unravel the historical:

> *In seinem Insichgehen ist er in der Nacht seines Sebstbewußtseins versunken, sein verschwundenes Dasein aber ist in ihr aufbewahrt; und dies aufgehobene Dasein—das vorige, aber aus dem Wissen neugeborene—ist das neue Dasein, eine neue Welt und Geistesgestalt. In ihr hat er ebenso unbefangen von vorn bei ihrer Unmittelbarkeit anzufangen und sich von ihr auf weider großzuziehen, als ob alles Vorhergehende für ihn verloren wäre und er aus der Erfahrung der früheren Geister nichts gelernt hätte.*
> [Thus absorbed in itself, it is sunk in the night of its self-consciousness; but in that night its vanished outer existence is preserved, and this transformed existence—the former one, but now reborn of the Spirit's knowledge—is a new existence, a new world and a new shape of Spirit. In the immediacy of this new existence the Spirit has to start afresh to bring itself to maturity as if, for it, all that preceded it were lost and it had learned nothing from the experience of the earlier Spirits.][45]

The suggestion that the Spirit only matures when it begins again on the assumption that "all that preceded it were lost" is couched in terms that invite the phenomenological reader to imagine forgetting as return, not a return to historical origins but to the space in which the opening of history becomes possible.

To read Hegel in this manner is to make at least three distinct but related claims. First, the importance of disinvestment in the passage of self-consciousness to a new level of experience cannot be overestimated. Hegel dramatizes the despair of self-consciousness in a dark night that is not total (for otherwise the possibility of emerging from it would not be available) but coincides with a self-absorption that temporarily invalidates the distinction between inner and outer life. Second, the transformation of existence that occurs during this period of evacuation is a spiritual event and recalls the formal aesthetics we associate with Kant. In this case, however, a kind of forgetting pervades self-consciousness, simultaneously allowing an unprecedented imaginary to consolidate a new sense of life while the past appears to have been left behind. Third, this experience is less of a false dawn than a displacement of everything that occurred previously, constituting a repetition that does not merely reproduce the past but significantly varies a vital relation to previous experience.

It should be clear from this bald outline that repetition would not be a simple "falling behind" but an active reliving that would refute all "prior" constructions of the past as partial, limited, and basically, surmountable. What also needs to be emphasized here is the kinship of Hegel and Freud, not in a manner that would assimilate a dialectical phenomenology to psychoanalysis, or conversely, but that would challenge standard readings of both authors.[46] Such a challenge in Freud's case would free the usual interpretation of repetition from its dependence on a classical model of the death drive and as implying the eventual return to stasis through the termination of all vital functions. This new reading would not deny the basically metaphysical framework to which Freud was committed in his major theoretical formulations, early and late.[47] However, it would provide another way of situating Freud's discoveries that would no longer confine them to the theoretical model in which they were first articulated. This repositioning of Freud could not be sustained within a classical framework but would enable the aesthetic implications of dialectical thought to be explored in their complexity.

AESTHETICS AND THE FIGURAL

The combination of a Hegelian thematic with a new interpretation of key psychoanalytic concepts should provide deeper insight into the role of the unconscious in textual production. Crucial in this regard is the dimension of language that perhaps first becomes evident when *writing* acquires an importance that goes unacknowledged by mainstream linguistics and that classical dialectics does seem to anticipate.[48] The semiotics of writing, however, resembles dialectics in enabling thought to be loosened from the traditional categories of the understanding. Benjamin was perhaps the first to seize on this possibility in his provisional but highly suggestive essay, "On the Mimetic Faculty" (*"Über das Mimetische Vermögen,"* 1933), which goes beyond a representational approach to mimesis in a manner that might be read as looking forward to Kristeva's semiotic appropriation of Jacques Lacan. For both Benjamin and Kristeva, mimesis is newly defined in relational terms, rather than as the faded copy of empirical realities. Mimesis in this sense is not restricted to the apprehension of visual appearances but involves a grasping of what is not perceived to be the same. Benjamin refers to how writing as script evokes "opaque similarity" that only begins to make sense when it is viewed from a new perspective. Writing as language, therefore, cannot be isolated from its semiotic transformation: "Rather, the mimetic element in language can, like a flame, manifest itself only through a kind of bearer. This bearer is the semiotic element. Thus, the coherence of words or sentences is the bearer through which, like a flash, similarity appears."[49] In proposing that the mimetic in writing is not to be conceived apart from the semiotic carrier that supports it, Benjamin enables us to develop an interpretation of repetition that no longer depends on a direct mirroring process. Instead, repetition is what occurs in the space *between* two objects, rather than as a secondary phenomenon that maps onto an original.

J. Hillis Miller has suggested in more literary terms that Benjamin's "opaque similarity" clarifies how nonclassical repetition can be related to Freud's early trauma theory and to Benjamin's approach to the Proustian image, which ultimately returns us to our reflections on Hegel. Even the early trauma theory did not posit an original, discrete event that was simply repeated in the traumatic experience; instead, it endeavored to show how trauma itself needs to be defined in relational terms, not as the repetition of what occurred previously but as a psychic event that occupies a third space. Miller resituates trauma in this third space: "The trauma is neither in the first nor in the second but between them, in the relation between two opaquely similar events."[50] In "The Image of Proust" (*"Zum Bilde Prousts,"* 1934), Benjamin claims that Proust's writing is the counterpart to Penelope's weaving, rather than its mere likeness, citing the author's habit later in life of working at night to produce a record of what is usually revealed to us only in our dreams.[51] Memory in this case shapes the textual web that would quickly unravel if it were exposed to the full light of day and deprived of the nocturnal element on which it depends. Literary composition for Proust would be the occasion for repetition to the degree that it occupies the space of writing as conscious and unconscious at once. At the same time, this occasion would involve a reliving of the past that, as Hegel contends, constitutes an aesthetic sphere in which reflection can encompass appearances and rethink their deeper meanings.

Miller is able to suggest in this way that the Proustian text is not constructed on the basis of comparisons between objects but through "opaque similarities" that echo differences that are then reconfigured: "They create in the gap of that difference a third way, which Benjamin calls the image [*Das Bild*]."[52] Image in this sense is not to be confused with anything to be found in empirical psychology. In defining the image in this manner, Benjamin no doubt had Biblical tradition in mind, where the notion of being created in God's image requires a leap of the imagination before it can be said to cast light on man's inner being. However, in relating this notion of image to literary texts, we might say as well that the objects that Proust evokes in writing and that bear only opaque resemblance to one another are what produce the images that cannot be seen but only thought. They partake of the reality and unreality of dreams, rather than testifying to logically ordered, self-conscious reflection. They compare for this reason to what transpires in children's games, where the same object can be assigned two or more meanings that are often contradictory.⁵³ Such a conception of the image is figural and not merely figurative; it breaks with purely verbal modes of expression, drawing on the vast resources of language but also on graphemic possibilities that may require visual experience to be fully realized.

Moreover, Proust's work can be related to patterns of trauma and repetition as well as to the Hegelian narrative that was discussed previously as an interruption of the past, rather than as a mere gathering together of what previously happened. In *Swann's Way*, the reader is invited to relive the narrator's sense of how past and present reconfigure, not in a chronological passage from one experience to the next, but in a repetition that transforms the past, producing an image that is neither a copy of an earlier experience or an ideal form that can be detached from temporal existence. Benjamin has crucially suggested how the moment of reconfiguration introduces a third possibility through an image that is not to be confused with a concrete synthesis but combines similar ways of seeing, perhaps in an ambiguous manner, without constituting a unified whole. From this standpoint, Rancière's argument that the conclusion to Proust's masterwork resolves the conflict between the everyday and the transcendental could be seen as premature; instead, this moment would simply look forward to a possible resolution that had to be achieved on an aesthetic basis because life would have to be raised to this level before it could be transformed into a work of art. Of course, we might want to argue that the novel is precisely what achieves this aesthetic synthesis, but the novel also includes Marcel who cannot grasp the aesthetic significance of what he witnesses. At the same time, this model for reading Proust would contest the standard way of interpreting the opposition between the young narrator who begins in Combray and the mature writer and creator of the complete masterwork.⁵⁴ In reading the novel, we are invited to repeat Marcel's imperfect gasp of circumstances, just as Proust repeats this imperfection by including it in his novel.

Let us consider for a moment that famous early scene in which Proust's narrator recounts his experience with tea and the "petite madeleine" as first offered to him by Aunt Léonie during the years in Combray, before he retires to bed, and then later, on his return home, by his mother whose presence seems to guarantee the possibility of retrieving the past. The narrator records his frustration in trying to conjure the same experience and finally comes to feel that only his own mind has the capacity to recreate the past as it was lived long ago. And then he hesitates: "*Grave incertitude, toutes le fois que l'esprit se sent dépassé par lui-même; quand lui, le chercheur, est tout ensemble le pays obscur où il doit chercher et où tout son baggage ne lui sera de rein*" ["What grave uncertainty, whenever the mind feels overtaken by itself; when he, the seeker, is at the same time, the dark region through which he must go seeking and where all his baggage will be nothing"].⁵⁵ The metaphor of leaving behind what one owns and of moving through dark space combines with the idea of losing oneself and having to contend with the contents of the unconscious. Moreover, the experience of abjection (as Kristeva has presented it through the lens of psychoanalysis) evacuates the self and precedes any future transformation: "*Maintenant je ne sens plus rien, il est arrêté, redescendu peut-être; qui sait s'il remontera jamais de sa nuit?*" ["Now I feel nothing; it has stopped, has perhaps sunk back into the night; who can say if it will ever arise from it again?"][56]

Proust's narrator emphasizes how the things of the past can reemerge in "*l'édifice immense du souvenir*" ["the immense edifice of memory"], even when the people with whom they are associated are long dead, because the one who remembers retains a vital relationship to the world.[57] While the past is crucial to this process of memory, Kristeva questions the wisdom of identifying the author too strongly with retrospection when such a relationship is inseparable from the use of the imagination as its operates through the sensibility. From this standpoint, Proust is "in search of an 'embodied' imaginary, a space where works, along with their unconscious and obscure emergences, knit the unbroken flesh of the world I belong to."[58] Moreover, this search engages language as the vehicle through which a productive belief in the imaginary implies a unique mode of time: "Time regained would then be the time of language as an imaginary experience. What is perceived and what is said are separated by a distance, an incompatibility, an inadequacy that somehow brings them together."[59] Noting Proust's indebtedness to major figures in the history of aesthetics, Kristeva emphasizes how the French writer "rejects psychology precisely because it is restricted to the subjective," while the notion of "involuntary memory" combines with time to mark a more original sense of the psyche.[60]

In evoking both the possibility of an embodied imaginary as well as the impossibility of bridging the gap between what is seen and what is said, Kristeva briefly refers to the work of Maurice Merleau-Ponty, whose notion of reversibility enables him to argue that living beings not only possess sensibility but are sentient as well. On a practical level, this means that the act of touching also initiates the process of being touched, enabling "a carnal adherence of the sentient to the sensed and of the sensed to the sentient" that provides a new significance to the fact of belonging: "For, as overlapping and fusion, identity and difference, it brings to birth a ray of natural light that illuminates all flesh and not only my own."[61] Merleau-Ponty is of course not referring to matter in evoking this realm, nor does he wish to imply that some sort of original disorder is subdued by the constructions of the mind: "The flesh (of the world or myself) is not contingency, chaos, but a texture that returns to itself and conforms to itself."[62] To the degree that ideas are invisible, they cannot be separated from their sensible appearances and assigned a privileged meaning. Language as well as music are integral to this process of giving expression to this vital sphere that is inscribed with ineffaceable qualities.

Merleau-Ponty contends that the modern novel gives witness to how this expression occurs: "No one has gone further than Proust in fixing the relations between the visible and the invisible, in describing the idea that is not the contrary of the sensible, that is its lining and its depth."[63] Proust demonstrates reversibility in turning the invisible into a source of aesthetic satisfaction, which has nothing to do with establishing an equivalency between what is seen and what is intangible, or even of discovering in more concrete terms what is originally cognized as abstract. Hence, the "little phrase" of Verteuil that Swann encountered during his visit to the Verdurin's home is not to be fully understood *either* in terms of that encounter *or* reducible to a formal bareness that might be derived from an analysis of musical notation. Instead, that phrase allows Swann to discover an inner depth through the richness and variety that is hidden from him in *"cette grande nuit impénétrée et décourageante de notre âme que nous prenons pour du vide et pour du néant"* ["the great unpenetrated and discouraging night of our soul which we take for emptiness and nothingness "].[64] This is why Merleau-Ponty can say that the worlds or entities in which this depth wells forth "have been acquired only through its commerce with the visible, to which they remain attached."[65] Hence, the older philosophical distinction between the transcendental and the empirical, although not completely overturned in Proust's literary practice, is radically revised when experience itself becomes necessary for the realization of an inner predisposition that enables the signs of aesthetic expression to assume artistic form, while, at the same time, experience is no longer to be identified strictly with an everyday occurrence in which the germ for that realization was planted.

Benjamin, Miller, Kristeva, and Merleau-Ponty all provide different but related versions of textuality that support Rancière's approach to Proust, who argues that the "aesthetic unconscious" performs a crucial role in enabling the French author to compose a work of art. However, unity in Proust is achieved only in perspective, rather than in the utterances of a narrator who, while aesthetically engaged, is unable to produce an artistically satisfying novel. In view of Kristeva's later reflections, we might say that a lingering maternal presence, enabling the subject-in-process to navigate beyond the binary opposition between the symbolic and the imaginary as promoted in Lacanian traditions, might explain how Proust was able to employ literary form in composing his masterwork. It is perhaps ironic (in view of canonical readings) that Hegel's phenomenology, which includes the possibility of radical disinvestment, also suggests how this passage can occur. The self that dissolves as it strains to shape the literary work occupies an imaginal space that prepares the reader for the work to come, which is also the work that the author has left behind. Hence, rather than understand the work as organically unified, perhaps in a manner that might enable the masterful conception of the author to provide the justification of a greater whole that acquires its form only when the original narrator recedes and makes way for this future work, the reader is able to glimpse the truth of a self that is forever in search of what it cannot find, but for that reason, testifies to a break in consciousness that allows the aesthetic to emerge as an essential component in the reader's experience of the text. From this standpoint, Schelling's remarks on art during the Age of Idealism acquire a special significance, especially when read in the light of Proust's remarkable achievement: "The work of art merely reflects to me what is otherwise not reflected by anything, namely, that absolutely identical which has already divided itself even in the self." Finally, and as a consequence, what is divided even in consciousness "comes, through the miracle of art, to be radiated back from the products thereof."[66]

NOTES

1. Jacques Rancière, *The Aesthetic Unconscious*, trans. Debra Keats and James Swenson (Cambridge, UK: Polity Press, 2009), 7.
2. Ibid., 28–30.
3. Figuration in G. W. F. Hegel could be assigned a narratological meaning that seems to argue in favor of a kinship between Hegel and Aristotle, which was often suggested by Hegel himself. For Rancière, however, Aristotle's system of reversal and recognition represses the figural dimension and, for this reason, marks the beginning of classical thought, which was revived and systematized in the wake of Voltaire from Batteux to Harpe. Rancière, *The Aesthetic Unconscious*, 19, 51. We might argue that Hegel preserves an unconscious dimension in dialectics, even if, in the end, the unconscious is subsumed under the directives of speculative reason. Symbolic art is not an art that is immediately unified but one in which unity is "reestablished out of difference and therefore not just met with but *produced* by spirit." See Hegel, *Aesthetics*, 1:351. A sort of break occurs between nature and spirit that opens a "space" in which the figure acquires a discontinuous, and unavoidably unconscious, meaning.
4. More strongly than Arthur Schopenhauer, Friedrich Nietzsche in his first major work tends to foreground pathos over Logos: "The artist has already surrendered has subjectivity in the Dionysian process. The image that now already shows him his identity with the heart of the world is the dream scene that embodies the primordial contradiction and primordial pain, together with the primordial pleasure, of mere appearance." See Nietzsche, *The Birth of Tragedy*, p. 49. Such statements problematize Nietzsche's later attempts in the same work to read the Dionysus/Apollo polarity in Kantian terms as an opposition between noumena and phenomena.
5. Ibid., 11–17.
6. Ibid., 86.
7. Julia Kristeva, *Time and Sense: Proust and the Experience of Literature*, trans. Ross Guberman (New York: Columbia University Press, 1996), 211.
8. Jacques Rancière, *Mute Speech*, trans. James Swenson (New York: Columbia University Press, 2011), 156. Kristeva echoes this analysis of "doubleness" in Proust in claiming that this "flashing" event always evokes pairs: "Two spaces, two times, and two sensations become merged in the narrator's desire. This appears to be *a primal metaphorical condensation*." Kristeva, *Time and Sense*, 193.
9. Ibid., 157.
10. Walter Benjamin, "The Image of Proust," in *Illuminations* (New York: Schocken Books, 1968), 158
11. Ibid., 162.

96   Chapter 5

12. Kristeva argues that metaphor performs a disjunctive (as well as conjunctive) role in Proust's work, perhaps suggesting the need to rethink the Hegelian notion of contradiction on a linguistic level: "Indeed, the essence of the Proustian metaphor is closer to the reciprocal relationship or the sustained contradiction between two terms that some more recent authors believe underlies the ambivalent character of the metaphor." See Kristeva, *Time and Sense*, 213.

13. Rancière, *Mute Speech*, 159.

14. Ibid., 163.

15. Ibid., 156.

16. See Stéphane Mallarmé, "Hérodiade," "L'Après-midi d'un faune," "Plusiers sonnets," *Oeuvres complètes*, ed. Bertrand Marchal (Paris: Gallimard, 1998), 17–22, 22–25, 36–46.

17. The possible conjunction of the two ways, as well as their ability to merge conscious and unconscious motivations, is announced in Marcel Proust, *Du Côté de chez Swann*, (Paris: Éditions Gallimard, 1992), 1:175–79.

18. Platonic readings of Proust abound. The most sophisticated is perhaps that of Gilles Deleuze, who emphasizes how Proust evokes a "plurality of worlds" in which verbal signs can be interpreted, even when their appearance is not always unitary. See Gilles Deleuze, *Proust and Signs*, trans. Richard Howard (New York: George Braziller, 1972), 5. Deleuze's semiotic reading of Proust, which tends toward Platonism, differs considerably from Rancière's aesthetic reading and should be distinguished from it. This reading sometimes combines semiotics and essentialism and then opposes them along Nietzschean lines, but it is generally at odds with Rancière's historicism. Closer to Rancière, Kristeva argues that for Proust, "[i]mpressions, which are *sensory hieroglyphs or figured truths,*" may have Platonic strains but that Deleuze's reading tends to 'derealize' human referents. See Kristeva, *Time and Sense*, 256.

19. Amid a somewhat macabre scene of reunion, the narrator brings together Combray and the world of the Guermantes in referring to these significant, if not always happy, marriages. See Proust, *Le Temps retrouvé*, in *A la recherche du temps perdu*, 7:314–16.

20. See Gérard Genette, "Metonymie chez Proust," in *Figures* III (Paris: Editions du Seuil, 1972), 39–67.

21. Ibid., 42.

22. Ibid., 63.

23. Paul de Man, "Reading (Proust)," in *Allegories of Reading: Figural Language in Rousseau, Nietzsche, Rilke, and Proust* (New Haven, CT: Yale University Press, 1979), 57.

24. Ibid., 59.

25. Ibid, 60.

26. Ibid., 60–61n5. De Man's notion of the unreadable is not equivalent to a kind of opacity that might have been avoided, or simply equated with meaningless reading, but with the discovery of how familiarization becomes impossible when it has lost its structural basis in natural experience. The term, therefore, could be interpreted as a radicalization of phenomenology's suspension of the natural attitude, except for the fact that it no longer "brackets" the outside world, in a skeptical spirit, but overturns the linguistic "meaning" of that world and, in this way, makes figuration in the strict sense impossible. What I refer to as *the figural*, however, would not reinstate referentiality as fully determinate but would describe the space in which the figure could be read, misread, or simply *not* read, depending of the situation in which interpretation unfolds.

27. Ibid., 62–63.

28. Ibid., 63.

29. Ibid., 64–65.

30. Proust, *Du Côté de chez Swann*, 1:103.

31. de Man, "Reading (Proust)," 71.

32. Ibid, 72.

33. Proust, *Du Côté de chez Swann*, 1:100–1.

34. de Man, "Reading (Proust)," 76.

35. Joshua Landy, *Philosophy as Fiction: Self, Deception and Knowledge in Proust* (Oxford: Oxford University Press, 2004), 68–75. Marcel, according to Landy's reading, fantasizes that everything possesses a common essence, a property that binds it to other elements. This

common essence allows each individual thing to constitute a "world" that gives desire its object. Although these worlds are plural, "metonymphors" provide windows on Marcel's mind, which is therefore easier to comprehend than that of Proust himself.

36. Ibid., 83.

37. De Man notes that Giotto himself named this figure, as if to suggest that the meaning of the figure could not be secured through visual means but needed to be linked to a "system" that was verbal, rather than graphic, to become intelligible. Moreover, the act of naming evoked a system of meaning that was external to visual representation, thus inserting the figure in an institution (presumably both religious and cultural) whose "permanence" concealed a hidden break between nomination and artistic content. For details, see de Man, "Reading (Proust)," 77.

38. Friedrich Schiller, "Twelfth Letter," in *The Aesthetic Education of Man*, trans. Elizabeth M. Wilkinson and L.A. Willoughby (Oxford: Clarendon Press, 1982), 78–83.

39. See Kant, *Critique of Judgment*, 140–41.

40. Schiller, "Fourteenth Letter," in *The Aesthetic Education of Man*, 95-99.

41. Gadamer contends that Kant contributes to the long tradition of aesthetics that was originally political and is only later "subjectivized" in transcendental philosophy. For details, see Gadamer, *Truth and Method*, 42–81. Gadamer's argument does not require that we see aesthetics as politics but as related to a history that was originally in tune with political experience and might be revisited within this framework, assuming that aesthetics can be interpreted in a hermeneutical context.

42. Jacques Rancière, "Aesthetics and Politics," in *Aesthetics and Its Discontents* (Cambridge, UK: Polity Press, 2009), 30–31.

43. Ibid., 29–30.

44. See Schiller, "Eighteenth Letter," in *The Aesthetic Education of Man*, 122–25.

45. Compare Hegel, *Phänomenologie des Geistes*, 590–91; *Phenomenology of Spirit*, 492. I am indebted to Rebecca Comay for having suggested the importance of this passage in her reading of Hegel.

46. After briefly discussing the passage from Hegel that I cite more fully, Comay argues for the pertinence of Freud's late notion of repetition as variable rather than as the shorthand for psychic regression. I am once again indebted to her insightful suggestions and persuasive exposition that enables Freud to be related to Derrida and, in this way, establishes a relation to the semiotic approach to dialectics that is more specifically explored in my references to Benjamin. See Comay, *Mourning Sickness*, 147–48.

47. Concerning the basic terms of psychoanalysis in general, Derrida argues that "all these concepts, without exception, belong to the history of metaphysics" and cannot be translated into a thematic of *différance*, or trace, even when Freud himself seems to be on the verge of achieving this remarkable transmutation. See Jacques Derrida, "Freud and the Scene of Writing" in *Writing and Difference*, trans. Alan Bass (Chicago: University of Chicago Press, 1978), 197.

48. Although clearly working in the structuralist tradition, Gérard Genette discusses how Proust gives us examples of how "a suddenly aberrant character, incapable of functioning in the same way as those around it," reveals an ideogram or pictogram that needs to be read in the manner of a rebus so that a process of negation is sometimes instated in passages that (even in combining different kinds of writing, like a polygraph) must be inverted to be understood. See Gerard Genette, "Proust and Indirect Language," in *Figures of Literary Discourse*, trans. Alan Sheridan (New York: Columbia University Press, 1982), 268–69.

49. Walter Benjamin, "On the Mimetic Faculty," in *Reflections: Essays, Aphorisms, Autobiographical Writings*, trans. Edmund Jephcott (New York: Harcourt, Brace Jovanovich, 1978), 335.

50. J. Hillis Miller, *Fiction and Repetition: Seven Engsh Novels* (Cambridge, MA: Harvard University Press, 1982), 9.

51. Benjamin, "The Image in Proust," 202.

52. Miller, *Fiction and Repetition*, 9.

53. Ibid., 204–5. We might also recall the "fort/da" game involving little Hans as discussed in Sigmund Freud, *Beyond the Pleasure Principle*, 18:14–17. It should be noted, however, that this narrative is used to support the hypothesis of the death drive, which arguably transforms

psychoanalysis from a relatively "classical" theory of ego constitution into a symptomatology in which the discourse of the unconscious forever overflows the possibility of total interpretation.

54. Pippin argues that even though Marcel sometimes suggests the world of Proust himself, "the novel does nothing to support the view that there is or even can be any point of view 'outside' the narrative flux and instability described," so that it needs to be read as a series of moments that never terminates in a Platonic reading that would invalidate social and historical complications. See Robert Pippin, "Proust's Problematic Selves," *The Persistence of Subjectivity: On the Kantian Aftermath* (Cambridge, UK: Cambridge University Press, 2005), 316–17.

55. Proust, *Du Côté de chez Swann*, 1:59.
56. Ibid., 1:60.
57. Ibid., 1:61.
58. Kristeva, *Time and Sense*, 169.
59. Ibid., 204.
60. Ibid., 309.
61. Maurice Merleau-Ponty, *The Visible and the Invisible*, trans. Alphonso Lingis, ed. Claude Lefort (Evanston, IL: Northwestern University Press, 2000), 142.
62. Ibid., 146.
63. Ibid., 149.
64. See Proust, *Du Côté de chez Swann*, 1:412. While Merleau-Ponty takes his readers to the highpoint of Swann's meditation, this entire discussion is significant in modulating a reading that navigates between two false positions, namely, the attempt to view the whole experience as the mere aftereffect of an empirical event (i.e., the visit to the Verdurin's home) or to interpret it as a purely spiritual event that does not require a retreat into the dark night of consciousness whereby *difference itself* has been lodged in some inexplicable fashion. What I am implying here is that a Hegelian reading would enable us to read this passage more productively.
65. Merleau-Ponty, *The Visible and the Invisible*, 150.
66. F. W. J. Schelling, *System of Transcendental Idealism*, trans. Peter Heath (Charlottesville: University of Virginia, 1978), 210.

Chapter Six

Space in Blanchot

Orphic Testimonies

Maurice Blanchot tends to be identified with the intellectual movement that culminates in Roland Barthes and Jacques Derrida as opposed to the Hegelian current that contributed to early twentieth-century German thought and underwent a resurgence in postwar France. Indeed, Blanchot demonstrates that the notion of *writing* implies a new thematic that is difficult if not impossible to assimilate to Hegelian models of criticism as a sophisticated mode of historical reflection. However, in this chapter, I first explore how Blanchot adopts the quasi-Heideggerian theme of reversal as a way of criticizing the role of the ego in standard art theory and criticism. Blanchot's use of reversal also calls attention to the place of the imaginary in contrast to what Martin Heidegger would identify more strictly with an ontological problematic. Thus, Blanchot's reading of modern literature is shown to be crucial to the notion of literary space, enabling him to employ a specific myth as a figure of aesthetics. The problem of history emerges at this point in Blanchot's critical trajectory and suggests the reading of G. W. F. Hegel that informs the present study. Blanchot's poetics is shown in my conclusion to engage both history and writing in a manner that invites us to reconsider modern literature and, from this perspective, to reassess the Hegelian legacy.

BLANCHOT'S REVERSAL

The possibility of approaching literature through philosophical resources performs an implicit, if not clearly acknowledged, role in Blanchot's early masterwork, *The Space of Literature* (*L'Espace littéraire*, 1955). While clearly concerned with the concept of the work of art that often emerges in early hermeneutics, Blanchot profoundly modifies the role of this concept in describing the experience of literature in terms of a radical reversal. Such a reversal is conceived as a disinvestment of the self, rather than as a triumph of the subject, just as it opens an infinite space that cannot be represented. Without referring to Heidegger's work as an important influence, Blanchot develops a dialogue between literature and philosophy that reminds us of how the theme of language was always central to phenomenology.[1]

It is evident that Heidegger's philosophical essays, particularly after the publication of *Being and Time* in 1927, can be read in a manner that questions the standard ways of interpreting philosophical modernity.[2] "The Origin of the Work of Art" ("*Der Ursprung des Kunstwerkes*" (originally composed during the 1935–1936 period) was presented during the same period that Walter Benjamin composed his own seminal essay, "The Work of Art in the Age of Mechanical Reproduction." But in contrast to Benjamin, Heidegger can be read as demonstrating how the space of writing is opened when an experience of "world" is introduced through a poetic discourse. From the perspective of a thematic of writing that is suggested but never developed, Heidegger's discussion of art, language, and truth acquires an inaugural status in demonstrating how the question of being is related to the way that words are used, even in everyday contexts.[3] Heidegger's essay on art also engages the reader in an ontological quest that is implied through a written description of a work of art that constitutes a "text" in its own right.

In an attempt to retrieve the work of art as a thing that bears the world within it, Heidegger famously employs one of Vincent Van Gogh's paintings of shoes to evoke the wearer, an ordinary peasant woman who belongs to a specific place but also alters the rural landscape of which she is a part. Heidegger in *Being and Time* had already explicitly examined how the phenomenological conception of world differs from that of René Descartes, providing a positive version of "world" on the basis of spatiality as a nonsubjective mode of being.[4] We might read Heidegger in the later essay on art as merely continuing the project of *Being and Time*, which already explained how the world comes into focus at the critical moment when an instrumental complex breaks down and forces us to reexamine our immediate environment as somehow integrated, if not entirely familiar to us. And yet, "The Origin of the Work of Art" provides us with a way of understanding Heidegger's world concept that is different from what the more systematic treatise provides in disclosing the world that it evokes.

Although Van Gogh's painting does not provide much information concerning the wearer of the shoes depicted, Heidegger takes us from the things that appear in the lifeworld of an imaginary woman who might have occupied the empty shoes themselves. An interesting transformation occurs in his description as the shoes, which evoke a poetic response to the rural environment and then become the useful "equipment" that enables the composition of a partial biography:

> *Unter den Sohlen schiebt sich hin die Einsamkeit des Feldweges durch den sinkenden Abend. In dem Schuhzeng schwingt der verschwiedgene Zuruf der Erde, ihr stilles Verschenken des reifenden Korns und irh unerklärtes Sichversagen in der öden Brache des winterlichen Feldes. Durch dieses Zeug zieht das klaglose Bangen um die Sicherheit des Brotes, die wortlose Freude des Wiederüberstehens der Not, des Beben in der Ankunft er Geburt und das Zittern in der Umdrohung des Todes.*
> [Under the shoes slides the loneliness of the field-path as evening falls. In the shoes vibrates the silent call of the earth, its quiet gift of the ripening grin and its unexplained self-refusal in the fallow desolation of the wintry field. This equipment is pervaded by uncomplaining anxiety as to the certainty of bread, the wordless joy of having once more withstood want, and trembling before the impending childbed and shivering at the surviving menace of death.][5]

This description evokes a silent landscape that somehow "speaks" to us through poetic reflection. But what is perhaps more plausible is that the woman has entered the texture of the wintry landscape, just as the landscape—which otherwise would lack the features that have been worked over it—has been transformed through the persistent activity of a human host into a site of need and withdrawal. The "world" of the peasant woman is evoked through a visual image that becomes a written response to what would have remained inexpressible in a purely philosophical discourse. But now the word "writing" is being used to indicate what cannot be assimilated to philosophy as generally conceived. Moreover, the figure stands out as a graphic reminder of how the text evokes an alterity that cannot be assimilated to a purely conceptual argument.

The ironic aspect of Heidegger's description becomes evident when we juxtapose poetic language and visual image in the narrative of a "world" that is visible and invisible at once. The verbal elaboration of "world" requires two media, namely, painting and poetry, to unify a reality that may be sundered. Nonetheless, this entire account is also a description of a certain Van Gogh painting that Heidegger has already mentioned to underscore the relative stability of the work of art in an antisubjective thesis. However, in contrast to what can be found in Heidegger's previous analyses, the thesis now involves a written account of a world that provides no heroic options to a peasant laborer who has survived many hardships. The work of art brings to light something that cannot be seen and deepens the meaning of reversal to involve the possible collapse of human subjectivity and measurable time. From this perspective, Heidegger's discourse on finitude can be interpreted as an instance of severe ontological limitation, which prevents the truth of being from coinciding with timeless presence. Moreover, this discourse might even be related to a critique of the natural attitude that was always central to Husserlian phenomenology, while in a different way, it might be related as well to Edmund Husserl's assertion that human accomplishments can be anonymous, even when classical phenomenology is generally resistant to Heidegger's ontological turn.[6]

The possibility of approaching literature through philosophical resources performs a crucial role in Blanchot's critical exposition, *The Space of Literature*. While concerned with the concept of the work of art that often emerges in early hermeneutics, Blanchot profoundly modifies the role of the work in describing the experience of literature in terms of a radical reversal that is neither ontological nor personalist. This reversal is conceived as a disinvestment of the self, rather than as a triumph of the subject, and opens an infinite space that cannot be represented. Blanchot's reversal might be read as a radicalization of what is already suggested by Heidegger. Thus, although Heidegger's reversal can be traced back to *Being and Time*, "The Origin of the Work of Art" redefines it in announcing "the possibility of impossibility" (Lévinas) that emerges in the forlorn mood that the work expresses.[7] Blanchot was clearly responsive to this variation in meaning that counters more optimistic claims. Perhaps in a different way, Blanchot also revives the phenomenological notion of anonymity as a neutral term that describes in a formal idiom the impersonal aspects of intentional life. His view of the writer challenges traditional subject-based criticism: "The writer belongs to a language that no one speaks, which is addressed to no one, which has no center, and which reveals nothing."[8] Thus, in looking forward to the early criticism of Barthes, Blanchot discusses how the anonymous site of creativity often coincides with the construction of third-person narratives from which the author is entirely absent.[9]

Blanchot's understanding of reversal also negotiates a new sense of aesthetic appearance that largely bypasses the Heideggerian problematic. Hence, the figure of Orpheus performs a crucial role in enabling Blanchot to specify how reversal carries us from a centered notion of the human subject to a process-oriented event of aesthetic ambiguity. To the degree that Orpheus gazes directly on Eurydice, he ruins the work and loses what he seeks to master. However, in simply refusing to observe his approaching lover, Orpheus demonstrates infidelity to the profound impulse to encounter her as an ineluctable other. Heidegger wrote "The Origin of the Work of Art" in the attempt to move beyond the constraints of philosophical aesthetics to retrieve our access to truth. Hegel moves beyond Immanuel Kant's assessment of the (aesthetic) subject, particularly in demonstrating how the sense of the sublime is a text, rather than primarily an experience of nature.[10] The question now becomes: How does Blanchot revive aesthetics in a way that provides new insights into the cultural imaginary, even when he employs mythic figures to communicate these insights in a way that is distinctively modern?

ORPHEUS AND AESTHETICS

Blanchot's interpretation of the Orpheus myth in *The Space of Literature* provides a key to the meaning of visibility as a quasi-aesthetic category that clarifies the way that literary texts can be read as testimonies to a unique order of experience. In discussing Heidegger's approach to the work of art, we encountered a discussion of "world" that was built out of a mysterious conjunction between person and place, but the nature of this conjunction remained unclear, perhaps because the whole notion of being-in-the-world occluded the movement between two zones of contact. Maurice Merleau-Ponty provides an eloquent critique of Henri-Louis Bergson in which he explains that my encounter with the visible world pervades the structure of experience itself: "There is an experience of the visible thing as pre-existing my vision, but this experience is not a fusion, a coincidence," so that I am already within the world with which I make contact. Moreover, the visibility that is woven into my experience of things allows me to discover "a Being of which my vision is a part, a visibility older than my perceptions or my acts."[11] Hence, instead of arguing that subject and object achieve a sort of higher synthesis that perfects self-reflectivity, Merleau-Ponty identifies the space in which I move and experience the world as one that allows me to enter into the domain of the things themselves, just as it allows the things to enter into my state of consciousness as other to myself. This dual movement is called "double reference" because of the way that it preserves the condition of being *lived through* as well as the sense of distance that prevents co-mingling from becoming a simple act of coinciding.[12]

To return to the myth of Orpheus, we might relate this analysis to Blanchot's appropriation of a classical narrative that seems to partake more strongly of the imaginary but also indicates how "double reference" pervades an aesthetic framework that suggests how the artist's gaze both responds to an appearance as an appearance and accepts the fading of an apparition into a distance that cannot be mastered. Orpheus cannot remain indifferent to an appearance that haunts him just as he is deflected from the special task of guiding Eurydice without observing her. And yet, the visibility that is momentarily achieved through his gaze is suddenly lost in the abyss of night. Blanchot reveals the paradoxical nature of this unveiling when he recounts the significance of the narrative in terms of the work of art. The Greek myth clearly demonstrates that the work cannot be pursued directly: Orpheus turns back, ruins the work, and Eurydice returns to Hades. However, this fateful movement becomes unavoidable as soon as Orpheus begins to understand that "not to turn toward Eurydice would be no less untrue."[13] Fidelity to what is immeasurable and to the force of circumstances require that a risk be taken, but the truth of the matter is that "only in song does Orpheus have power over Eurydice."[14] This power, nonetheless, is strictly limited. Eurydice has ceased to be present in the voice of the poet, while her mode of appearance cannot be separated from an encounter that once took place and continues to inform the memory of what now appears only as lyric poetry.

Blanchot's interpretation of the Orpheus myth can be related to the dual nature of aesthetic appearance and invites us to question what sort of work actually emerges through the vehicle of the artistic gaze. The gaze of Orpheus is said to be an "ultimate gift to the work," no less than it is the moment when the work is lost.[15] Heidegger places the origin of the work of art in art, rather than in the artist, and provides an alternative to aesthetic experience in reminding us that nothing can be accomplished in a creative vacuum. Blanchot, in contrast, identifies ontological instability with the transformation of the work of art into a "text" that lacks continuous presence and bears a kinship to evanescent appearances.[16] Moreover, while Heidegger provides examples of how the work of art projects a "world" that discloses truth, Blanchot anticipates Jean-Luc Nancy in discussing how the world of sense dissolves when the artist undergoes temporal displacement in an experience of solitude.[17] At the same time, Blanchot's recourse to a certain mode of appearance when describing the impossibility of the work exposes him to the criticisms that Heidegger's approach was designed to counteract; it no longer depends on the work concept that implicitly limits the aesthetics of subjectivity in a poetic ontology.

For Blanchot, however, the dissolution of the stability of the world does not undermine the possibility of art, or even the existence of the world, to the precise degree that the artist is always already related to an alterity that prevents him from being assimilated to self-sameness. Blanchot specifically refers to a "radical reversal" in which the artist perceives a certain object as "the point through which the work's requirements pass," thereby effacing all notions of value and utility in apparent world loss.[18] It is important to acknowledge that this procedure includes two aspects that prevent the loss of stability from resulting in subjective chaos. First, the artist in producing the work of art remains a quasi-subject who views the ordinary world in a new way. For this reason, the artist never simply rises from the ordinary world to the sphere of art but invariably enters a negative relationship to everyday life before providing a different perspective on his goals and values. Moreover, Blanchot does not merely describe how this process occurs but seeks to explain the artist's capacity to move beyond a given world and alter our understanding of the familiar. Hence, the second aspect of this process combines with the first in bringing about a compelling transition: "It is because he already belongs to another time, to time's other, and because he has abandoned time's labor to expose himself to the trial of the essential solitude where fascination reigns" that the artist emerges as relatively unscathed from the initial experience of world loss and includes what is unlike in his account of existence.[19]

Blanchot employs the literature of Franz Kafka to cast light on the artist's exile but also to demonstrate the artist's ability to pass beyond the limits of his own experience. Kafka is the writer who feels banished from any homeland and ultimately discovers that literature alone can offer him something that cannot be identified with the notion of a timeless world. Art is a sign of an "unhappy consciousness" (Hegel) and an antidote to the illusory satisfactions that are the refuge of weak souls. Blanchot identifies Kafka with one of the basic traits of art, which is the capacity to link us "to what is 'outside' the world, and it expresses the profundity of this outside bereft of intimacy and of repose," so that the life of the artist can seem like a perpetual misfortune.[20] The experience of being cast out can be related to a singular discovery. The choice between the homeland before us and the desert beyond does not permit recourse to metaphysical consolations. Kafka understood that his own options were limited and did not allow him to remain at home in a changeless world that possessed overarching significance and sheltered him in this way from the condition of banishment. The artist is the "poet" for whom this world has ceased to exist: "For there exists for him only the outside, the glistening flow of the eternal outside."[21]

Although insisting that art provides access to an outside or sense that is irreducible to inner experience, Blanchot also emphasizes how the artist promotes an encounter with death that assumes many forms in a general economy of creative expression. The example of Stéphane Mallarmé serves the purpose of highlighting the role of death as well as absence and negativity in artistic production. The poet who remarked on the power of words to make physical things absent was also the author of *Igitur*, a verse drama in which the protagonist confronts the midnight of freely chosen death. Blanchot notes that the final version of Mallarmé's poetic drama assumes the form of a soliloquy in which the protagonist, like another Hamlet, becomes a speaking presence who directs us to the ordeals of consciousness.[22] The opposition between pure consciousness and a midnight that threatens to obliterate all thought does not admit of a possible resolution. The problem is that Igitur has never known chance. The dice are only cast at midnight, which is also the hour that does not arrive. Blanchot keenly observes that the successor poem of Igitur is necessarily *Un Coup de dés*, a literary work that gives chance its due. The first poem passes beyond the nothingness of pure consciousness to become a game of chance that compares to an inconclusive narrative, whereas the work that remains evokes the element of uncertainty and risk that inheres in all uses of language. The play between the visible and the invisible only achieves stillness when the poem emerges as a literary object that shines in the portals of being.

Blanchot's approach to Rainer Maria Rilke is consistent with a concern for the relationship between death and writing that pervades his reading of Kafka and Mallarmé, but it also provides a coda to the way that the visible passes into the invisible in the reading process. Mallarmé's poetry brings us to the brink of death in the consciousness of Igitur and in the transformation of the work into a site of dispersal and a mark of limits. Rilke's early attitude toward death is perhaps similar to what can be found in Friedrich Nietzsche when read as a precursor to existentialism. A well-stated abhorrence for the modern depersonalization of death is a constant theme in the poet's only novel, *The Notebooks of Malte Laurids Brigge* (*Die Aufzeichnunger des Malte Laurids Brigge*, 1910). And yet, Rilke's late poetry commemorates "the fruition of the visible in the invisible for which we are responsible," just as it epitomizes "the very task of dying."[23] This task is analogous to the translation of things into verbal realities that takes place in the silent world of poetry. Blanchot contrasts the role of change in life and its more profound role in art as memorialized in Rilke's *Duino Elegies* (*Duineser Elegien*, 1923), the testament of the poet's final years, a sequence that demonstrates how "in imaginary space things are transformed into that which cannot be grasped. Out of use, beyond wear, they are not in our possession but are the movement of dispossession which releases us both from them and from ourselves."[24] The space that provides the basis for this change both exceeds and occasions the things that change, reconciling the world of things and the language of nonbeing.

Blanchot's meditation on literature assigns the poem the task of constituting a space that allows the passage between the visible and the invisible. The possibility of this passage occurs in the space of the Open, which is not to be confused with the site of the poet: "This is the Orphic space to which the poet doubtless has no access, where he can penetrate only to disappear," so that any intimacy that he brings to this opening is only achieved at the cost of silence.[25] The disruption of the world that occurs in the creation of the work of art opens a "space" in which things can newly appear because "absence is also the presence of things" in their being.[26] And yet, the work of art radiates a "being" that is not the being of things but contains inside and outside at once; it refers to a space that is "prior" to everyday life experience and serves as the starting point for world-constituting practices. Blanchot is less interested in placing the work before us as the setting for truth than in foregrounding the open as the productive space in which the work of art quietly unfolds: "The Open is the work, but the work is origin."[27]

A NEW HERMENEUTIC

Blanchot's account of art and literature allows us to assess the broader implications of a hermeneutical theory that challenges received notions of modern culture. Various hermeneutical motifs foreground the interactive nature of text, reader, and community in terms of the opening of the work as a gateway to time and alterity. In this part of the discussion, I will be concerned with how Blanchot anticipates but also surpasses the position of Hans-Georg Gadamer, whose major treatise, *Truth and Method* (*Wahrheit und Methode*, 1960), develops modern hermeneutics in a systematic form largely as a response to Heidegger's ontological concerns. Blanchot, in contrast, goes beyond Gadamer in his conception of the literary reader and the "language" of writing, in his view of the historical significance of works and, finally, in his own way of saying that the literary work is an "event" rather than an object.

Blanchot's emphasis on the reader in constituting the work of art might be compared to Gadamer's position on how a "fusion of horizons" mediates between the perspectives of reader and author in literary reception.[28] Without denying that a text possesses hermeneutical value that cannot be revealed through a narrowly historical analysis, Gadamer argues that interpretation occurs somewhere between the intentions of an author and the motivations of a reader who approaches the text in a contemporary setting. Subsequent to Gadamer's elaboration of this concept, Hans Robert Jauss develops a more historically oriented approach to literary reception that allows us to study a text in terms of the history of readings that transform its meaning in time. Roman Ingarden had previously demonstrated in detailed analyses that literary reception is temporally layered and allows us to correlate the reader's motivations with the production of the literary work of art as a harmonious structure. Blanchot's contribution to the problem of reception is even more strongly antihistoricist and anticipates the thought of Barthes, Michel Foucault, and Derrida, whose poststructuralist thematic derives from Sausurrean linguistics. For Blanchot, the act of reading does not primarily establish contact with sedimented meanings but liberates us from original intentions: "The reader does not add himself to the book, but tends primarily to relieve it of an author."[29] Rather than contend that literary meaning is negotiated in a middle zone that mediates original intentions with contemporary directives, Blanchot conceives of the literary text as an impersonal manifestation in which writing appears *as* writing. The literary text in this sense is a phenomenon that does not simply pair the reader's subjectivity with that of the author but introduces a sphere of knowing that tests the limits of the unthought.

The author therefore "dies" in a precise sense when the reader constitutes a work that no longer coincides with the intentions of the author who produced it. On this basis, Blanchot "affirms the new lightness of the book" and displaces the role of the author in the reception of meaning. But does this imply that the reader can construe any meaning in disregarding the real or apparent intentions of an imputed author? Blanchot answers this question when he compares the role of the reader to the process of shaping a sculptural work: "Reading gives to the book the abrupt existence which the sculpture 'seems' to get from the chisel alone."[30] This does not mean that the book would cease to exist if it went unread, but that, like the sculpture shaped from stone, the book acquires standing existence when reading isolates it from the flow of meanings that might allow us to situate the work in the past and, thus, to finalize interpretation. Blanchot does not conceive of the literary work as an ideal object that can be grasped as either a timeless mental entity or as the concretization of universal schemata. Instead, he posits the radical difference between a work that is always partially concealed but contains limited meanings and *a work to come* where "everything which does have meaning returns as towards its origin."[31] For Blanchot, literary reception is less of a "fusion of horizons" than a liberation from sedimented meanings that are no longer part of an ongoing interpretation.

By detaching the literary work from the intentions of the author, the reader can join the origin of the work with the movement that carries us beyond the meanings that are initially evident. Because this act of detachment is possible, Blanchot can reenvision the literary work as capable of resituating us in life, just as it possesses the power to alter existence in innumerable ways:

> The book, the written thing, enters the world and carries out its work of transformation and negation. It, too, is the future of many other things, and not only books: by the projects which it can give rise to, by the undertaking it encourages, by the totality of the world on which it is a modified reflection, it is an infinite source of new realities, and because of these new realities existence will be something it was not before.[32]

The reception of the literary work is therefore inseparable from an effort to vary the given precisely because the work derives from a world that is undergoing change on a continual basis. At the same time, we should not attempt to naturalize this process of change, which requires what we might call a phenomenology of language. With reference to Mallarmé, Blanchot emphasizes how the poet undergoes a reduction in presence that corresponds to a decisive displacement: "The poet disappears beneath the pressure of the work, by the same impulse that causes natural beauty to disappear."[33] Both the poet and the natural world are transposed into a movement that occurs in language and nowhere else, since language is "the only initiator and principle: the source."[34]

By implicating the literary work in the process of change, Blanchot also helps us understand how the reader responds to art's vocation in historical terms. History provides us with the second point of possible convergence with modern hermeneutics, but once again Blanchot departs from what might have been a simple agreement. Gadamer's stated preference for mediatory over historicist approaches to art suggests an opposition to antiquarianism that seems to echo Blanchot's notion of the work to come. However, although Gadamer's notion of the classic was not intended to conflate normative and Greco-Roman conceptions of art, this same notion enshrines the past in the mode of continual presence, particularly when it argues that the canonical work can speak in a contemporary context.[35] Blanchot emphasizes in contrast that the fragmentary experience of history is essential to what remains true of traditional conceptions of art. The reader, thus conceived, experiences the work's distance, but this is what allows him or her to consider the work's genesis as a displaced origin. In Blanchot's account of literature, history possesses a divisive meaning and, more strongly than Gadamer, indicates how the past is only recovered in the "space" where alterity informs interpretation anew.

Blanchot willingly acknowledges that art can become an enduring reality when it is interpreted according to a plurality of cultural values and across varied circumstances. The historical aspect of reception is what guarantees the integrity of an "endless conversation" that draws on many perspectives and ceaselessly initiates a dialogue with the past. Gadamer refers to how the work is encountered in a "history of effects" that might have the cumulative significance of implying an immediate totality. Blanchot argues that the continual search for new interpretations is what gives the work its historical future. Art has a public significance, which is not predicated on the presence of a past achievement that has been reaffirmed as a canonical value. Blanchot acknowledges that the Greek dramas contain meanings that have become opaque in time, signifying a reality that is no longer accessible. The Eumenides will never speak again, but from another standpoint, "each time they speak it is the unique birth of their language that they announce."[36] Their first utterances occurred in the primeval night of myth, whereas they later became synonymous with the ascendancy of law and order. When they speak tomorrow, their words may be part of a literary work in which the language of origin has acquired a more intimate meaning.

Blanchot also shows us that the work of art is an event in the radical sense of providing a basis for new beginnings. The notion of the work as an event constitutes the third possible area of convergence between Blanchot and modern hermeneutics as conceived in the wake of Gadamer's critique of Romantic historicism. One traditionalist approach to art turns away from the process character of what comes to us from the past and reaches us in the here and now. Gadamer's critique of the Romantic approach to history as remote and inaccessible (which can be used to support the traditional view) is consistent with Blanchot's suspicion of academic historicism, but more importantly, the hermeneutical rehabilitation of art as a possible source of knowledge draws on the notion that "the language of art is an encounter with an unfinished event and is itself part of this event."[37] Gadamer cautiously affirms Hegelian models of historical research, which in his interpretation foregrounds the present, over Romantic ones that value the past for its own sake. Blanchot also acknowledges the power of Hegel's arguments, and yet, in a different spirit, Blanchot returns to the work of art as historical in a way that is irreducible to any survey that would minimize the importance of the work's beginning. The trained historian may be too methodologically encumbered to grasp the event-like quality of artworks, but the work does not lack historical resonance because "it is an event, the event of history itself, and this is because its most steadfast claim is to give to the word beginning all of its force."[38] In a style that might evoke a nonclassical reading of Hegel's aesthetics, Blanchot's inaugural poetics invites us to interpret all of art as an ongoing encounter with a history that remains forever in process.

WRITING AS BEGINNING

In the early part of my discussion, I compared Blanchot's approach to the literary work and Heidegger's understanding of the work of art, broaching the possibility that Merleau-Ponty's notion of visibility clarifies the mode in which the space of literature opens our sense of works. What I wish to do now is to examine some of the deeper aspects of this space, particularly in terms of what Blanchot has called writing. Blanchot's approach to the literary text opens the significance of writing, as opposed to a purely verbal understanding of what constitutes the literary. Timothy Clark has discussed how this approach required the development of modern poetry to become theoretically compelling: "The space of text, with Mallarmé, becomes no longer one of voice, but of writing, whose force is always to break away from narrowly representational constraints."[39] This notion of literary or textual space does not map onto external reality any more than it participates in the regime of everyday speech. Blanchot refers to an "essential language" that appears when the poet occupies a space that opposes our mimetic expectations:

> Sounds, rhythm, number, all that does not count in current speech, now become most important. That is because words need to be visible; they need their own reality that can intervene between what is and what they express. Their duty is to draw the gaze to themselves and turn it away from the thing of which they speak. Yet their presence is our gauge for the absence of all the rest.[40]

Without depriving poetry of its visible dimension, Blanchot also emphasizes how writing is the crucial term that expresses "a rupture with language understood as that which represents," just as it breaks with the manifestations of sensible appearance.[41] Writing in this sense must be conceived in a concrete way as a kind of "other" that provides the space within which thinking can occur: "Uncontained by any system or any conceptual or empirical limit, it is a species of infinity, or, better, of infinitizing."[42] The word of the poet is thus an appearance of what no longer appears, evoking "the imaginary, the incessant, the interminable."[43]

Early in our discussion, Blanchot's adoption of the Orpheus myth as a paradigm for considering the poetic imaginary was examined in terms of Heidegger's use of the work of art, which provides a model for assessing the concept of "world" in phenomenological terms. What is easy to overlook in both cases is the modern contribution to our understanding of the matter at hand. In Blanchot's case, the myth of Orpheus is elaborated in terms of Rilke's poetry rather than simply as a classical myth that had its home in ancient Greek tradition. For Heidegger, in a similar way, the "world" of the peasant women derives from reflections on Van Gogh's painting of peasant shoes, a modern work of art that reveals hermeneutical possibilities that are expressed in language. Blanchot's recourse to the myth of Orpheus is also a paradigm for interpreting the reversal that occurs when appearance passes into disappearance but also produces a work that is other than anything else in the world. His literary work of art is difficult to assimilate to any ontological project, even the most generous, to the degree that it evokes a "space" that is noncontinuous and perpetually inaugural. Writing is the name that describes the semiotic process through which the subject is disinvested of its personal features but also enables encounters with an alterity that is potentially transformative.

In coming to terms with these claims, we might briefly compare what Blanchot calls writing to what Derrida has discussed under the heading of *différance*, which places writing in the foreground of a new theory of linguistic functioning. In the early essay, "Différance," Derrida argues that the space *between* signs, rather than the phonemic structure of verbal units, forms the site where language acquires its distinctive features. Although acknowledging that "there is no purely and strictly phonetic writing," Derrida reminds us that writing contains graphic features, but also that writing is produced through an inaudible play of differences that do not allow us to reduce individual marks to discrete sounds.[44] Inaudibility would be what guarantees the play of signs in a fully differentiated model of language, which could never be free of silence even though what cannot be heard is rarely acknowledged as an aspect of verbal utterances. According to this model, verbal utterances would always bear a relation to the movement of graphic signifiers that give spoken language its distinctive features, just as written language is never reducible to the audible expressions that accompany it. As readers of Derrida, we need to rethink the possibility of writing so that *neither* writing nor speech can be assigned the meanings that were adequate to them in the tradition. Writing in Derrida's sense implies "semiotic" motility and would not be "indifferent" to variation; it would spur a transformation of meanings, allowing speech/writing to become a play of opposites.

Writing in this sense also undoes the experience of a pure present that was already under critique in Hegel but does not exhaust Derrida's recourses. Surely this possibility could not be based on the metaphysical notion that language is grounded in a presence that precedes the "text" of language, which would conceal how language presupposes "a retention and protention of differences, a spacing and temporalizing, a play of traces—all of this must be a kind of writing before the letter, an archi-writing without a present origin, without archi-."[45] And yet, would this mean that the traditional Logos—as a lived unity that brought together a complex verbal heritage of spiritual meaning—has been abandoned in favor of a diffuse substratum that never could be known or given historical significance? In his critique of Jean Rousset's structuralism, Derrida discusses how language only comes into its own when it cannot be conceived along the lines of communication but becomes instead "a sign without signification," as well as an inscription, because "paradoxically, inscription alone—although it is always far from always doing so—has the power of poetry, in other words, has the power to arouse speech from its slumber as sign."[46]

Are we entitled on this basis to argue that writing has a dialectical future? Julia Kristeva has questioned the viability of Derridean *différance* as "a nonrenewable, nonproductive redundancy" in contrast to the resources provided by Hegelian dialectics.[47] My suggestion is that *différance* performs a role in Derrida's philosophy that compares to that of negation in the philosophy of Hegel, which is not to argue that the two terms are equivalent. Blanchot's use of writing was presented previously as a reversal of subjectivity, which was prefigured in Heidegger's poetic ontology that anticipates, without clarifying, a *textual* approach to literature. Moreover, the role of layering in the formation of texts is what allows writing to be read as a social performance, that is, as a drama that presupposes a "system of relations between strata" rather than the nucleus of a homogenous accomplishment.[48] Because the literary work is also an event, the community that it implies would be complimentary to the heterogeneity that it evokes and requires a rethinking of what it means to be a singular being in the midst of plurality. Agreeing but modifying the older Aristotelean dictum that being is said in many ways, Nancy casts light on how ontology must undergo a decisive transformation once it ceases to be identified with the totality of what is present: "The multiplicity of the said (that is, of the sayings) belongs to Being in its constitution. This occurs with each said, that is always singular; it occurs in each said, beyond each said, and as the multiplicity of the totality of being."[49]

Moreover, if writing is the other of speech, this other remains an aspect of speech in all instances, and the Logos must already always retain features that modify whatever limits interpretation to the sayable and the known. In a late meditation on the thought of Emmanuel Lévinas, Derrida even argues that Logos would remain "indispensable" within the context of a movement that negotiates a new space and according to a new logic:

> It is not, then, a thought of the limit, at least not that limit all too easily figured forth by the word "beyond" so necessary for the transaction. The passage beyond language requires language or rather a text as the trace of the place of a step that is not (present) elsewhere. That is why the movement of that trace, passing beyond language, is not classical nor does it render the *logos* either secondary or instrumental.[50]

The text to which Derrida refers inscribes the trace of a certain movement; however, such a movement compares to a step that is somehow incomparable. This analogy returns us to the trace of writing as the condition for the possibility of (re)interpretation that enables the community to dwell in time. And yet, rather than being constructed through boundaries that guard its absolute integrity, any community that belongs to this space will enlist what is irrevocably outside; it exceeds the limits of the everyday, while preserving the poetic in our own midst. Instead of being reducible to any appearing sign, the trace would be precisely what allows the member of the existing community to maintain that the instituted is *merely* instituted, rather than provided by nature as the limit of personal identity.

Hannah Arendt has discussed how the possibility of beginning anew exceeds the limits of knowledge and cannot be understood apart from the question of who I am. This possibility is as old as the Augustinian belief in the possibility of claiming a new origin in the mode of a recurrent recollection, but what Arendt emphasizes in this case is not so much the role of memory in enlivening the past as the ontological conditions that allow the beginning to be made: "This beginning is not the same as the beginning of the world; it is not the beginning of something but of somebody, who is a beginner himself."[51] Blanchot is closer to this viewpoint than he is to the Gadamerian notion of affirming the truth of art as an alternative to Kantian and post-Kantian aesthetics. He underscores the role of beginnings in history without depriving inaugural poetics of its meaning as a space in which the past is seized on as novelty, thus allowing the self to be disinvested of its stable features as it crosses a threshold that cannot be anticipated in advance. Literature for Blanchot is uniquely situated in its evanescence to present a kind of truth that calls attention to our mortality, thus pointing back to a reversal in which subjectivity is longer defined primarily through interior meaning. The work of art provides us with a reminder of a death that all of us share, but it also unfolds in the fragile space of an infinite conversation, suggesting that no community is more difficult to preserve than the community to come.

The question of community is once again central to the work of major thinkers who have contributed to the Continental tradition, including but not limited to Blanchot, Derrida, Giorgio Agamben and Nancy. What is less clear is that the Hegelian tradition still has something to add to the ongoing debate over the *possibility* of community as an ideal that is not exhausted by totalizing accounts of how social life often appears to be organized as a transparent object of knowledge. My two final chapters are concerned with how literature in the wake of Proust explores an interiority that not only indicates how the subject is constructed in a process where unity is no longer present to immediate experience but is also torn between conflicting loyalties and personal interests. Nevertheless, while Proust and the modernists who came later focused on the situation of the individual as a being of conflict and desire, the authors whose works form the basis for my concluding studies are more concerned with the systemic meanings that derive from sharp encounters with historical institutions. The challenge that is faced in each case can be related to the place of language and writing in an open economy of signs, but the result is never uncomplicated. Transformation occurs, or becomes a possibility, only when historical institutions are confronted through refection, irony, and self-criticism. Each study will therefore demonstrate how figural space provides the setting for whatever alterations assume an ongoing, if not dialectical, character. The outcome of both studies is a vindication, however qualified, of "Hegelianism" to the degree that this term can be assigned a new, and not a merely historical, significance.

NOTES

1. The role that Edmund Husserl's conception of categorial intuition performs in Martin Heidegger's ontology is examined in Jiro Watanabe, "Categorial Intuition and the Understanding of Being in Husserl and Heidegger," *Reading Heidegger: Commemorations*, ed. John Sallis (Bloomington: Indiana University Press, 1993), 109–17. The influence of Husserl's *Logical Investigations*, particularly the Sixth Investigation, on Heidegger's attempt to disclose the limitations of the propositional theory of truth was crucial to the hermeneutical tradition, beginning with Gadamer, who argues that language is the horizon of ontology in *Truth and Method*, 438–91.

2. Reiner Schürmann argues that the first eight sections of *Being and Time* constitute a sort of prolegomena that draws on Plato and Aristotle, rather than modern philosophy, in the effort to retrieve the question of being. In Schürmann's reading of Heidegger, intuition is under critique to the degree that it is concerned primarily with the cognitive status of objects as opposed to the understanding of *Dasein*. For details, see Reiner Schürmann, "Heidegger's *Being and Time*" in *On Heidegger's "Being and Time"* (London: Routledge, 2008), 56–131.

3. The status of language as everyday discourse as well as the role of language in the expressive disclosure of truth are both discussed in Martin Heidegger, *Being and Time*, translated by Joan Stambaugh (Albany: State University of New York, 1996), I.5A, section 34, 150–56; I.6 section 44, 196–212.

4. After developing a comprehensive criticism of Descartes's concept of world, Heidegger works out a phenomenological understanding of world on the basis a new approach to spatiality in *Being and Time*, I.3, sections 22–24, 94–105.

5. Compare Martin Heidegger, *"Der Ursprung des Kunstwerkes"* in *Holzwege, Gesamtausgabe* (Frankfurt am Main: Vittorio Klostermann, 1977), 5:19; "The Origin of the Work of Art," *Poetry, Language, Thought*, trans. Albert Hofstadter (New York: HarperCollins, 2001), 33.

6. The formation of the lifeworld by "anonymous" subjective phenomena is discussed in Edmund Husserl, *The Crisis of European Sciences and Transcendental Phenomenology: An*

Introduction to Phenomenological Philosophy, translated by David Carr (Evanston, IL: Northwestern University Press, 1999), IIIA, section 29, 111–14. From this standpoint, the task of philosophy is to investigate "anonymous" subjectivity as existing prior to what we accomplish in more limited spheres: "Before all accomplishments there has always already been a universal accomplishment, presupposed by all human *praxi*s and all prescientific life." Husserl, *The Crisis of European Sciences*, IIIA, section 29, 113.

7. Under the heading of the radical reversal, Blanchot implicitly refers to Immanuel Lévinas after discussing Heidegger's "possibility of impossibility," thus inviting us to consider finitude in a new way. See Maurice Blanchot, *The Space of Literature*, trans. Ann Smock (Lincoln: University of Nebraska Press), 140. A discussion of the full implications of this shift can be found in Lars Iyer, *Blanchot's Vigilance: Literature, Phenomenology and the Ethical* (New York: Palgrave Macmillan, 2005), 16–20. Clearly, the Lévinasian term, "impossibility of possibility," radically qualifies the possibility of all human projects and no longer allows being-toward-death to open a future in Dasein's present.

8. Blanchot, *The Space of Literature*, 16.

9. For a critical discussion of the use of third person narrative in modern novels, see Roland Barthes, *Writing Degree Zero*, trans. Annette Lavers and Colin Smith (New York: Hill and Wang, 1968), 29–40.

10. In Hegel's aesthetic theory, the process whereby substance becomes other than nature is described as involving religious intuition: "Only through this intuition of the being of God as the purely spiritual and imageless, contrasted with the mundane and natural, is spirit completely wrested from nature and sense and released from existence in the finite." See Hegel, *Aesthetics*, I:371. For Hegel, religious monotheism, as enshrined in the Hebrew scripture and Persian lyric poetry, expresses the sublime in texts that no longer require the vehicle of nature.

11. Merleau-Ponty, *The Visible and the Invisible*, 123.

12. Ibid.,124.

13. Blanchot, *The Space of Literature*, 172.

14. Ibid., 173.

15. Ibid., 174.

16. See Roland Barthes, "From Work to Text," in *Image Music Text*, trans. by Stephen Heath (New York: Farrar, Straus and Giroux, 1988), 155–64.

17. Jean-Luc Nancy argues that, under conditions of late modernity, the world is largely deprived of sense in a postreligious situation that threatens the survival of the world as an ontological constant. This event, however, does not means the end of sense but that the world's sense has become immanent. See Jean-Luc Nancy, "The End of the World," in *The Sense of the World*, trans. Jeffrey S. Librett (Minneapolis: University of Minnesota Press, 1997), 4–9. Blanchot seems to have embraced the literary implications of world loss but does not, for this reason, accept the solipsistic outcome that might have resulted from this predicament. His phenomenology of art and artist enacts a transformative meaning that enables the world to be recuperated on both pragmatic and aesthetic grounds.

18. Blanchot, *The Space of Literature*, 47.

19. Ibid., 47.

20. Ibid., 75.

21. Ibid., 83.

22. Ibid., 115–16.

23. Ibid., 141.

24. Ibid.

25. Ibid., 142.

26. Ibid., 158–59.

27. Ibid., 142.

28. We should note here that Gadamer's notion of a "fusion of horizons" presupposes two interpretive horizons, rather than a process whereby past and present completely merge. In clarifying this historical concept, Gadamer asks why there is the need to speak of *fusion* instead of *one horizon*, when understanding always occurs with the setting of a given tradition. Significantly, he then discusses how interpretation requires *texts* that introduce alterity into historical

consciousness, at least before fusion enables the horizon to be (re)formed as traditionary. See especially Gadamer, *Truth and Method*, 306–7.

29. Blanchot, *The Space of Literature*, 193.
30. Ibid., 193.
31. Ibid.,196.
32. Maurice Blanchot, *The Work of Fire*, trans. Charlotte Mandell (Stanford, CA:: Stanford University Press, 1995), 314.
33. Maurice Blanchot, *The Book to Come*, trans. Charlotte Mandell (Stanford, CA: Stanford University, 2003), 228.
34. Ibid., 229.
35. Gadamer distinguishes this conception of the classic from Greco-Roman models of normativity but also attempts to ground the notion in an experience of timelessness according to which the past is experienced in the mode of the present. See Gadamer, *Truth and Method*, 285–90. Because this notion of the classic might not be able to acknowledge how disjunction can overtake temporal experience, Gadamer restores continuity in a manner that grounds canonicity in an interpretive self. Blanchot's model of reading would not reject canonicity on principle, but it would allow us to imagine "other worlds" as posing hermeneutical problems to any interpreter, and, for this reason, as offering ongoing challenges to any settled reading.
36. Blanchot, *The Space of Literature*, 206.
37. Gadamer, *Truth and Method*, 99.
38. Blanchot, *The Space of Literature*, 228.
39. Timothy Clark, *Derrida, Heidegger, Blanchot: Sources of Derrida's Notion and Practice of Literature* (London: Cambridge University Press, 1992), 68.
40. Blanchot, *The Work of Fire*, 31–32.
41. Maurice Blanchot, *The Infinite Conversation*, trans. Susan Hanson (Minneapolis: University of Minnesota Press, 1993), 261.
42. Clark, *Derrida, Heidegger, Blanchot*, 80.
43. Blanchot, *The Space of Literature*, 40.
44. Jacques Derrida, "Différance," in *Margins of Philosophy*, trans. Alan Bass (Chicago: University of Chicago Press, 1982), 3–15.
45. Ibid., 15.
46. See Jacques Derrida, "Force and Signification," in *Writing and Difference*, trans. Alan Bass (Chicago: University of Chicago Press, 1978), 12.
47. Kristeva, *Revolution in Poetic Language*, 145.
48. Derrida, "Freud and the Scene of Writing," 285.
49. Jean-Luc Nancy, "Being Singular Plural," in *Being Singular Plural*, trans. Robert D. Richardson and Anne E. O'Byrne (Stanford, CA: Stanford University Press, 2000), 38.
50. Jacques Derrida, "At This Very Moment in This Work Here I Am," in *Re-Reading Lévinas*, edited by Robert Bernasconi and Simon Critchley (London: Athlone, 1991), 20.
51. Hannah Arendt, *The Human Condition* (Chicago: University and Chicago Press, 1958), 177.

Chapter Seven

Revisiting Jean Rhys

Postcolonial Aesthetics

The difficulty of defining a human community in unambiguous terms is heightened when the cultural sphere is riven by historical conflicts. During the colonial era, the problem of establishing the boundaries for community becomes acute when colonizer and colonized occupy different worlds in the wake of immense cultural disparities. The idea of the political in such instances is hard to reconcile with standard interpretations of how universality is represented through legitimate governance. My strategy in this regard is to demonstrate how aesthetic experience is the terrain where the question of political legitimacy is contested, not through discursive opposition but through a sense of radical displacement that has been brought to light in Julia Kristeva's account of abjection. In this regard, I first explore Jean Rhys's early experimental fiction and then proceed to discuss her acknowledged masterpiece, *Wide Sargasso Sea*, a literary work that indicates how the unstable opposition between the symbolic and the semiotic occurs in figural space, thus enabling the question of norms to assume special importance. My approach to Rhys's fiction is inflected by psychoanalysis but also considers the role of figural space as a locus for reading, just as it ultimately suggests the movement from aesthetics to political reflection that G. W. F. Hegel's own philosophy more strongly foregrounds.

ABJECTION IN VIRTUAL LIFE

Rhys's early novels acquire special complexity when explored as texts that suspend the usual distinction between autobiographical and impersonal meanings. The result is what I would like to call a "virtualization of experience," which becomes increasingly evident in the fiction that Rhys begins to produce during the 1930s. But virtualization contains a deeper meaning that is not to be limited to the phenomenon of derealization but suspends the protagonist's relationship to a largely mythic past. By implicitly questioning the mythic world view on which colonization depends, Rhys's early novels already prepare the reader for a postcolonial standpoint, even when they unfold in colonial contexts. In *Voyage in the Dark* (1934), for instance, Rhys presumably tells the story of her own journey to England as a young art student from Jamaica.[1] Rhys dramatizes Anna Morgan's journey through rapid transitions in point of view and indeterminate references to the past. In passages that anticipate the novels of Nathalie Sarraute, Rhys presents her characters from the subatomic standpoint.[2] The time of the Constance Estate is shown to be overwhelmed by the unending threat of material disintegration: "That's how the road to Constance is—green, and the smell of green, and then the smell of water and dark earth and rotting leaves and damp."[3] This image enacts a subversion of origins through which the journey to safe haven is caught up in patterns of death and decay.

Anna's arrival in England is characterized by a kind of metaphysical reversal: "The streets looked different that day, just as a reflection is different from the real thing."[4] In the dream of a return voyage, Anna's perception of "nature" begins to depend more on mirror images than on the things themselves: "These were English trees, their leaves trailing in the water."[5] Unstable reflections provide clues into the process of dissolution through which the subject struggles to survive loss and abjection. The metaphor of darkness that underlies this narrative does not simply refer to a condition of ignorance but reminds us of an absence that haunts a disoriented protagonist, who neither discovers the past in the signs of semiotic doubling nor meets the present as a port of arrival. The darkness that overwhelms the present invalidates a vaguely Edenic beginning and disturbs a present that is unmoored and inhospitable. It is as if the surrounding world, instead of protecting the protagonist, provides the occasion for an impending disaster that prevents the journey itself from reaching its goal.

The highpoint of virtualization is reached in *Good Morning, Midnight* (1939), a novel in which Rhys combines modernist technique with scattered allusions to a barely accessible, colonial world. This novel provides details of social life and suggests the role of illusion in the quest for self-knowledge. After her lover reminds her that deception performs a crucial role in life experience, Sasha Jensen learns that truth is more likely to be revealed in the aesthetic imaginary than through a disinterested reflection on objects: "You imagine the carefully pruned, shaped thing that is presented to you is truth. This is just what it isn't. The truth is improbable, the truth is fantastic; it's in what you think is a distorting mirror that you see the truth."[6] Sasha's truth might be compared to T. S. Eliot's evocative description of exhausted life in *The Waste Land*, where the metaphor of the Unreal City might be interpreted as a continuation of Charles Baudelaire's Romanticism in sustaining the opposition between nature and artifice. However, Rhys's novel also argues in a different way that a virtualization of the cosmopolitan setting is a precondition for the rearrangement of the sensible and the *possible* emergence of a new order of truth. While Eliot's poem testifies to an unreality that pervades the surface of modern life, with its recently interned casualties of war and the turmoil that results from ongoing dislocation, Rhys's novel uses virtualization to refer to a sharp contrast between rival groups and the "truth" that is entangled in fateful encounters.

Good Morning, Midnight is inscribed with historical conflict in its basic concerns, juxtaposing various cultural attitudes with the realities of a colonial world that comes to light in images that reveal and conceal underlying tensions. A painter named Serge shows Sasha a set of African masks whose expressions are difficult to distinguish from those of the white colonists with whom both are deeply familiar. Later, we learn about a woman from Martinique whose biracial marriage has incurred the disapproval of the white community: "She said that every time they looked at her she could see how they hated her, and the people in the streets looked at her in the same way."[7] The opposition between oppressor and oppressed, which emerged in the Caribbean world during the period of slavery, structures a gaze that reminds us of how otherness was instituted by the white oppressors as a rigid designate that inhibits fluid communication.[8]

The specter of a female protagonist, as excluded from *both* the colonial and metropolitan world, emerges in the conclusion to *Good Morning, Midnight*, which becomes semiotically empty just as the reader begins to search for spiritual resolution. Through symbolic gestures, Sasha tries vainly to give a place to the ancient gods on the streets of Paris. Even this effort becomes meaningless as she reflects on a series of deities who have failed her, now that love, knowledge, and redemption have revealed themselves to be illusory: "But I know quite well that all this is hallucination, imagination is dead. Venus is dead; Apollo is dead; even Jesus is dead."[9] Unreality, however, is less a matter of losing grip on reality than the hollowing out of divinity at a time when the gods have fled and their traces are no longer to be found in the world at large. In this moment of abjection, the protagonist loses the capacity to integrate concrete experience into symbolic meaning and is overwhelmed by spiritual emptiness. In subverting the traditional reading of James Joyce's *Ulysses* as an application of "mythic method" to modern writing, Rhys constructs the figure of Sasha as a rejoinder to familiar cultural representations of women as fecund, unified and instinctually whole.[10]

Chapter 7
NARRATIVE AS POLYLOGUE

The publication of *Wide Sargasso Sea* (1966) marks the end of a long period when the author refrained from publishing new novels. In this final novel, the author draws on her own past as a time when she sought to rediscover herself in an alien milieu, while also providing a new framework for transmitting her knowledge of colonial history. It is perhaps no accident that, as a literary outsider, Rhys composed a work that would assume the form of a polylogue, or play of voices, rather than a linear narrative, and that the voices that compose this novel would be consoling, poetic, threatening, and violent by turns, depending on the setting and situation of the speaker. This three-part novel concerns life in Jamaica in the 1840s and includes references that mark the era as one that has only begun to emerge from the ordeal of slavery. The narrator in Part I is a female voice, providing a poetic account of a vanished childhood, whereas Part II is largely, but not entirely, narrated by a male voice who speaks in a monotone that sharply contrasts to the voice that opens the novel. Other voices fill the novel—those of minor characters that are sometimes accusatory but at other times merely inform the reader of how we should view those who often run at cross-purposes and are perhaps destined to remain in conflict, due largely to profound cultural differences that are only exacerbated by the colonial system.

Antoinette is the first voice to emerge in a semiotic tour de force that provides the reader with brief but telling glimpses into a cultural imaginary shaped by images, metaphors, and memories in which the past is recreated, even when its space is fragmented. Significantly, the novel opens with Antoinette's statement: "The Jamaican ladies had never approved of my mother, because 'she pretty like pretty self' Christophine said."[11] Christophine is the Black servant from Martinique who was brought into the parental marriage by the mother's first husband, but the image that she doubles brings together Antoinette and Annette, the mother whose life the daughter will repeat as the words of Christophine innocently suggest. Gayatri Spivak has discussed how the myth of Narcissus, as it first emerges in Ovid's *Metamorphosis*, is adopted to the novel and serves a crucial role from beginning to end, with Antoinette generally failing to recognize her own closure in various images, whether as mirror image or image of the other woman whose dehumanization is guaranteed by the process of colonization.[12] To read in this way, however, is to remain too much within a thematic of representation. If the novel is conceived as a polylogue, the role of multiple discourses in an unfolding narrative prevents us from assuming that any one discourse is entirely flawed, even when it is mystified. The problem is simply that the voice of an unreliable narrator may be misleading, not that it is incapable of offering us insights into a medley of voices that are difficult to separate.

Antoinette's narrative, especially as presented in Part I, is entangled in myth and memory but can be read as a projection onto a past that cannot be recovered. The account that she provides of childhood in Coulibri sharply contrasts to the idyllic natural setting with the remote, imaginary, and incredible world of English emblems and cultural references. *Wide Sargasso Sea*, like Rhys's previous novels, also makes use of the myth of nature, but this time Rhys weaves dense historical material as an ironic foil to the Jamaican landscape of presumably natural experience. Antoinette's description of Coulibri has ominous overtones:

> Our garden was large and beautiful as that garden in the Bible—the tree of life grew there. The paths were overgrown and a smell of dead flowers mixed with the fresh living smell. Underneath the tree ferns, tall as forest tree ferns, the light was green. Orchids flourished out of reach or for some reason not to be touched. One was snaky looking, another like an octopus with long thin brown tentacles bare of leaves hanging from a twisted root.[13]

From one standpoint, this natural setting is inscribed in a textual lesson that underscores the impossibility of sustaining innocence as separation from life. However, the introduction of ambiguity into this ideal place also seems to be out of keeping with the world of colonial rule and its culture of static artworks. Antoinette always stares into a clouded mirror, which alters her gaze so that the image that comes back to her is not that of a changeless self. The myth of Eden, like that of Narcissus, is marked with opposition as well as variability. A reproduction of "The Miller's Daughter" may refer to a child's view of the mother country, but it also foregrounds the difference between Antoinette's stepfather, Mr. Mason, and her own mother, a Creole now remarried to an Englishman.[14]

Longing for contact and immediacy, Antoinette turns to Tia, a native Jamaican, for companionship. The possibility of an interracial friendship in the colonial world has been questioned by Edward Braithwaite, who comments on the Antoinette/Tia relationship in terms of the enduring legacy of racial inequality.[15] Rhys herself suggests that a harshly oppositional dress code quickly undoes whatever friendship might have flourished between them. Taking Antoinette's dress from her, Tia gives her own dress to her accepting companion. After discussing the matter with Christophine, Antoinette's mother burns the dress that her daughter wears in exchange for her own.[16] Veronique Gregg has argued that this same episode dramatizes how relations between Creoles and native Blacks in postemancipation Jamaica were still governed by a system that required external signs to function socially.[17] The limitation of this argument is not that some sort of middle term is readily available as a means for reworking an opposition; on the contrary, the opposition is historical and needs to be confronted in all of its harshness and intractability. However, even if friendship cannot be envisioned as a concrete possibility, we need to ask ourselves if new social relations can be *thought* within the limits of the text that the writer has composed.

The burning of Coulibri sets up a scene of instruction in which Antoinette's ambiguous place in the colonial system seems to be regulated by a fateful opposition. As a literary representation of native violence, the burning of the ancestral estate in postslavery Jamaica could be said to perpetuate the old myth of innate ferocity that the author may have given a racial twist.[18] Nonetheless, this burning also precipitates a crisis in Antoinette's identity as a native colonial when it involves a sudden rupture in her relationship with Tia. After Tia assaults her, Antoinette begins to recognize her own role in instituting colonial oppression: "We stared at each other, blood on my face, tears on hers. It was as if I saw myself. Like in a looking-glass."[19] But the looking glass in this case does not return the image of someone who is in any way complacent. Antoinette's world has been disrupted. The gaze of the other is no longer located outside the space of self-awareness; it offers clues as to how the subject has constructed a self that has been divided along racial lines throughout the period of colonial history.

At the same time, this revelatory moment can be interpreted as an experience that neither contains the future, as a time of violence, nor does it trap the subject in a circular condition from which there is no escape. If we cannot confidently evoke the solidarity of friends as the key to release from colonial constraints, we do not lack reasons for believing that repetition can assume many forms in this complex novel. The parrot who cries "*Qui est là?*" repeats this question in the voice of Antoinette's mother and is heard again before Antoinette wakes from the dream that recapitulates the destruction of Coulibri during her final captivity.[20] The parrot who repeats is an emblem of a recurrent past but also an ontological clue to the subject who must speak from some position to be heard as an interruption of the same. The mother who adopts this voice is perhaps the least capable of assuming such a role, being the agent who transmits a trauma that the daughter repeats in a marriage to a colonial who, like Mr. Mason, continues the mission that buttresses cultural and material dominance.

Antoinette's narrative yields to that of her husband and his deceptively simple account of Coulibri and its aristocratic heritage. Although unnamed, the husband who parallels Rochester in Charlotte Brontë's *Jane Eyre* does not act entirely on his own and is not clearly animated by malevolent intentions. Spivak has discussed how his role in the novel evokes the figure of Oedipus, who emerges when the son addresses the father in two versions of letters that call attention first to the transactional and then to the arranged nature of his marriage to Antoinette.[21] Because the revised letter is not even sent, Spivak equates its nondelivery with the erosion of paternity as a proper name, and then cites the small collection of literary works that line the shelves of the Granbois estate as evidence of how decomposition has invaded the cultural sphere as well.[22] The reader may note that this booklist would have been dated reading in the 1840s, with the visible works of Lord Byron, Sir Walter Scott and Thomas De Quincey emerging prominently on the shelves.[23] It also indicates, as Homi Bhabha suggests, that a specific literature, namely, English, has been processed in the guise of natural authority but also serves as an allegory of loss when authority loses its binding power.[24]

Although the unnamed husband may not be entirely responsible for his own predicament, his world is one that reflects the anonymous discourse of the traditional state and its accompanying institutions of control and surveillance. Nancy Harrison's distinction between the two kinds of texts to be found in the novel refers back to the structural difference between two types of social organization. This means that the reader is only able to recognize "Rochester" with reference to Brontë's novel that encodes patriarchy more directly when it preserves the patronym and also positions Jane Eyre and Bertha Mason as distinct characters.[25] The husband's narrative inscribes the false neutrality of patriarchal law in an anonymous text while opposing the trace of orality that adheres to Antoinette's discourse. Daniel Cosway's letter to the husband provides an overview of Antoinette's family history, but his denunciations of her father, mother, and stepfather ironically disclose how "lies" and hypocrisy are repeated in the husband's mission.[26]

Considerable irony surfaces in the husband's discussion of Antoinette's deepening unhappiness and allegations concerning her perceptions of England and the Europe that is only known at secondhand: "Her mind was already made up. Some romantic novel, some stray remark never forgotten, a sketch, a picture, a song, a waltz, some note of music, and her ideas were fixed."[27] Resigned to an inability to change her way of thinking, he drifts into a casual relationship with Amélie, the servant girl, and receives Daniel Cosway, who reinforces his suspicions. Attempting to communicate with Antoinette more directly, he calls her Bertha, rather inexplicably, unless the reader recalls the intertext that frames this novel as an image of divided worlds. As he moves closer to her, he also enters into the space of Christophine, who is responsible for drugging the unsuspecting couple to induce lovemaking. Moreover, much like the one-time slave owners of Coulibri, he is haunted by the thought of betrayal and projects this possibility on those around him. Indeed, Antoinette is said to resemble many other women who need to be watched because they might turn against him as well: "She's one of them," he tells himself as he plans his escape.[28]

The unnamed husband's narrative employs standard rhetoric to express his social background and ostensibly logical habits of mind. At the same time, the story of how the estranged couple becomes increasingly disoriented contributes to an atmosphere of mayhem and disorder that turns the Caribbean setting into a nightmare rather than a scene of liberation. Both Antoinette and her husband occasionally wake from this nightmare to discover that violent dislocations prevent them from fully constituting themselves as either colonials or as concretizations of some third option that would mediate colonists and colonized. Antoinette's Creole ancestry certainly provides her with a special function, but she cannot occupy this third position as long as her husband's imperial interests dominate her life. The text of voices therefore becomes as abject as any failed subject, unless a new standpoint on colonial experience can be introduced from the outside.

The imprisonment of Antoinette in the third part of the novel blurs the difference between the protagonist and some other being who has been even more forcefully excluded from the legal sphere. The attack on Grace Poole that occurs in the third part of the novel recalls the behavior of Bertha Mason in *Jane Eyre*, but it also presupposes the "zone of indistinction" that has been elucidated by Giorgio Agamben as a kind of neutral space in which sovereign power traditionally exercises authority over defenseless subjects.[29] Antoinette apparently turns on this woman when the word "legal" is broached, as if to suggest that the law cannot function as law unless it first produces a division in the human community by transforming the other person into an animal.[30] And yet, even before this act of defiance, Antoinette has begun to grasp how an internal division has come to block self-transparency: "The girl I saw was myself but not quite myself."[31] The dream of a perfectly undivided self, like the myth of natural authority, involves a failure to recognize the supplementary nature of all texts that present themselves to us as both sufficient and self-contained.[32]

Nonetheless, the conclusion invites us to glance back to a previous moment in the narrative if we wish to better grasp the position that interrupts colonial experience through which the subject begins to emerge in a new way. Spivak reads this conclusion as a scene in which Antoinette, imprisoned in a "cardboard house" in England, finally wakes from a dream only to act out a ritual of conflagration in which she immolates her fictive self, thus guaranteeing the production of *Jane Eyre*, a future text that both furthers the colonial mission and guarantees the victory of the feminist heroine over Bertha Mason, her rival in marriage.[33] The problem with this reading, I will argue, is that it restricts significance to the oppositions that the novel places in question when it is read as, in some sense, postcolonial. My suggestion is that these oppositions are indeed shown to be problematic on the basis of the *aesthetic* construction of a novel that provides us with a basis for revisiting the colonial world as modern—and also from the standpoint of that world's inversion.

INTERROGATING MODERNITY

Like Rhys's earlier novels, *Wide Sargasso Sea* alludes to a previous world that continues to haunt and perhaps distort adult experience over the course of three narratives. Moreover, although in many ways Edenic, this first world falls into decay as soon as it appears and constitutes the scene of repetition in a novel of repetitions. The reader soon comes to suspect that the past is more of an imaginary projection than an ideal place and, thus, reveals more about the protagonist's desire for solace and harmony than about the historical realities that the novel inscribes. However, in partial contrast to many of the authors who dominated her own literary period, Rhys turns away from assigning a central role to nostalgia in her final novel and suggests what Jean-François Lyotard has identified with the aesthetics of the postmodern, just as she affirms the possibility of moving beyond sexual and racial repression in a traumatized but intertextual vision of colonial history.[34] Antoinette herself often stumbles into what is sometimes called the "postcondition condition," particularly when the traumatic events of her childhood recur and block her ability to navigate through life as a free agent. At vital junctures, Rhys employs the Victorian precursor novel in constituting an intertext that is unstable but, perhaps for this reason, fully exploits unconscious dynamics in enabling repetition and severely limiting the control that characters have over their conduct. What this means is that *Wide Sargasso Sea* is a novel that invites us to decisively *rethink* the category of the postmodern as generally conceived, particularly in the way that it provides a moving image of a postcolonial world that is still in the process of formation.

More precisely, we might say that this novel is a literary event that challenges every attempt to place the colonial/postcolonial rupture in a purely chronological narrative that preserves the postmodern moment for a later, presumably avant-garde, phase of cultural history. On the contrary, it is also a postcolonial text and, in the words of postcolonial theorist, Bhabha, might call attention to "a colonial contramodernity at work in eighteenth- and nineteenth-century matrices of Western modernity that, if acknowledged, would question the historicism that analogically links, in a linear narrative, late capitalism and the fragmentary, simulacral, pastiche symptoms of postmodernity." This weak link does not always enable us to recognize "the historical conditions of cultural contingency and textual indeterminacy" that shape the postcolonial subject in a manner that "transforms, in the process, our understanding of the narrative of modernity and the 'values' of progress."[35] And yet, in revising the usual parameters that define modernity, Bhabha indicates that the so-called underdeveloped world, prior to the twentieth century, is no longer to be conceived as simply premodern, in contrast to the modern European and North American metropoles, but can be shown *on a textual basis* to prefigure the postcolonial as well as the postmodern when viewed through an aesthetic that is inseparable from the unfolding dynamic of the modern as such. Such an aesthetic would enable a critical response that demonstrated how the premodern and colonial, if viewed from a certain standpoint, contained incentives for overturning many of the leading assumptions of modernity itself.

In *Wide Sargasso Sea*, Rhys provides an index on "colonial contramodernity" when she offers an oblique reading of *Jane Eyre*, which she revises and transforms into a criticism of patriarchy and colonial oppression. Harrison discusses how the relations between *Wide Sargasso Sea* and *Jane Eyre* call attention to a singular displacement that the latter novel often conceals but becomes evident in the strategy of revision. Rhys's reading of the precursor novel foregrounds the colonial background and simultaneously problematizes the traditional distinction between colonial and colonized, which also sustains the subordination of women: "In responding to her reading of Brontë's text, Rhys sought not only to correct an omission, but also to correct what she considered a misreading of 'Creole women,' part of whose identity was shaped by the British exploitative context."[36] Antoinette Cosway, the protagonist, is neither equivalent to Brontë's Jane Eyre nor to Bertha Mason, Edward Rochester's legal but abused and imprisoned wife. Antoinette is the Creole daughter of Alexander Cosway, the deceased plantation owner whose alcoholism and profligacy contributed to the misfortunes of a once-privileged family in postslavery Jamaica. In contrast to Brontë, Rhys constructs a three-part narrative in which the *effects* of racial and colonial exclusion are brought to light in the imaginary history of Antoinette, who is "doubled" as both the colonial victim of a manipulative husband and, later on, as the captive of his maneuvers to imprison her.

Rhys obviously invites the reader to consider modernity from an alternative point of view, which engages the aesthetic to the degree that literary form can accommodate the disruptive material that often composes the fictional narrative. The degree to which the aesthetic is limited by the subject matter of the novel is debatable, and surely the category of the postmodern, especially as employed by Lyotard, is not easy to construe *as* aesthetic once the status of the philosophical subject has been placed in question. Bhabha, in contrast, indicates how the colonial needs to be interrogated as an aspect of modernity that has been evaded in Eurocentric accounts of the modern project. At the same time, Bhabha's version of the postmodern would not exclude the possibility of aesthetics or of reading colonial texts as postcolonial because coloniality itself would no longer depend on a rigid time frame that used formal independence to mark the difference between colonial and postcolonial. Hence, just as the postcolonial might be conceived through the lingering effects of colonization, the postmodern could be envisioned as an afterimage of the modern. Such a description of the postmodern, however, would preserve a sense of the subjective, perhaps in the disappearance of the traditional subject, which would no longer be understood through the analog of the observer but instead would acquire the meaning of an interpreter. The postmodern subject, therefore, would be more of a reader than an observer and her aesthetic proclivities would be more literary than visual.

A POSITION IN READING

As a narrative that is largely concerned with the undoing of a marital relationship, *Wide Sargasso Sea* can be experienced as morally empty, particularly once Antoinette and her husband begin to drift into a zone of indistinction where communication becomes impossible. However, the persistent tendency for readers, even in the wake of structuralism, to look for the moral center of literary works in the actions of major characters prevents *texts* from being read as ethically significant, that is, as organized according to ethical possibilities that sometimes can be found in the peripheral directives that inform verbal sequences. In Rhys's novel, the reader needs to turn away from the two characters who define the marital drama at the heart of the text before the question of ethics can be broached as one that engages the postcolonial as an interruption of coloniality, rather than merely as a phase of history that comes after the colonial era. Moreover, this turning away from what presents itself to us as readable in an immediate sense must entail a new position, an "abstract" or speculative moment that would be "Hegelian" to the degree that it would transcend the particular without, however, denying the particular its due. Is there a way that the processual character of interpretation can be respected and also linked to a movement beyond the domain of the given?

In answering this question, we would be loath to neglect the role of the aesthetic in the reading process, which is not to be understood as an unbroken continuum. Wolfgang Iser has described how this process calls into question the vertical structure of conventional validity, insofar as "it disrupts this vertical structure and begins to reorganize conventions horizontally."[37] Iser argues that this process presupposes a basic asymmetry between text and reader, allowing certain "gaps" in the text to be filled in by the reader. The reorganization of conventions, however, cannot be achieved within a system that the reader identifies through the original repertoire: "They cannot, of course, be filled in by the system itself, so it follows that they can only be filled in by another system."[38] The emergence of another system requires a *space* that must be empty, or must become empty, if the vertical structure is to be challenged as natural and inherent, which means that the transformation of meaning that occurs through the text is a performance, rather than a value that is formulated by the text itself. Moreover, the performances that enable transformation are aesthetic in their play: "Their aesthetic quality lies in this 'performing' structure, which clearly cannot be identical to the final product, because without the participation of the individual reader there can be no performance."[39] Aesthetics in this sense would presuppose the active use of the imagination in the production of systemic transformation.

It is not difficult to see how this reading model can be related to the ethical concerns of *Wide Sargasso Sea*, which emerge in a decisive encounter that is only misread if the performative element is not held rigorously in mind. Indeed, the unnamed husband's conversation with Christophine constitutes the ethical core to what otherwise would unfold as an anomic spectacle in which domination retains the upper hand. But Christophine's importance is not to be measured in terms of didactic messages that can be derived from her petulant discourse. Spivak is correct to underscore that Christophine is not a major character in a novel that is unable to transform the other into a self when the former has been marked as integral to imperialism.[40] Nonetheless, the binary of self-other is not impermeable but a fluid opposition that can be thought through *as* ethical—as well as political—even before it is frozen into the rigid hierarchies of colonial rule. Furthermore, the role of *language* in this process cannot be underestimated.[41] Language alone, rather than physical acts, can loosen the foundations of a system that has become sedimented with past injustices and for this reason cannot offer the chance of a new beginning.

Christophine does not perform this function as a free agent who is untainted by corruption insofar as her status as "good servant" is compromised when she attempts to drug Antoinette and the unnamed husband, and while her attachment to voodoo is not simply to be condemned as "backward" from the standpoint of the advanced religions, we cannot argue that her use of magic is unrelated to her willingness to intervene in an unsatisfactory relationship.[42] Christophine's games with Obeah might bring to mind what Marx identified as the capitalist codification of the commodity form, which invariably excludes the time of labor from market value.[43] Fetishism as a theme cannot be assigned an economic significance in Christophine's discourse, but it is woven nonetheless into her insistence that the unnamed husband, rather than the one who speaks, is the fetishist who engages in practices that are unacceptable. From a certain standpoint, we might even say that her entire discourse reverses the colonial order of things through a metaphorical shorthand, but in this case the operant metaphor is not a figure of speech but a spatial reconfiguring where suddenly the native perspective is brought to bear on that of the colonizer, and the two perspectives provide a contrast from the standpoint of a counternarrative.

To understand how this works, we also need to understand that Christophine is not primarily a didactic speaker, however easy it is for the reader to confuse her stance with that role. Being compromised, she is not to be taken as a standard for moral rectitude but constitutes a profound gesture, a solemn sign through which the unnamed husband's conduct is allegorized as a narrative that combines "primitive" religion with the analytical dismemberment of the native woman's defenseless body. Christophine speaks to him with "her judge's voice" in a way that allows her to refer to his deeper intentions: "All you want is to break her up," she exclaims, while repeating Antoinette's name and allowing it to slip into *Marionette*, a cognate for doll, and reminding her husband of his deceit and unfaithfulness.[44] And yet, repetition performs a dual role in this scene of instruction in which the husband is condemned and the *absence* of Antoinette speaks to the possibility of some future subject. Christophine accuses the husband of repeating the crimes of Antoinette's father as he carries his conception of marriage as a financial exchange to new extremes and prepares to depart from the island. At the same time, Antoinette's uncanny disappearance from this encounter is not only noted but also constitutes an indictment of the husband, just as it isolates him as a crucial link in the colonial process.

While the state as an institution is not figured in Christophine's discourse, we might read this discourse as political to the degree that it lacks content but prepares us for the translation of moral agency into a response to the social and marital injustices at issue. We might argue that Christophine's gestures are merely idealistic in that they seem to be oblivious of material realities and therefore disqualify her as an emissary of some future resolution that cannot be achieved apart from a transfer of power, which the colonial situation prevents from occurring. Nonetheless, even if her gestures do not translate into direct action, they put in question the existing (colonial) state as an institution that has replaced the bond of marriage with the rule of exchange and underwrites the transformation of a feudal, slave-owning system into a protocapitalist one that reigns in the free movement of persons (whether Black, Creole, or female) in the interests of economic consolidation. Christophine's dispute with the unnamed husband can be read as a critique of the contractual view of marriage that Hegel abhorred and that Rhys parodies by taking it to precarious extremes. Her discourse can also be read as expressing the need for *purifying* the natural drives so that marriage as an institution is no longer grounded in an ethical rigorism that would be "formalist" but would enable particular contexts to give birth to universality itself, instead of being opposed to it.[45]

At the same time, although Christophine cannot accomplish a political reversal that would overturn the colonial relationship, we might try to imagine her as initiating a dialectical rethinking of how the private space that has been carved out of the colonial regime is merely an extension of the system that privileges man over woman, the former masters over the former slaves, as well as colonizer over native.[46] If we go behind this interrogation, however, we do not find either religious truth or even the possibility of a more equitable mode of production that might usher in a new age of justice. Instead, we find little more than the will to question someone who at first seems to be free of violence and corruption but has succumbed to both, even before he invaded the colonial world with the intention of mastering it. And yet, this same effort is also a challenge to the colonial system and enables the reader to step outside the oppositions that constitute inside and outside, subject and object, self and other. These are the oppositions that are inscribed in the text and maintain it but also can be found in the world at large, which lies on the horizon of consciousness as we read and take into account what continues to take shape before our eyes. It is fitting that Christophine should perform this role precisely because, in suspending the oppositions on which the colonial system depends, she opens up an imaginary space that enables the reader to recover the novel in an aesthetic sense, allowing the woman in the cardboard house to pause, and then briefly light a way into the unknown.

NOTES

1. Rhys describes her first arrival in London and early training in drama in "Smile Please," and then, in "The Situation Began to Grow Cold," reminds the reader of the basic situation of the protagonist in *Voyage in the Dark*. For details, see Jean Rhys, *Smile Pease: An Unfinished Autobiography* (New York: Harper and Row, 1979). *Voyage in the Dark* (New York: Harper and Row, 1982) is Rhys's third novel, but it provides the best starting point for a brief discussion of the emergence of an aesthetic dimension in her early work, which concerns the semiotic to the degree that it also testifies to the prevalence of erotic loss in the early fiction.

2. Nathalie Sarraute's early novel, *Tropismes* (1939), which employs a neorealist technique, compares humans to microorganisms and challenges various conventions of plot and character. This calibrated description of Sarraute's novels might be applied to *Voyage the Dark*, among Rhys's early novels: "We seem to see an endless and inconclusive effort to maintain a constantly threatened equilibrium in a world where every version of the self, of other people, of experience and of reality, is open to question, and frequently meets conflicting versions." Valerie Minoque, *Nathalie Sarraute and the War of the Words* (Edinburgh, UK: Edinburgh University Press, 1981).

3. Rhys, *Voyage in the Dark*, 161.
4. Ibid., 29.
5. Ibid., 164.
6. Jean Rhys, *Good Morning, Midnight* (New York: W. W. Norton, 1982), 74.
7. Ibid., 96.
8. These remarks are not intended to argue that alterity is *merely* an institution but that the empirical project of sequestering others can be internalized in a manner that prevents an internal alterity from enabling change. At the same time, what I would like to call "internal alterity" is not an original or natural alterity but an otherness that presupposes some sort of quasi-dialectical relationship between self and other because the self has been reconceived as always already other in its potential to become different.
9. Rhys, *Good Morning, Midnight*, 189.
10. Gardiner contrasts Sasha and Joyce's Molly Bloom. See Judith Gardiner, "Good Morning, Midnight; Good Night, Modernism," in *Boundary* 2 II.2 (1988): 247–49. According to this reading, Joyce's celebration of archetypal, female unity gives way to Sasha's "split self" in a world that presupposes but also negates the mythic style of *Ulysses*. This reading of Joyce becomes problematic, however, once we place *Ulysses* in a poststructuralist thematic.
11. Jean Rhys, *Wide Sargasso Sea* (New York: W. W. Norton and Company, 1982), 15.
12. Gayatri Spivak, "Three Women's Texts and a Critique of Imperialism," *Critical Inquiry* 12, no. 1 (1985): 250–51, 252.
13. Rhys, *Wide Sargasso Sea*, 17.

14. Ibid., 32–33.
15. Edward Kaman Braithwaite, *Contradictory Omens: Cultural Diversity and Integration in the Caribbean*, Monograph 1 (Mona, Jamaica: Savacou Publications, 1974), 36.
16. Rhys, *Wide Sargasso Sea*, 23.
17. Veronique Gregg, *Jean Rhys's Historical Imagination: Reading and Writing the Creole* (Chapel Hill: University of North Carolina Press, 1995), 89–91.
18. Ibid., 94.
19. Rhys, *Wide Sargasso Sea*, 41.
20. Ibid., 38, 42, 170.
21. See ibid., 63–64, 68–69; Spivak, "Three Women's Texts and a Critique of Imperialism," 251–52.
22. Spivak, "Three Women's Texts and a Critique of Imperialism," 252.
23. Rhys, *Wide Sargasso Sea*, 68.
24. Homi Bhabha, "Signs Taken for Wonders," in, *The Location of Culture*: Questions of Ambivalence and Authority under a Tree outside Delhi, 1817" (London: Routledge, 1994), 157–58.
25. Nancy Harrison, *Jean Rhys and the Novel as Woman's Text* (Chapel Hill: University of North Carolina Press, 1988), 195.
26. Rhys, *Wide Sargasso Sea*, 68–90.
27. Ibid., 85.
28. Ibid., 156.
29. Giorgio Agamben identifies the "zone of indistinction" with the sphere of the sovereign ban, enabling us to identify the sacred as what can be killed but not sacrificed. See especially, Giorgio Agamben, *Homo Sacer: Sovereign Power and Bare Life* (Stanford, CA: Stanford University Press, 1998), 81–86. From this standpoint, Antoinette as bare life is "sacred" and must be killed; however, in reliving the destruction of Coulibri, she also suggests on the contrary how the imagination enables her to transcend (self)murder and thus to sublate the preoccupation with the religious that pervades the novel as a whole.
30. Rhys, *Wise Sargasso Sea*, 165.
31. Ibid., 162.
32. For details on supplementary, see Jacques Derrida, *Of Grammatology*, trans. Gayatri Chakravorty Spivak (Baltimore, MD: Johns Hopkins University Press, 1967), 163.
33. Spivak, "Three Women's Texts and a Critique of Imperialism," 250–51.
34. Lyotard's argues that the postmodern not only problematizes nostalgia but emerges as a way of describing the traumas of life and history, which are "unpresentable" and inassimilable to a conventional appropriation of the dialectic. Lyotard's view of the postmodern looks back to Kant rather than to Hegel and subscribes to the view that the speculative use of reason (as limited by Kant himself) is basically illegitimate. This basically Kantian view of the postmodern to be found in Jean-François Lyotard, *The Postmodern Condition: A Report on Knowledge*, trans. Geoffrey Bennington and Bian Massaumi (Minneapolis: University of Minnesota Press, 1984).
35. See Homi Bhabha, "The Postcolonial and the Postmodern," in *The Location of Culture* (London: Routledge, 1994), 248. Bhahba's argument is that the "time-lag" between colonial and postcolonial is precisely what has been missed in conventional theories of the postmodern, which juxtapose the signs of a stylistic break and the linear narratives that typify modernity. For Bhahba, who temporalizes what is usually thematized in purely spatial terms, the focus on First-World narratives in most postmodern theory goes along with an inability to acknowledge a mode of temporality that is *already* in place in advance of its modern apprehension.
36. Harrison, *Jean Rhys and the Novel as Woman's Text*, 128.
37. Wolfgang Iser, *The Act of Reading: A Theory of Aesthetic Response* (Baltimore, MD: Johns Hopkins University Press, 1980), 61.
38. Ibid., 169.
39. Ibid., 27.
40. Spivak, "Three Women's Texts and a Critique of Imperialism," 253.
41. An approach to Hegel's later philosophy that brings language into prominence is explored in Hans-Georg Gadamer, "Hegel's Idea of Logic," in *Hegel's Dialectic: Five Herme-*

neutical Studies, trans. P. Christopher Smith (New Haven, CT: Yale University Press, 1976), 75–99. The general thrust of this study is to claim that language performs a major role in demonstrating how rigid categories are loosened in the sphere of what Hegel has discussed as logic, helping us to understand dialectics as a nonfoundational discipline. Hence, we might say that in Rhys's novel, Christophine occupies the position of the one who asks questions and sustains the possibility of dialectics, if not in the mind of the unnamed husband, who is unable to respond to her denunciations and criticisms, but rather in the mind of the reader herself.

42. Spivak's description of Christophine, however valid from certain standpoints, does not imply that she is morally ambiguous, even when she performs an exemplary role: "Taxonomically she belongs to the category of the good servant rather than that of the pure native." Spivak, "Three Women's Texts and a Critique of Imperialism," 252. This description is surprising because it prevents us from viewing Christophine as a strong example of the *pharmakon* as both remedy and poison. See especially Jacques Derrida, "Plato's Pharmacy," in *Dissemination* (Chicago: University of Chicago Press, 1981), 95–115.

43. See especially, Karl Marx, *Capital, Volume 1*, translated by Ernest Mandel (New York: Penguin Books, 1990), 164–69, 983, 1046. Marx's indebtedness to various nineteenth-century anthropologists is noted in W. J. T. Mitchell, *Iconology: Image, Text, Ideology* (Chicago: University of Chicago, 1987), 185–90. Without denying that Christophine offers a description of the unnamed husband's *ritual of dehumanization* through its kinship with fetishism—and, in this way, provides an ironic defense of her own interest in voodoo—we need to distance this reading from a sort of Marxist economism *avant la lettre* because the whole project of industrial commodification lies in the future, as Rhys would have known as a late twentieth-century postcolonial author.

44. Rhys, *Wide Sargasso Sea*, 138–40.

45. Hegel indirectly refers to the economic materialism of modern civil society when he strongly objects to the contractual theory of marriage, which for him acquires a "shameful" meaning in Kant's *Philosophy of Law*. See G. W. F. Hegel, *The Philosophy of Right*, trans. T. M. Knox (Oxford: Clarendon Press, 1965), 58–59. We might argue that the contractual theory no doubt signifies Kant's failure to confront the problem of intersubjectivity, particularly in his moral theory. In Hegel's theory of the drives, purification refines the will as nonnatural (thus supporting Kant's belief that ethics should be empty of content) without, however, destroying its natural origin. A detailed assessment of Hegel's rejection of Kant's ethical rigorism can be found in John McCumber, *Understanding Hegel's Mature Critique of Kant* (Stanford, CA: Stanford University Press, 1913), 118–22, 159–63.

46. The possibility that Hegel had the abortive Haitian Revolution in mind while writing his *Phenomenology of Spirit*, and that he may have attempted to understand the relationship between lord and bondsman on this basis, has been thoughtfully, if somewhat inconclusively, explored in a recent short study. For details, see Susan Buck-Morss, *Hegel, Haiti and Universal History* (Pittsburgh: University of Pittsburgh Press, 2009). "Lordship and Bondage" is conventionally historicized as a narrative about two individuals, the medieval lord and his servant, rather than about later class conflict. However, even this reading is flawed to the degree that it misses how the Hegelian narrative functions as a key to the development of self-consciousness in a social setting. This narrative does not necessarily exclude the Haitian example any more than it can be reduced to the struggle between labor and capital.

Chapter Eight

Ishiguro's Imaginary

Figures of History

Literary texts would be difficult to identify as literary if the imaginal component were removed from how we receive them. Although nonliterary texts are valuable and perhaps true for similar reasons, literary texts often have the distinct advantage of presenting the imaginary in narrative frameworks that are unique to literature. This chapter examines how the contemporary author, Kazuo Ishiguro, employs the literary imagination in two novels, *An Artist of the Floating World* (1986) and *The Remains of the Day* (1989), that are perhaps differently concerned with historical experience. In emphasizing the hermeneutical importance of the literary imagination in Ishiguro's work, I also discuss the need to engage with the nonliterary problem of ideology in the former novel, where ethics and politics emerge in an aesthetic matrix that proves to be crucial to the possibility of figural meaning. In my argument, the idea of the political is shown to require an absent space, enabling figuration to unfold in a world without foundations. I then examine how the second novel explores the limitations of morality, understood as a formal system that is unable to define agency in clear terms. My conclusion argues that the critical response to history that the novel encourages is inseparable from the way that the past becomes the theme of aesthetic reflection.

HERMENEUTICAL BORDERS

In *Truth and Method* (*Wahrheit und Method*, 1960), Hans-Georg Gadamer argues that the role of reading in the constitution of literature is precisely what prevents literature from becoming a purely aesthetic phenomenon. On the basis of the normative claims that derive from the practice of reading, literature becomes world literature just as it begins to be recognized in the mode of literary history.[1] The possibility of world literature, however, should not be confused with the idea that literature loses its integrity once it is taken out of the "world" to which it first belongs. "Thus it is by no means the case that world literature is an alienated form of what originally constituted the work's mode of being."[2] Gadamer argues further that the historicity of literature, particularly as exemplified in world literature, is pertinent to the constitution of all texts, not only literary ones, and that an underlying linguistic quality is also pertinent to texts that provide the basis for the human sciences. Texts for Gadamer cannot be thought apart from the founding aspect of language, which means that textuality does not remain separate from the dimension of communication and the existence of other persons. At the same time, although the distinction between poetry and prose is undeniable, we should not allow this difference to obscure the essential kinship between literature and a discipline like history, which employs texts in a manner that recalls literary expression and includes an imaginal component in a seemingly objective mode of exposition.

The "borderline" condition of literature therefore provides the key to the function of the literary, broadly conceived, in the construction of many disciplines that employ texts as their subject matter. Gadamer notes that, for this reason, even scholarly texts can be compared to works of art insofar as they attest to a way of conveying delimited meanings and are not simply aesthetic objects. Indeed, literary texts are not to be conceived as marginal phenomena but share with all (written) texts the property of having been formed in language. Nevertheless, while literary texts are somehow always indebted to verbal performances, they also convey a sense of strangeness that can be attributed to the nature of writing, which is inseparable from the experience of encountering the mind in an alien medium: "Nothing is so strange, and at the same time so demanding, as the written word."[3] Gadamer argues that writing allows a transformation to take place when the mind confronts its own alien being in an external medium that enables the past to speak, not simply as past, but almost magically, overcoming the historical distance that obscures the meaning of physical objects and reduces them to shadows of an earlier time. Hence, Gadamer's willingness to underscore the strangeness of writing does not prevent him from placing texts amid the evolving interpretations that serve a mediatory function in historical understanding.

However, what Gadamer does not so clearly demonstrate is how a mediatory discipline like history can also function as a border discipline, a possibility that is entailed when the role of the imaginary in historical reflection is clearly acknowledged. The signs that enable historical interpretation are unstable, even if a factual core can be identified as a crucial aspect of historical meaning. This means that a discipline like literature does not simply assist the historian in providing a rhetorically driven analogue to a more scientific discipline. On the contrary, history itself is "literary" to the degree that it involves ambiguity, indeterminacy and instability of reference in functioning as a semiotic, contesting the allegedly natural oppositions that structure social perception in general. This does not mean that history is devoid of factual evidence but that a margin of uncertainty necessarily clings to historical data. Perhaps nowhere is this more crucial to the historian than when politics presents itself as an indubitable source of incontestable values. The historian's task is at least in part to criticize the assembled constructions of the political imaginary, not from an absolute or more perfect standpoint but to avoid confusing the imaginary with the ontological.

Hence, although hermeneutics enables us to envision the imaginal component in literature as running across various disciplines that appear to be utterly unlike one another, semiotics not only allows us to acknowledge this shared trait but also to affirm the critical potential of the imagination to overturn any positions that sustain an ideological mirage of natural unity. Paul de Man has explained how ideology attempts to naturalize linguistic categories so that hierarchical constructions end up being presented as intrinsic to the order of things: "What we call ideology is precisely the confusion of linguistic with natural reality, of reference with phenomenalism."[4] The function of the intertext in the semiotic of literary texts is to introduce an unforeseen psychic dimension to reading, a dimension that can be used to confront the constructions of hegemony with a remnant of historical difference that explodes ideological closure. The goal of psychic disclosure would not be to end up with a completely "transparent" statement that substituted ideology with scientific truth but to demonstrate how the literary text contains openings beyond the constructions of ideology itself, thus providing the reader with insights that are irreducible to conceptual generalizations.

Once again, our critical adventure will bring together semiotics and aesthetics, but it will also indicate how the aesthetic aspects of literary texts are difficult to separate from the ethical and inherently political meanings that are foregrounded by literature, especially when literature interfaces with a situation that in no sense remains separate from the construction of the text as a reflection on historical circumstances. Thus, if semiotics engages the sensibility in a manner that is almost necessarily aesthetic in the largest sense, the aesthetic experiences that literature activates cannot be considered in isolation but are part of a social milieu that the literary text encodes and enables us to apprehend on multiple levels. The political questions that are raised by literature are therefore not extrinsic to the production of literature but emerge out of the issues that the work addresses as a response to both the possibilities and inadequacies of finite social arrangements. When the literature in question explores situations that are remote in time, these questions need to be considered reflectively, particularly when the literary text has been designed to communicate a complex understanding of historical experience.

IRONY AND THE MEMORY OF ART

Ishiguro's novel, *An Artist of the Floating World*, is concerned with the perennial conflict between art and ideology, just as it demonstrates the importance of semiotics to the literary imagination. However, this brilliant and evocative literary work makes use of intertextuality in situating the reader in a sphere that is not that of the protagonist's immediate reality; instead, it invites a backward glance over an ancient world and a more recent time that has been displaced by historical circumstances. At various junctures in the novel, Ishiguro subtly alludes to Shen Fu's famous short work, *Six Records of a Floating Life*, a Chinese classic that combines pastoral romance, social commentary and autobiographical elements in a somewhat loosely structured narrative that enables the reader to imagine a poorly positioned government functionary who was indeed the author himself, a literary dreamer in flight from the Confucian bureaucracy of his own period. However, while Shen Fu's memoir was written during the period of the Ch'ing Dynasty, Ishiguro's protagonist, Masuji Ono, lived through the period of Japan's increasing politicization during the 1930s that entailed the attempt to construct an overseas empire through tactical alliances that resulted in the Second World War.

The difference between Shen Fu's "floating world" and the Migi-Hidari, the district where Masuji worked and lived as a young artist, encodes historical distance but should not conceal underlying similarities. Although the contrast between ancient and modern is inherent in Ishiguro's appropriation of the Chinese text, Masuji's evocation of his local environment suggests that the two "worlds" might share undisclosed aesthetic possibilities that are mutually enabling. Arguing that "our pleasure district" had nothing illicit about it, he elaborates on the cultural space within which he would gather with friends and discuss various matters which were often preliminary to his own artistic pursuits: "It drew a lively but respectable crowd, many of them people like us—continuing into the night. The establishment my own group frequented was called "Migi-Hidari," and stood at the point where three districts intersected to form a paved precinct."[5] While Shen Fu provides various settings within which he conducts his life as a young lover and adventurer, Masuji constructs a world in which his youthful artistic aspirations have a productive, if precarious, home.

Masuji fashions this image of a "floating world" that provided him and his artistic colleagues with the setting for the artistic pursuits that would continue until the ideological turn of the 1930s, which plunged Masuji into an artistic crisis from which he did not emerge unscathed.

Masuji's floating world is not to be identified with dissipation and irresponsibility because it enabled him and his artistic friends to produce works of art that may not have been masterpieces but were the condition for aesthetic experience in which life emerged as complex figural expression. Perhaps the notion of "firstness" as originally explored by Charles Sanders Peirce, the founder of modern semiotics, provides the more accurate description of this utopian space, which might be useful in identifying the backdrop for the adventures and artistic endeavors of a Japanese artist who did not initially follow ideological promptings but remained faithful to the life of the senses, which is not to be morally condemned as corrupt or impure but functioned as a kind of imperfect origin for artistic work. The key in this case is the manner in which this world was a spur to creativity, a contributing factor to the use of the imagination that the artist enjoyed and that links him, however indirectly, to the literary aspirations that animate Shen Fu and his surrogate author.

During the war, the Migi-Hidari is slowly destroyed; smoke rises from the rubble as Masuji, in October 1948, observes and nostalgically looks back over his fatefully compromised career. His in-laws offer him little support as he struggles to come to terms with a past in which his artistic career was politicized to the detriment of his personal integrity. He also remembers how the old pleasure district was transformed around 1931, which marks a sudden shift from one set of values to another: "Whole districts seemed to change character overnight; parks that had always been busy with people became deserted; long-established businesses suffered severe losses."[6] The new proprietor is Yamagate, who subsequently linked the Migi-Hidari to "a celebration of the new patriotic spirit emerging in Japan today."[7] The fear of "decadence" enters Masuji's mind at this moment in the narrative, suggesting how ideological themes would eventually supplant artistic ones. Later in this reconstruction of the past, Masuji relates how Kuroda, a talented colleague, is responsible for producing "The New Patriotic Spirit," an ideologically charged painting that suggests the subtle transformation that overtakes the Migi-Hidari during this transitional period.[8] This painting does not stand for the aesthetic concerns of Masuji's youth but for the nationalistic ambitions that soon come to dominant his life and the lives of his artistic colleagues, who are all, to varying degrees, swept away in a powerful political current.

In the next sequence of reflections, dated April 1949, Masuji provides more details on this moment of transformation that offered false hope to a young artist whose artistic designs were distorted and deformed by the politics of the day. The so-called China crisis involved the production of propaganda posters by a compliant pupil, Shintaro, under Masuji's supervision. While expressing reservations about wanting to produce the posters in the first place, Shintaro also wants Ishiguro to inform a cultural committee in postwar Japan that the posters were never his idea. Masuji will not comply to Shintaro's request, which he considers to be deceptive.[9] In the domestic context, Masuji helps negotiate details involving the marriage of Norika, his daughter, to Taro Saito. He also visits Kuroda, who suffers from a serious war injury, and he learns while in the Yanagawa district that his old friend has been beaten in prison. Nonetheless, during this period, Masuji begins to acknowledge that his role in the war was hardly praiseworthy: "I accept that much of what I did was ultimately harmful to our nation, that mine was part of an influence that resulted in untold suffering for our own people."[10] In the meantime, Shintaro, who apparently avoided combat, appears to have relinquished his stance on the China poster affair. Masuji and Shintaro, in a brief moment of intimacy, regret the passing of the "floating world" but also acknowledge that its effects were not always beneficial.[11]

The reflections dated November 1949 provide a telling record of how a small community of Japanese artists gradually moved from a position of aesthetic indeterminacy, which had the advantage of sustaining multiple forms of artistic expression, to a more strongly ideological stance in which art ceased to dwell in the borderland between percept and concept but was subordinated to specific political agendas. The open space that is at least suggested by the Migi-Hidari turned out to be a fragile one; it begins to close as Masuji falls under the influence of a new instructor, whose political orientation adds a fateful twist to his pupil's career. Mori-san, his earlier instructor, constantly sought to "modernize" Utamaro tradition but dispersed Western elements that were not present in Japanese tradition. Mori-san's artistic ambition was to alter the identity of painting as pursued locally in a way that allowed his students to explore the city's floating world. This open space should not be conflated with crass hedonism because its evanescent nature is the gateway to sublime possibilities: "I could see numerous silhouettes dancing behind the paper scenes, and a single voice came drifting out through the night to me," Masuji exclaims.[12] And yet, even Mori-san has doubts concerning the validity of this aesthetic refuge. The transitional instructor in this case was Matsuda, an ultimately persuasive pedagogue who brought Masuji over to the ideology of protofascism.

The decisive change in Masuji's work is foretold in the revision of a single painting that was initially revealing in its partial embrace of the enveloping ideology. We learn that one of Masuji's artistic colleagues accused him of being a traitor on viewing "Complacency," his first painting to employ the new political style. This graphic work, painted under Matsuda's influence, goes beyond any attempt to represent the growing poor who the new instructor had pointed out to him during one of their urban walks because the city boys depicted did not wear "defensive scowls" but instead "would have worn the manly scowl of samurai warriors ready to fight." Masuji goes on to say, "It is no coincidence, furthermore, that the boys in my picture held their sticks in classic kendo stances."[13] Although only beginning to suggest the artist's political transformation, this painting also conveys ideological instability whereby an evidently socialist position begins to gravitate towards an overtly imperial stance. "Eyes to the Horizon," a print dating from the 1930s, reworks the same painting, merging two images while making use of Japan's coastline. Three of the faces depicted in the later painting resemble the faces of prominent politicians, indicating the use of allegorical motifs in a work that adopts the Japanese state as essential to its subject matter. In this painting, the image of stick-bearing boys has been replaced with soldiers carrying rifles, led by a sword-bearing officer who points westward towards Asia: "Behind him, there was no longer a backdrop of poverty; simply the military flag of the rising sun."[14]

Masuji's memories of this period mingle a consciousness of Matsuda's increasing influence with some understanding of the repression that began to grip the country as the new ideology became stronger. Matsuda embarrasses Masuji by revealing his pupil's ignorance of modern ideas. Discussing Karl Marx, he also uses a crisis-laden vocabulary to prompt his impressionable listener to develop unprecedented resolve. However, Matsuda does not argue for a revolution but for a return to older ways in which traditional authority is restored and a new empire is constructed to rival that of the British and the French. Observing the change in artistic style that occurs around him, Masuji momentarily celebrates the passing of decadence and closure. Before the outbreak of the war, however, he visits Kuroda's home as an emissary of the government only to discover that a police officer is monitoring the house. Learning that Kuroda's paintings have been destroyed, Masuji finally begins to recognize the nature of the regime that he uncritically supported and to which he contributed his modest artistic talents.

The final set of reflections unfolds in June 1950, after Matsuda has died. Masuji recalls a conversation that he had with his old instructor in a time that only the two of them are able to clearly remember. Postwar optimism has become the order of the day; Noriko is happily married. Matsuda's comments are not remorseful but summarize the minor role that the artist and his instructor played in the events of history: "It's just that in the end we turned out to be ordinary men. Ordinary men with no special gifts of insight."[15] Matsuda regrets only the misfortune of having lived in those times, which already have grown dim in contemporary minds. Masuji remembers the bestowal of a prestigious award on him in May 1938, when Mori-san, his earlier mentor, had been labeled unpatriotic. On a trip to the villa, he finds the pleasure district unrecognizable but nonetheless expresses the thought that the renewal of his nation will surely occur in the energies of its youth.

Ishiguro's poignant and engaging novel, *An Artist of the Floating World*, not only demonstrates the borderline condition of literature, poised between aesthetic awareness and historical experience, but it also constitutes a cautionary warning against many varieties of ideological reductionism that stem from the eradication of the open space in which political thinking more properly dwells. This space is not a ground but as a location where the signs of the political can be negotiated, not in the service of abstract concepts but as subjective elaborations of a "conceptual" sphere that enables mutuality and recognition. Ishiguro's Masuji captures the sense of groundlessness that pertains to all political reflection and decision in depicting the Migi-Hadari as a place of errancy and perceptual indeterminacy, while the rush into ideological certainty that blights his artistic career is not the result of illicit pleasure but the end product of a shift from aesthetic openness to doctrinal rigidity. Matsuda's amalgamation of socialist sympathies, conveyed through a few superficial remarks, and imperial ideology fills a space with figures that are neither inevitable nor drawn from subjective life. These figures are little more than ideological signs, rather than an engagement with figurality that might have forestalled the automatic application of conceptual schemes to aesthetic experience. In the end, Masuji's embrace of a composite synthesis, falsely merging art and life, does not lead him headlong into an abyss but fades in time, bringing him to his senses once he finally begins to discern the pernicious effects that it had on an entire generation.

What enables us to distinguish ideology from dialectical experience is the role of political coercion in blocking the path from aesthetic abundance to social fulfilment. Gadamer has suggested that hermeneutics enables us to appreciate how literature is a borderline discipline, engaging the imaginary at the precise juncture where conceptual generalities might otherwise prevent mediation. Literature, or perhaps art in general, is what that keeps the imaginary open for different uses, not just political ones. The danger of foreclosure is amply demonstrated in Ishiguro's novel, where the slippage from socialist orthodoxy to imperial ambitions does not go unobserved. My argument, in this case, is that the model for Hegelian politics would not be any existing state but presupposes a gap at the heart of whatever political order G. W. F. Hegel suggests might approximate, but never equal, the universal. Such a model presupposes a quasi-ethical conception of the political, which in turn begs the question of how ethics is to be rethought in the post-Kantian context. To suggest how this rethinking might be carried out, we need to turn to another one of Ishiguro's novels—a novel that enables us to address the question of ethics more directly.

MORALITY'S CRUEL DEMISE

Ishiguro's widely acclaimed novel, *The Remains of the Day*, can be read as a study of manners in midtwentieth-century England, impacted as it was by the events leading up to the Second World War, where the Darlington estate and its old traditions provide the background for the events at hand. This description, however, prevents the profoundly tragic aspect of those years from being clearly acknowledged, even if the word "tragedy" does not strictly to the outcome of an impending international confrontation and its aftermath. In presenting the memories of Stevens, an ordinary butler who performs his household duties conscientiously and in the service of Lord Darlington, Ishiguro produces a fictional account of an institution that bears the marks of an earlier period to model a critical perspective on a conflict that is recurrent in human affairs. The main actions presented in this narrative are relatively simple, but the conflict between rectitude and a credible response to domestic injustice alerts us to the need to rethink the meaning of morality when defined through rules of conduct. Without oversimplifying Immanuel Kant's contribution to moral philosophy, I would like to discuss the novel as a critique of the same mentality that Kant would have us develop as moral subjects. It is unlikely that Ishiguro had Kant in mind when he wrote this novel, but his argument at least implies that moral rigorism can easily lapse into an abdication of responsibility for systemic wrongs. The underlying argument of the novel, nonetheless, is not that formalism is necessarily flawed but that its larger context needs to be deepened if it is to enact meaningful purposes.

The novel begins in July 1956 and unfolds in the mind of Stevens himself, who travels for six days in the West Country at the suggestion of Mr. Farraday, the American who now owns the Darlington estate and has assumed responsibilities that were once those of Lord Darlington. He speaks of possibly visiting Miss Kenton, now Mrs. Benn, who was a close associate of Stevens during the period remembered. Readers learn that the numbers employed in domestic service have declined but that Stevens does not wish to champion tradition for tradition's sake; he accepts this situation as more or less inevitable. On the first day of the journey, Stevens visits Salisbury Cathedral and offers reflections on the surrounding landscape, allowing English and Continental character traits to be fully contrasted: "I would say that it is the very *lack* of obvious drama or spectacle that sets the beauty of our land apart."[16] Stevens proceeds to discuss what makes a butler "great" and lends him "dignity," while adding that his own father enabled him to assess the latter quality. In illustrating dignity, Stevens tells the story of how his father, also employed in Darlington Hall, performed the duties of butler when required to wait on a certain military commander—the same officer who led a disastrous campaign that resulted in the death of his elder brother in the Boer War.[17] For Stevens, the ability of a butler to hide his feelings is the clearest sign of "dignity" and provided exemplary standards as he carried on in the same house.

The second day in Salisbury also concerns both memories of Stevens's aging father and the use of the Darlington House for a diplomatic conference that took place in March 1923. We learn that Stevens's father, in his seventies and suffering from arthritis, is gradually losing his ability to perform his job flawlessly. On one occasion, the father suffers injury while carrying a dinner tray, claiming that the steps outside were in disrepair to excuse his fall. Stevens mentions that the conference marks a turning point in his own life, the first time when the meaning of "dignity" became clear to him.[18] During this same period, various dignitaries but also many disreputable people became frequent visitors of Darlington Hall. A main purpose of the conference was to discuss a possible revision of the Versailles Treaty, which Lord Darlington considered to be unfair, especially concerning war reparations involving Germany. During the meeting, the interaction between a French dignitary, Monsieur Dupont, and Mr. Lewis, an US Senator who is generally skeptical of the pro-German sentiment that soon begins to dominate the conference, is crucial to how the conversation proceeds. After Monsieur Dupont arrives and greets Mr. Lewis, Sir David Cardinal calls for a freezing of German payments and the withdrawal of French troops from the Ruhr region.[19] Lewis argues somewhat later that Dupont is being manipulated, but when Dupont has a chance to speak, he not only agrees with Darlington and most of those in attendance but also denounces Lewis as disloyal and deceptive. Lewis in turn claims that Darlington is a naïve amateur, like everyone else at the conference, while Darlington claims that his amateurism marks him as a man of honor.[20] We learn toward the middle of this episode that Stevens's father has suffered a stroke that proves to be fatal. Stevens responds to this personal crisis simply by proceeding and insists that his father displayed "dignity" under duress and that he has modelled his own actions accordingly.[21]

The second afternoon of the excursion take us to Mortimer's Pond in Dorset, where Stevens discusses what constitutes "greatness" in a butler, especially when this quality is no longer linked to employment in a great household. Stevens argues that the Hayes Society erred in too directly linking the greatness of the butler to the prestige of the household that employed him. For Stevens, the greatness of the employer, rather than the household as such, provides the key for assessing the butler, who contributes to the course of history when he works under those who make the decisions that shape human destiny. Thus, if the Hayes Society conceived of the world as a ladder, Stevens and his generation came to view the world through the analogy of a wheel: the turning of a wheel, rather than the ascent up a ladder, involves uncertainty but also creates new options that can be seized on in the drift of time. Private negotiations seem to provide the means for soliciting outcomes that no longer require public discourse: "Rather, debates are conducted, and crucial decisions arrived at, in the privacy of the great houses of this country."[22] Stevens's discourse continues to teem with the words "greatness" and "dignity" as he recalls the most problematic episode in the history of Darlington Hall. His unquestioning allegiance to Lord Darlington allows him to believe that his service to the great man is nothing less than service to humanity at large, a position that blinds him to his own role in furthering dubious aims.

In a manner that seems almost defensive at times, Stevens then goes on to explain, if not fully justify, Darlington's cooperation with various individuals who were complicit with fascism, at least for a short period. On the third day of the excursion, Stevens visits Taunton, Somerset in the morning and Moscombe, Devon, later in the day. While in Somerset, Stevens states that Darlington was not personally anti-Semitic but had only a brief association with the British Union of Fascists. At the same time, he continues to emphasize how he made a modest contribution to history when he functioned as butler at various conferences that continued in Darlington Hall for several years. In Moscombe, Stevens mentions Mrs. Barnet, a politically connected socialite whose brief influence on Lord Darlington in summer 1932 resulted in the dismissal of two Jewish housemaids.[23] No credible reasons were given for their dismissal; however, Stevens was delegated the responsibility of dismissing them: "It was a difficult task, but as such, one that demanded to be carried out with dignity."[24] Miss Kenton, his long-term colleague, was deeply outraged and momentarily withdrew from the household. Darlington privately expressed his regrets. One year later, Miss Kenton explains to Stevens that she wanted to leave but had no relatives who could take her in and no further chance of employment if she simply left Darlington Hall.

Moscombe is also important because it provides the setting in which Mr. Harry Smith, a local personage, expresses a view of dignity that is opposed to the definition that Stevens has been proposing throughout his long excursion. "Dignity's not just for gentlemen," Smith insists.[25] Nonetheless, Steven rejects Smith's arguments but evokes another incident from Darlington Hall. Stevens remembers how in 1935, one of Darlington's friends asked him three pointed questions to prove that ordinary people cannot be trusted to direct public policy. Stevens was incapable of answering these questions. Within this same context, we also learn that Lord Darlington finally apologized for dismissing the two Jewish servants, suggesting that this reprehensible deed was a departure from his usual management style.[26] Nonetheless, Stevens continues to maintain an unchanging definition of "a butler's duty" and his notion of "good service" as if this evident inconsistency does not require him to rethink the understanding of greatness on which his whole argument depends.

Days four and six bring us to the conclusion of the narrative. Day four unfolds in Little Compton, Cornwall, in which Stevens remembers how Mr. Cardinal warned Lord Darlington that he was in considerable danger from becoming the tool of the German government abroad. Cardinal's insights are followed by an image of Miss Kenton crying. This image signals the end of the journey on day six, which is set in Weymouth. When Stevens meets Miss Kenton, now Mrs. Benn, he discovers that she has aged and that her marriage seems to be in disarray. She speaks with some regret of having left Darlington Hall years ago but then acknowledges having been reconciled to her husband; indeed, she has become resigned to a life that might have been different. Stevens relates a peculiar discussion with a man in Weymouth who has helped him understand that the evening is especially enjoyable to many people. This observation is coupled with the advice to maintain "a more positive outlook and try to make the best of what remains of the day."[27] He considers in this late context that he might become somewhat more disputatious, but this is just a passing thought since he has only begun to enter into his reflections on life at Darlington Hall.

ISHIGURO IN A HEGELIAN FRAME

The Remains of the Day is a heart-breaking novel that demonstrates how moral constraints prevent the traumas of history from inducing a subjective response to temporal dislocation; it also inscribes an underlying emptiness that potentially foregrounds action itself. Stevens is radically disconnected from what might have enabled him to think through his political responsibilities, even if his practical options were severely limited. In coming to terms with this problem philosophically, we might do worse that return to Hegel's disagreements with Kant, whose rigorist morality can be interpreted, in some respects, as an uncanny precursor to Stevens' own position. Hegel argues that the empty space that transcendental freedom projects in Kant's moral philosophy is basically teleological and merely disguised as deontological.[28] This argument is informed by Hegel's reading of Kant's *Critique of Judgment*, Part II, which suggests that a modified version of teleology is implicit in the processes of nature. Hegel accepts the intimate connection between willing and thinking, but unlike Kant, he argues that actions have goals and that natural drives provide "content" to the ethical will. Such drives, however, are not unalloyed; they need to be purified to perform a role in ethical life, which is not based on abstract law but on the good, which provides the general criterion for determining what is a duty and what is not. In *The Remains of the Day*, Miss Kenton is perhaps the figure who most strongly suggests the indeterminate (but crucial) nature of the good as such.

Ishiguro's situated approach to moral dilemmas allows to glimpse how Hegelian ethics would differ in fundamental ways from what Kant proposes to be ethical, particularly when the idea of the good is proposed as the basis for morality. In a comprehensive discussion of dialectical logic, Geoffrey Mure explains how for Hegel, the goodwill must be "rooted in the nature of Reality, with which the subject in Will identifies itself, *prior* to an identification of it in immediate external Being."[29] This contrasts to the goodwill in Kant, which is only hypothetically good. At the same time, Kant is correct in emphasizing how goodwill is good for itself but not yet in itself, even when this distinction cannot overturn goodwill's absolute validity. Hegel also acknowledges that the external world confronts the will as a barrier, which can only realize itself against a background of contingency, and hence, evil: "Evil, though contingent and unactual, is not illusory; it is the unrealized self which conditions the subject's self-realization in Will—just as error is the other-being of truth and dynamic element in the self-conquest of the subject."[30] Nonetheless, Hegel argues as well that goodwill requires a transition to another sphere before evil can be turned into good, that is, before the practical idea, which Kant uses to express the idea of the good, can be enlightened on a theoretical level.[31] Of course, Hegel is not proposing here a return to pre-Kantian rationalism: the movement from goodwill to this more enlightened stance would not only transform externality but would involve doing what is right to produce good, which presupposes Kant's position on the essence of human reason.

Ishiguro's novel also strains the limits of antinaturalism, which performs a basic role in Kant's morality and in Hegel's rearticulation and transformation of Kantian themes. Of course, Hegel can only be called a naturalist with some qualification; his position would be hard to imagine without the prior example of Kant, whose transcendentalism he does not reject by returning to empirical conceptions. Nonetheless, Hegel's dialectic is irreducible to mechanism and engages nature itself, which argues that ethical action is capable of organizing inclinations into a rational whole, instead of simply extirpating or marginalizing them. Kant's mistake, therefore, is not to say that the will is formal but that it must *remain formal* with respect to its ethical and political possibilities.[32] Hegel proposes that culture (*Bildung*) permits the instincts and passions to assume determinate form, and this sphere cannot be understood if the Kantian opposition between moral and nonmoral criteria is maintained as a binding thesis. Hegel also argues that Kant imports content instead of keeping the law empty whenever claims are made about how transgressive actions contradict legitimate claims. For instance, it would be inconsistent to assert that deposits are valid and then to permit deposits to be stolen. However, Hegel also notes that in this example, which is used to condemn theft, Kant has made an assertion about the existence of deposits in the first place; hence, the alleged contradiction depends on a prior assertion about norms and practices that are assumed to be socially justified.[33] This prior assumption is what Kant as a moral philosopher cannot properly acknowledge or assess.

The social world that gradually overtakes Darlington Hall at a crucial moment in history is perhaps civil society at its worst, but precisely for this reason, the novel dramatizes the danger of falling back on a purely empirical phenomenon for moral guidance. Stevens evokes the metaphor of the wheel to describe the social process through which he maintained his faith in the great man who stood above him, permitting him to proceed with "dignity" while others were thrust aside, apparently for reasons of expediency. The formal law that he obeys may be little more than a parody of Kant's categorical imperative, but the role of coercion in the regime that he accepts indicates the moral bankruptcy of civil society, which is assumed to provide ethical guarantees that go without saying. Hegel argues, in contrast, that a fully articulated State requires the development of civil society but also presupposes a break with the private interests that are adequate to the construction of social life, narrowly considered. Far from supporting political tendencies that were only beginning to emerge in the wake of the Napoleonic wars and in subsequent European history, Hegel defended the universality of the civil servant class as a bulwark against nationalist passion and cultural provincialism. However, we can see how Hegel's political stance in this regard largely extends Kant's formalism into another sphere, instead of abrogating it. The world that Ishiguro's Stevens inhabits is no longer in touch with the subjective motivations that might have transformed contingency into a public response to moral aberration. Recalling Hannah Arendt's ontological claims concerning selfhood, we might even say that Sevens is unable to make a new beginning and thus provide a basis for his own actions that might stand some chance of acquiring public significance. Understood within the narrower sphere of how Hegel transforms Kant's formalism into a unique theory of the modern state, Ishiguro's novel demonstrates how the failure to advance beyond the arbitrary separation between civil society and government power can result in immoral actions, which cannot be justified, even within the limited framework of Kant's ethics.

In returning for a moment to Ishiguro's novel as a literary performance, we might also consider how Stevens briefly gathers together the remnants of the past in some new way, just as the owl of Minerva, as Hegel contended, only takes flight at dusk.[34] The relationship between aesthetics and ethics is crucial to Kant's *Critique of Judgment*, where the sublime performs a bridging function that may be overextended but is certainly fundamental to his aesthetic project. Without producing a separate treatise on political philosophy that might have taken its place among his major works, Kant opened the space for a new understanding of the active life, particularly when he indicated how the sense of the sublime marked the transition from an aesthetic mode of apprehension to ethical universality. Such a transition requires a revised conception of the active life, wherein the standpoint of the whole comes to replace the more abstract position that would be stipulated if Kant's formalism were to be given the final word on what lies on the other side of pure theory. In his use of irony, Ishiguro shows us how private intentions are compromised by contingent circumstances, instead of remaining untainted by the empirical residues that threaten autonomy, but this demonstration is not carried out for its own sake. The reader of Ishiguro's novel is invited to grasp the ironical aspects of Stevens's rigorism and then, in the end, to understand that this same irony has pushed Stevens into a more reflective mode that might even lead to moral and political awakening.

The reader of Ishiguro's novel is also occasionally invited to consider the discrepancy between intention and outcome from a position that looks forward to a fuller apprehension of ethical life and a different arrangement of human institutions. This position would be recollective in allowing irony to unfold in a broader context and permit past actions to be part of a longer journey where the errors of time suggested the need for a different history. It would not be aesthetic in the Kantian sense but would take the "remains" of what is no longer whole as the beginning of another journey, one that might be melancholy but also contained the promise of a more credible apprehension of rectitude, duty and intersubjective experience. This place of recollection would not justify the past as past but allow the flow of time to be thought about in much the same way that the floating world became the occasion for Masuji's reflections on his own belatedness and offered a kind of aesthetic solace for one in need.

NOTES

1. Gadamer, *Truth and Method*, 161.
2. Ibid., 162. Gadamer's sketch of "world literature" is significant for many reasons. Perhaps most importantly, his use of the concept of "world" does not seem to be bound to a quasi-Heideggerian notion of rootedness, which some readers have discovered in the evocation of the peasant landscape as encountered in "The Origin of the Work of Art." It is as if Gadamer wishes to underscore how literature, perhaps in contrast to the visual arts, either implies a different sort of ontology or may need to be rethought on some new, postontological basis. But this possibility would have to involve a radicalization of the imaginary that, according to Gadamer, is present in all of literature and potentially destabilizes all disciplines that share this component, if only to a limited degree.
3. Ibid., 163.
4. Paul de Man, *Resistance to Theory* (Minneapolis: University of Minnesota Press, 1987), 11. In de Man's deconstructive criticism, linguistic categories replace phenomenological ones, even though referentiality has not been utterly banished from the scene of reading. It is perhaps noteworthy that reference makes a reappearance in de Man's very late work, where the concept of ideology begins to surface as a critical term that requires an analytic distinction between the phenomenal and referential. But even in the late work, de Man does not identify the referential unequivocally with the real, suggesting that his approach to language remains "transcendental" in some way.
5. Kazuo Ishiguro, *An Artist of the Floating World* (New York: Vintage International 1989), 24.
6. Ibid., 62.
7. Ibid., 63.
8. Ibid., 74–75.
9. Ibid., 100–4.
10. Ibid., 123.
11. Ibid., 127.
12. Ibid., 141.
13. Ibid., 168.
14. Ibid., 169

15. Ibid., 200. The transition from an aesthetic approach to art to allegorical coding provides us with a basis for contrasting the figural to the figurative, whereby a style that engages the whole sensibility is opposed to a more rigid type of visual representation that correlates the visible signs with ideological references. In this case, imperial ambitions underwrite the "progressive" art that has the hidden intention of furthering the aims of war, rather than encouraging amelioration. That art can have political implications is clearly suggested when Masuji abdicates aesthetics in favor of a more doctrinaire form of cultural activity.

16. Kazuo Ishiguro, *The Remains of the Day* (New York: Vintage International, 1993), 28.
17. Ibid., 40–42.
18. Ibid., 70.
19. Ibid., 92.
20. Ibid., 102–3.
21. Ibid., 106.
22. Ibid., 115. The entirely private nature of these conferences is underscored in this passage, compromising the possibility that the meetings were genuinely political in the sense of engaging the public sphere. The shrinking of the public sphere and the replacement of political deliberations with sheer chance are crucial aspects of the wheel metaphor that otherwise might be mistaken for an acceptance of genuine risk, which certainly has a place in all decisions. The metaphor of the wheel also implies a certain abdication of personal responsibility that enables Stevens to conceive of history as utterly beyond the reach of those who seek to alter the wheel's path.
23. Ibid., 145–46.
24. Ibid., 148.
25. Ibid., 186.
26. Ibid., 196–99.
27. Ibid., 244.
28. McCumber, *Understanding Hegel's Mature Critique of Kant*, 117.
29. G. R. G. Mure, *A Study of Hegel's Logic* (Oxford: Clarendon Press, 1950), 285.
30. Ibid., 286.
31. Ibid., 287–89.
32. McCumber, *Understanding Hegel's Mature Critique of Kant*, 159. A persistent criticism, which may be a reaction to Marxist appropriations, argues that Hegel seeks to replace form with content and thus favors a "concrete" approach to society and history, in sharp contrast to more theoretical approaches. Such criticism, however, overlooks how, in Hegel's system, concreteness is only achieved through the movement and deeper realization of the concept. Formal specifications allow content to emerge as a prerequisite for exploring ethical and political possibilities. Content is not inevitable but mediated through subjective freedom, which gives history a special role in the construction of institutions. Finally, content is not generated on the basis of purely logical determinations but presupposes an improvisatory (and historical) space in which freedom can be experienced and, to some degree, realized in time.
33. Ibid., 164–66.
34. Hegel, *The Philosophy of Right*, 13. Hegel's use of the Owl of Minerva metaphor is generally assumed to suggest that philosophical reflection is basically historical recollection, but history in this case is "the being of what was" and cannot be identified uncritically with a static record of unchanging facts. Moreover, because aesthetics is a type of reflection—that abandons art as traditionally conceived—we might detect traces of the aesthetic in the metaphor itself, which evokes the play of light and darkness in the passing of the classical age and its dream of perfect adequacy.

Conclusion

Negotiating the Figural

The present study has explored how writers from Edmund Spenser to Kazou Ishiguro have employed figuration in literature, not simply as an embellishment or rhetorical strategy but as a clue that demonstrates how the literary text negotiates psychic and social conflicts in creative ways. Nevertheless, because the role of the reader in this process of negotiation remains unclear, we need to take a closer look at the reading process, particularly in terms of its ethical and political implications. The conclusion to this study therefore takes up the question of what occurs when a literary text conjoins semiotics and aesthetics in a manner that lends figural space hermeneutical significance. After considering how Walter Benjamin engages both Karl Marx and Sigmund Freud in presenting a cultural version of trauma theory, I will clarify how Julia Kristeva carries this engagement to a new level, while suggesting the limitations of the psychoanalytic paradigm. This part of my discussion will also allow me to recapitulate how key literary works, previously under analysis, support Kristeva's theoretical position. G. W. F. Hegel's work in aesthetics, however, is subsequently shown to lend itself to hermeneutical readings in contrast to the approach favored by Kristeva. In returning to the issue of philosophical aesthetics, I will indicate in conclusion how Hegel seeks to recast the ancient controversy concerning the one and the many, thus justifying a tentative "return to Hegel" that has been one purpose of this study.

Conclusion
TRAUMA IN BENJAMIN

The literary texts that we have examined thus far are all narratives of one type or another and have assumed the form of works that were written in historical time. All of these texts include speakers or protagonists who evoke an earlier moment that has been encoded as a profound disturbance in personal experience. Spenser's great epic concludes with a long narrative romance that presupposes a colonial background and, partly for this reason, is difficult to read as the unambiguous restoration of natural perfection. Both William Wordsworth and Percy Bysshe Shelley provide different images of traumatic life that interfere with the conventional readings of their poetry as a tribute to natural abundance. Marcel Proust's narrator is only able to manage the traumatic effects of modern life through patterns of repetition that may be consoling but never quite banish a sense of how time itself is perpetually in flight. Maurice Blanchot has been presented as offering us a view of historical time that integrates rupture and discontinuity in a new interpretive framework. The two authors whose work conclude this study are concerned with historical catastrophe, which turns the past into more of a projection of the present, even if it cannot abolish what structures operate as a hidden cause that the reader can guess but not fully decipher. This backward glance can be located in cultural as well as individual history, unfolding in the human community to the degree that the transition from a relatively stable to an unstable world is difficult to ground in the external conditions that shaped it.

One way of imagining how this disjunction occurs is to examine a local but perhaps epochal instance that suggests the impact that various technological advances have had in the way that human beings process subjective life. Thus, in "The Work of Art in the Age of Mechanical Reproduction" ("*Das Kunstwerk im Zeitalter seiner technischen Reproduzierbarkeit,*" 1935), Benjamin invokes a narrative in which the origin of art is related to ritual practices that leave their mark on works that are only later assimilated to the canon of humanism during a secular age.[1] The aftereffects of religious rite seem to confer a distinctive aura on modern works, but only at the expense of disrupting an integral tradition that no longer survives as the works enter the world of commodities within which they are fated to be appraised and distributed. For Benjamin, auratic art, or the art of humanism proper, is thus a dim reflection of ritual practices that have become marginal to modern life, but it is also a transformation of those practices into something wholly different. This dual inheritance is precisely what gives Benjamin's analyses of works their historical depth because it enables him to both lament the inevitable demise of the aura due to the passing of medieval tradition but also to give credence to the fragility of modern art as an aesthetic achievement.

And yet, this cultural narrative becomes strained at the precise juncture that it allows for two equally valid, but no doubt contradictory, responses to auratic art: On the one hand, auratic art depends on a past that is threatened with extinction, and on the other hand, it also bulks against this past as rigid and distant from the quick pace that may be an aspect of all experiences that seek fluidity and freedom from external control. This tension reaches the breaking point in two areas at the same moment. First, Benjamin presents the advent of reproducibility as a technical event of signal importance that ushers in a new relationship between artist and spectator to cultural work. Once texts and images become reproducible on a vast scale, cultural production ceases to be defined primarily in terms of individual creativity, while the works themselves are no longer strongly linked to delimited sites of origin. Reproducibility thus becomes the occasion through which the traumatic effects of modern life can be said to surface, not only in the experience of art but also whenever the impact of modernity on consciousness deprives the urban inhabitant of connectedness to the past.

However, this rupture in continuity, which is hard to describe as an experience to the extent that it threatens to disrupt what seems to be integral to experience itself, raises epistemological issues that cannot be resolved through recourse to familiar models. From one standpoint, rupture is incompatible with the understanding because it radically decenters the subject whose stability is generally considered to be a prerequisite for truth. Such decentering would be unthinkable in classical and early modern systems of thought that adopt the stability of the knower as the basis for knowledge. Thus, how can Hegel, as heir to post-Kantian idealism, argue that the movement toward absolute knowledge is anything less than thoroughly "subjective" in requiring a conscious being whose itinerary is dialectical insofar as it allows the knower to grasp the contents of the mind in a process of growing complexity? Dialectics in this trajectory would be "classical" when it insists on the priority of subjective unity to a process that enables the subject to be realized in time. Nonetheless, this reading of Hegel is problematic to the degree that it assumes in advance what dialectics sets out to achieve, namely, a unity that is inseparable from a process through which the subject "recovers" what it loses when it gives up its status as a self-contained being.

A rather different reading of Benjamin not only enables us to revise the standard dialectical model but also to suggest how Hegel's contribution to aesthetics can be reconsidered in a similar manner. On a more basic level, the concept of the aura is a performative one, rather than the reflection of an ongoing history that provides Benjamin's narrative with its direction and impetus. Eva Geulen has objected to Jürgen Habermas's reading of Benjamin as a kind of late Weberian, who redeploys the "disenchantment of the world" as an historicist thesis that undergirds his interpretation of cultural history. The concept of the aura is crucial in this regard because it *presupposes* the shattering of tradition and acquires its meaning at the precise moment when the opposition between the original and the copy has been invalidated. What this suggests is that the idea of an earlier site no longer testifies to a more "authentic" cultural experience but is invariably a reconstruction of what the aura evokes as a sign that art itself has ceased to be auratic: "That is why the aura is not a concept in the classical sense, but rather in the Hegelian sense: act and result at once."[2] We can see how this reversal of conventional historicism is also at work in Hegel's so-called "end-of-art" thesis, which is often misinterpreted as nostalgic classicism. Thus, when Hegel refers to how philosophical thought is required if art is to be realized in its truth, he did not mean that art simply came to an end and thereby became a topic for modern reflection. On the contrary, he more strongly suggests how aesthetics faces a new problem once reflection advances to a higher level: "The real problem that is thus bequeathed to all post-Hegelian aesthetic reflection is not the end of the production of art, but rather the end of the possibility of a form of aesthetic reflection that *does not* bring about the end of art."[3]

In another manner, although the aura in this sense would be difficult, if not impossible, to assimilate to a dialectical method that insisted on phenomenological unity as the basis for grasping experience as a whole, Hegel's willingness to encompass heteronomy and negation in his system of thought never allows truth to appear as an *immediate* experience but continually insists on the role of division and incompleteness to a process that cannot be traced back to a simple origin. Hence, we might revisit Benjamin's peculiar version of cultural history—where reproduction threatens to undo the "truce" that temporarily subdues the conflict between religion and art—as a narrative that ultimately prevents truth from being defined in the "proper" sense. What is disconcerting is that, under conditions of late modernity, Benjamin's narrative apparently eliminates the claim for truth, so that emptiness and vacuity seem to insert themselves into the cultural register, replacing experience altogether, and thus annihilating the progressive potential of a dialectic that falls apart if it cannot retain some residue of an evolving self, the subjective kernel of an open process. At the same time, this same narrative can be read as ultra-Hegelian when truth becomes less a matter of subjective experience than an event that requires a system of mediation to be more fully articulated. When viewed from this perspective, whatever allows the disintegration of the aura to be registered as understandable acquires an aesthetic meaning that complements semiotic interpretation.[4]

However, without denying that the aura has the aesthetic significance of linking art to a perceptual background, Benjamin identifies the survival of subjectivity with the reduction of the person as well as the preservation of the subject in the work of art, reconceived as a social accomplishment. This transformative sense of the aura is explored toward the end of the Artwork essay, where Benjamin contrasts concentration and distraction, aligning the attempt to focus on what the work means with a man who disappears into it: "He enters into this work of art the way that legend tells of a Chinese painter when he viewed his finished painting."⁵ In this analogy, Benjamin sustains the difference between the masses who are merely distracted by films and the individual who somehow "produces" meaning just as he contemplates it, since the work itself is transformed into a new object at the moment that it provides the occasion for an abandonment of the self, and indeed, its very extinction: "The disappearance is a sacrifice, a pledge, which allows the aura to be retained and which is retained in the image."⁶ The advantage of this model over the old-fashioned Romantic one is inherent in the way that it restores the object to a new position of aesthetic pertinence. It would undo the more classical and contemplative view of the object, while retaining one meaning of trauma in containing the possibility of a transpersonal response to the work of art.

Benjamin's radicalization of psychoanalysis—and Hegelian thought by implication—enables him to attest to the role of materiality in the apprehension of cultural life at the exact moment when the "truth" of a previous cultural object begins to dissolve. Instead of banishing subjectivity from this process, Benjamin gestures toward a new mode of the subjective, not as a controlling factor but as a limit to conscious experience that is also the other side of a dialectical process. Although not able to be phenomalized, this other side cannot be reduced to an abstract movement that merely assimilates a preexisting subject to a more universal phase of knowledge. As truth ceases to be available in the usual forms, the subject that remains does not mark the impossibility of time (because of the role of repetition in traumatized life) but suggests how a new time can be recuperated. The subject can be recovered only as a transformed one that no longer recognizes itself in previous forms of truth because it has been forced to give up its earlier position and establish new relations to the cultural sphere. Nonetheless, certain questions remain unanswered in Benjamin's appropriation of Hegel, some of which concern the status of the dialectic in his synthetic reconfiguration. We might ask, for instance: How does change occur in a system in which negation no longer operates in a logic of continuity? Kristeva's own reading of Hegel and Freud provides a partial answer to this question.

KRISTEVA'S SEMIOTIC RESPONSE

It is thus in a comparative sense that we might reconsider Kristeva's post-Lacanian conception of the imaginary in terms of how the semiotic provides a new basis for enabling the subject to respond to the constraints that otherwise would be imposed on it by symbolic structures. In contrast to Jacques Lacan, Kristeva envisions a maternal background to the discovery of both dejection and bonding, thus constituting a sort of middle term that is also animated by negativity to reject paternal prohibitions, at least to some degree. This can occur largely because, for Kristeva, the semiotic and the symbolic are complementary aspects of a single process and therefore should not be interpreted as a dyad in which the symbolic emerges as the dominant term. Hence, for Kristeva, the role of the semiotic in cultural processes would go beyond anything that Benjamin envisioned, retaining a quasi-Hegelian meaning when considered as a ternary process but also implying the principle of negativity that is also the fourth term of the dialectic, in the words of Kristeva. Kristeva's challenge to the cultural dominant would also involve an artistic challenge, but in this case, the challenge would be launched by avant-garde poets, rather than by the emissaries of modern film.

However, just as Benjamin's model of trauma runs the risk of eliminating the individual and severely limiting if not disabling ethical and political agency, Kristeva's overreliance on trauma (whether it assumes the name of negativity, abjection or melancholy) runs a similar risk and, from some standpoints, ends up confirming symbolic authority to the degree that it stages a mere revolt that cannot alter the basic composition of whatever institutions that it attempts to resist. The latter critical assessment needs to be squarely confronted because it does have merit, particularly in suggesting the ethical and political limitations of psychoanalysis. For Judith Butler, for instance, the whole thematic of abjection refers back to the rigid process whereby subjects are politically regulated, whereas Kristeva argues that it invokes a sphere that admits of no boundary and emerges before the ego acquires its distinctive features. This contrast turns out to be crucial to how the two thinkers assess the value of dejection in the project of promoting social and political change. Butler criticizes Kristeva for apparently valorizing a mode of consciousness that only confirms symbolic structures, while Kristeva might reply by arguing that the space between semiosis and symbolism is what allows for a margin of difference, the location for destabilization and the concomitant opportunity to resist what sustains the binary opposition that presides over current arrangements.[7]

In summarizing how Kristeva and Butler disagree, Sara Beardsworth proposes that their dissimilar projects could be reconciled according to an insight that they seem to share. Butler offers a crucial basis for reconciling the two positions, however divergent they may be on a theoretical level, when she implies that subjectivity does indeed survive, even in prohibitive regimes that repress sexual diversity: "In sum, constraints on the constitution of sexed identity must be thought in terms of *repetition* not *ground*."[8] In short, Butler suggests that an active resistance to societal closure can assume a performative dimension when irony and parody contest symbolic hegemony, thus providing a counterpart to what Kristeva has identified as the space that lies between society and culture. We might say that both positions contain the insight that repression cannot be complete if performativity is possible or if the space of abjection remains open to cultural expressions that are informed by the imaginary. Moreover, when conceived in this way, the two positions also acquire proximity through a thematic of ritual that they explore differently. If Butler's conception of performativity has ritual aspects, we might say that Kristeva's exploration of abjection argues that, even in secular societies, ritual provides the analog for what enables a new position to reconstitute the symbolic order: "To be *like* ritual, to recall Kristeva's argument, is to accomplish the warding off of the abject without tying the logic of abjection to a founding instance: the Law."[9] This conception of ritual does not require that the semiotic analyst accept a specifically religious point of view on cultural material but instead suggests that practices that function like rituals be seen as attempts to cope with traumatic symptoms.

Along with this claim, Kristeva also stipulates the persistence of repression in symbolic regimes as well as a possible lessening of repression, not through a simple return to the semiotic but through the vehicle of memory and the acceptance of the past as past. If the memory of an originary loss—the loss that is mostly deeply felt in the state of abjection—is not commonly recalled under conditions of late modernity, then one of the most important aspects of Kristeva's project would be to acknowledge this loss. Benjamin is in many aspects ambiguous about our retaining a presentiment of the aura that both depends on nature and anticipates the moment when nature dissolves. Mechanical reproduction signifies the passing of the aura and is a figure of hope only if the new technologies have political implications that relate to matters of proximity and accessibility. And yet, Benjamin seems to be arguing at times that the conditions that enable art to become modern are forever in recession because nature itself is doomed to disappear, when it erases the last vestiges of auratic experience from the sphere of culture. Kristeva's cultural model, in contrast, is both less and more optimistic. It assumes a loss that cannot be recovered but also an experience that waits to be recuperated once the repression of loss is lessened, presumably through the aid of cultural memory and the many texts that flow from memory's use. A brief survey of the literary chapters in the present work supports Kristeva's sense of loss and well as the power of literature to innovate an aesthetic sphere through which history provides us with new styles of engagement.

In this study, I have discussed how several modern writers have achieved something of what Kristeva has recommended in her cultural model when they display how performance is interwoven with identity in a manner that has a "spiritual" quality, even though the situation of the writer is predominantly secular. Spenser in "The Book of Courtesy" introduces performative ceremonies after exploring the terrors of archaic sacrifice, while removing the protagonist from view in the middle scenes and requiring a political resolution, thus complicating what otherwise might be read as a strict Platonic allegory. Wordsworth's student-poet in *The Prelude* plays at appropriating a canon that remains beyond his grasp, and then, as a mature traveler, gazes back at a revolutionary moment that situates deep anxiety in another sphere. Shelley in *The Triumph of Life* reminds us that performance has a ritual aspect that is crucial to his work as a secular poet, without ceasing to affirm how modernity testifies to aesthetic loss. The difference between Renaissance and Romantic literature in this regard is sometimes rather stark, however, insofar as the former tends to assimilate the social model to a preconceived model of nature, which explains why traditional pastoral ends up reinforcing social values that are assumed to be "natural" when it stages their reconciliation in narratives that usually confirm moral certitudes and theological doctrines. Romantic literature, in comparison, suggests a crisis in the apprehension of nature itself, even when nature becomes a discourse that is used to support normative purposes, so that the function of performativity in the Romantic text often heightens this crisis, instead of resolving it.

Performativity in literature, beginning with Romanticism, also contains a semiotic element that serves as the precondition for the emergence of what Jacques Rancière has called the "aesthetic unconscious." Figural expressions in the poetry of both Wordsworth and Shelley double signs and a sense of the virtual that prevent familiarization and mark the emergence of a disruptive temporality through which the aesthetic unconscious makes its appearance as a discourse that cannot easily be given a disciplinary frame. The difference between psychology and history in Wordsworth's poetry was shown to generate a hermeneutical conflict, but this same conflict can be read in semiotic terms as necessary to the formation of a new horizon in which unconscious elements in human experience can be brought to the foreground. In figuring Jean-Jacques Rousseau, Shelley demonstrates how unconscious elements merge with naturalistic details to overwhelm Enlightened reason, but the figure of life that contrasts with this downward plunge has an aesthetic quality that alludes to Dante's divine vision without replicating his theology. In the longer view, the fading of life is a repetition of Rousseau's defeat and shatters the possibility of representation when an unanswerable question serves as the only plausible conclusion to a poem that remained unfinished. For Wordsworth and Shelley, performativity is not only interwoven with repetition but can be read as a sign that aesthetics continues to have a role in the aftermath of cultural oneness.

The motivation behind Proust's *In Search of Lost Time* may be religious in some vestigial way, combining the dream of completed time with an awareness of a past that remains forever inaccessible. However, the kinship between aesthetics and semiotics, as well as their creative divergence, becomes thematic in Proust's masterwork and demonstrates how a narrative sensibility gives the modern novel a special place in the history of literature. For Rancière, Proust offers a basis for charting the devolution of Schillerian aesthetics, whose key concepts are differently arranged in the history of French literature and then achieve a kind of symbolic truce in the conclusion to *Time Regained* (*Le temps retrouvé*). I suggested how Rancière's reading, without being rejected, can be developed and modified when the role of the interlocking roles of metonymy and metaphor support a reading that acknowledges the importance of singular moments to a narrative that carries the protagonist along with it, depriving him of a stable identity in which the past often overwhelms the present. This argument allowed me to trace the outlines of a critical debate that began with Stephen Ullmann's reflections on style and was clarified on the basis of Gérard Genette's structuralist analyses until it reached an impasse in Paul de Man's linguistic account of tropes in *Swann's Way*. After presenting de Man's argument in some detail, I was able to show how related critical positions converge in Kristeva's approach, which was opposed to de Man's insistence on unreadability. The outcome was an aesthetic reading of Proust that derived, indirectly, from Hegel's peculiar understanding of phenomenology, and the opportunity to suggest how Proust's use of the imagination is figural and processual, rather than linked to a transcendent order.

My reading of Proust also argues that semiotics combines with aesthetics in a manner that goes beyond a traditional humanistic reading, particularly one that would emphasize reconciliation as the telos of a fictional narrative. The departure from this reading is consistent with my suggestion that what Benjamin named the aura and applied to auratic art already implies a break with tradition, and that Proust's narrative is both continuous and discontinuous, full and broken, in a manner that lends itself to Hegelian readings. The fullness of the Proustian narrative is manifest at different moments but particularly when Marcel's memory provides the occasion for a sense of the maternal that Kristeva has theorized as a counter to symbolization, allowing the aesthetic imaginary to assume a new role in the reception of texts. Nonetheless, Proust can also be read as indicating how the repetition of sensuous moments is irreducible to aesthetic satisfaction but also presupposes an experience of disinvestment when the psyche is no longer in control of its contents. What this means is that the humanistic reading of Proust, although not always wide of the mark, fails to account for the duality that can be discovered in the novel whenever Marcel is both confused and elated by the tropes that he works through in daily life. My remarks on Maurice Merleau-Ponty's references to Proust, as examined in the context of Kristeva's reading, confirm this duality and once again indicate how repetition—as demonstrated in this case in Swann's reflections on the musical phrase—only embodies the imaginary after it passes through a stage of disjunction with empirical experience.

The vexing question of where literature has gone after Proust inevitably requires an investigation into how the imagination comes to terms with a sense of loss in a new literary situation. My exposition of Blanchot's critical treatise, *The Space of Literature*, began with a brief excursion into Martin

Heidegger's enunciative response to a work of art that inserts an element of writing into what is bring described. This response opened up the theme of reversal, which is sometimes used to describe the turn that occurs in Heidegger's later phase but performs a different role in Blanchot's criticism, where the subject is no longer at the center of the literary work either as narrator or internal agent. Nonetheless, Heidegger argues that aesthetics itself is problematic because of its abiding allegiance to a modern philosophy of the subject, whereas Blanchot, in my reading, renews the aesthetic tradition, even when he deploys ancient myth to give figural significance to this renewal. Hence, Blanchot's response to the religious myth of Orpheus was shown to be integral to a view of literature in which appearance and disappearance are both crucial to the experience of the work of art. It was at this point that Merleau-Ponty, rather than Heidegger, became a guide in reading Blanchot, and then allowed me, later in my argument, to suggest the kinship between Blanchot and Hegel on the basis of distinct criteria. The key to this kinship was taken to be the disruptive role of disinvestment in both the creation and reception of literature, as well as the understanding of history, thus precluding a return to either traditional or Gadamerian hermeneutics. The "return to aesthetics" also informed my account of Blanchot's discussions of Mallarmé, Ranier Maria Rilke, and Franz Kafka, who are generally classified as modernist and contrasted to Proust on the basis of a stylistic and historical difference. Blanchot's response to canonical European modernism needs to be interpreted anew once the question of being is interrupted on behalf of a radical historicity that is complementary to the impossibility of achieving homecoming in a time of need.

My final two chapters were concerned with how figural signs inscribe historical experiences in fictional narratives that elicit a new exercise of the aesthetic imagination. Focusing on *Wide Sargasso Sea* among Jean Rhys's novels, I discussed the instability of semiotic and symbolic modes of narration and argue that a process of decentering operates against viewing individual characters as morally unambiguous. The broader significance of the novel, however, is shown to engage the reader on an ethical level, but only after the reader has passed through a journey through repetition in which the past reappears as already *present as past*. This moment is revelatory and does not dispense with the aesthetic but complicates its meaning, containing political meanings that are anticipated in Hegelian thought. Nonetheless, in suggesting how the Hegelian reading provides insights into figural interpretation, I also stressed that the social thought of Hegel and the different thought of Marx are only applicable to the colonial situation in a manner of speaking; instead of arguing, as has been done many times before, that either or both of these systems can be used without respecting the historical distance between the age of colonization and the emergence of the postcolonial, my analysis of Rhys's most important novel was intended to show how figural space is most strongly explored in imaginary encounters that free the mind to grasp on a figural level how judgments become possible. This process necessarily occurs in an *aesthetic* framework, which enables the reader to experience a specific "time-lag" as already performing a role in the colonial world and as thus subverting the tendency to read the past as having vanished, once and for all, in a progressive history.

The novels of Ishiguro performed a similar role in my analysis. Moreover, my interest was not only in exploring the broader significance of two novels that approach modern history from the perspective of vanished time but, once again, in suggesting how the past continues to inform the present, just as the past lives as past in a present that is no more. Masuji's "floating-world" haunted the daily lives of those who would carry on in postwar Japan, but this same world provided new opportunities for art and perception when free spirits could gather and distance themselves from social pressures that otherwise might ruin their creative prospects. The descent of figural expression into rigid allegorical depiction in the political climate of the 1930s became, in this longer perspective, a betrayal of the aesthetic promise that materialized in post-Meiji Japan with its relative openness to combining Western influences and indigenous traditions. The imperial ambitions that thwarted creativity later on are the signs of an unbridled nationalism that had nothing to do with what Hegel explored in his philosophical argument that the modern state can serve as a bulwark against the floodtides of Romantic extremism. In a complementary manner, Ishiguro's exploration of various intrigues in Darlington Hall during roughly the same time period can be viewed in retrospect as providing us with a backward look on a past that had *already* begun to shift in meaning when the public world had begun to shrink in significance. Although opposing Hegel and Kant as moral philosophers, my final assessment of this second novel underscored the importance of irony and sought to demonstrate how an aesthetic point of view could introduce a measure of doubt and uncertainty in contesting the primacy of a more strictly *political* unconscious.

This brings us back to the question of how aesthetics provides the link between semiotic experience and the larger goals that lie on the horizon of conscious life and require a more comprehensive framework to become intelligible. Art, particularly when it maintains its traditional relationship to ritual, suggests how repetition can provide an opening beyond what Jacques Derrida has called the metaphysics of presence and that prevents time and history from assuming disruptive roles in a general economy of signs. Throughout this study, the role of the aesthetic has been clarified in terms of how this opening leads beyond the blind impulses that turn repetition into an unconscious process that psychoanalysis has generally identified with the incest taboo, a prohibition that is believed to be difficult to integrate into civilized life. In positing the idea of an aesthetic unconscious that exceeds representation, Rancière has suggested that a sharp distinction needs to be made between the explanatory tendencies that dominate psychoanalysis and the discourses that suggest the effects of the unconscious and show how art possesses a shaping power that can lend form to what it cannot fully master. To argue in this manner, however, is also to argue implicitly that psychoanalysis does not provide an adequate basis for moving from trauma, broadly conceived, to a more engaged mode of experience. This inadequacy takes us back to the contrast between Kristeva and Benjamin as cultural theorists who were both influenced by psychoanalysis but have different ways of assessing aesthetics as a possible key to how repetition can be given a place in the sphere of art and public experience.

The role of the aesthetic in Benjamin's Artwork essay remains unclarified to the degree that the mechanical work of art is residually traumatic in the account provided, and, for this reason, is contrasted with aesthetic appropriation.[10] Although it could be argued that a version of the aesthetic might survive the demise of subjectivity that results from Benjamin's analysis of modern film, we might question how this can occur unless the spectator is sufficiently rooted in lived experience to improvise a new relationship to the symbolic, rather than merely reproduce the depersonalized structures that abound in modern society generally. In contrast to Lacan, Kristeva argues on a developmental level that the subject acquires symbolic awareness through the maternal bond, which no doubt provides a paradigm for creativity in the cultural sphere. However, this does not clarify how a passage through dejection can be transformative of symbolic structures, thus reopening normative issues that psychanalysis is not always equipped to address. Kristeva's subject, fully revised along semiotic lines, does not have support in a past that has lost its binding power and is hard to locate in a context in which responses to present-day dilemmas might be imagined and negotiated.

This being the case, Kristeva does allude to the resources that might be employed for going beyond the limitations of psychoanalysis to cast light on ethical and political possibilities that are improvised in what has been called "figural space." One clue is provided in Kristeva's argument that the second overturning of the dialectic is more basic than the first; in other words, in the theoretical revolution that joins Marx and Hegel, the role of language should be given precedence over production. For Kristeva, the discovery of language required Freud and the thematic of the unconscious before it could acquire validity. In this sense, aesthetics follows political economy, certainly not as an embellishment or secondary accomplishment but as a starting point for grasping what occurs in the political sphere when language emerges as the crux of interpretation.[11] Rancière has argued that aesthetics is not an explanatory science but provides a way for identifying art as art in the wake of representation. To join these two positions is to reopen the question of hermeneutics as it applies to the Hegelian tradition, which also tests the limits of everyday understanding. This is a question to which I now turn.

HEGEL AND HERMENEUTICS

Particularly in his disagreements with Jürgen Habermas, Hans-Georg Gadamer argues that the social sciences are alienated through their recourse to method in a manner that exacerbates the break with tradition that is the precondition for their emergence.[12] At the same time, Gadamer argues that hermeneutics not only belongs to this same terrain but somehow counters the implicitly nihilistic and skeptical consequences that are implicit in the discourses of the social sciences. Gadamer's thesis concerning the historical origin of hermeneutics acknowledges the difference between hermeneutics and classical rhetoric but attempts to detach hermeneutics from the moment of rupture that precipitates it. The problem with this approach, however, is that it tends to underestimate the degree to which instability is an aspect of all interpretation and testifies to the modernity of hermeneutics as a discipline. It was for this reason that the nonclassical hermeneutics of Blanchot was presented in this study as more in keeping with the historical conditions that gave rise to hermeneutics initially. Indeed, Gadamer's phenomenological approach to language would need to be modified before various figures could be said to express and mark the limits of cultural hegemony.

Gadamer apparently discovers a philosophical ally in arguing that Hegel's focus on contemporaneity is superior to Friedrich Schleiermacher's historicism in going beyond nostalgia without denying our tragic inability to retrieve what is no longer living. Hegel agues for Recollection (*Erinnerung*) as a process of "inwardization" that does not attempt to reproduce the past but repeats it in mediating past and present.[13] However, in this crucial instance, Gadamer obscures the degree to which Hegel was part of the crisis that is coeval with the origin of hermeneutics. His phenomenological conception of language is no doubt partly responsible for placing Hegel in the "continuist" camp, whereas another conception of language would complicate this gesture. Hence, while one reading of Hegel suggests a denial of the past as past in favor of an "idealistic" monism, recollection, more deeply considered, would include the memory of conflict and division, pain, and dislocation. This process would be both hermeneutical and semiotic in engaging the sensuous imagination as a faculty that allows for presence and absence in reconfiguring the past as it vanishes, indicating how the signs of another time are no longer reducible to the restricted meanings that they once assumed. In such a situation, the interpreter would not be a subject who seeks a ground but an unstable position in a semiotic chain, occupying a space that would be aesthetic as it enables normative concerns to be assessed on the basis of ongoing practices.

We might consider for a moment how a shift from Gadamerian hermeneutics to a semiotics of language would accept the non-foundational as the starting point for viewing the products of late modernity as figural signs that unfold in a space that is not closed like the cosmologies of antiquity. Semiotic criticism would assert the priority of textuality to the legible signs that constitute the literary work as a cultural object so that the possibility of moving outside the literary work might emerge in an open reading. The inseparability of textuality and alterity would guarantee the passage beyond the (literary) signs at hand, not in a manner that would reinstate classical representation but enable the reader to glimpse a "world" that is not the immediate one in which the reader dwells. The world imagined would be one that assumes an aesthetic trajectory, constituting the locus for reassessing normative concerns as well as the provisional telos of textual inquiry. Semiotics, thus conceived, would offer an implicit critique of the ontological conception of language as well a pathway for avoiding the dangers of ontological closure.

At the same time, semiotics would not dispense with hermeneutics to the degree that hermeneutics might be reenvisioned in the mode of rupture, which, as even Gadamer admits, was the precondition for its entry into modern thought. From this standpoint, Kristeva's opposition between semiotic and symbolic structures might be viewed historically as a sign of modernity itself, exacerbated but also linked to an experience that is *lived* and therefore impossible to minimize as a manner of subjectivity that is social rather than individual, thus rekindling the possibility of relating it to the Hegelian tradition that Kristeva acknowledges in her analysis of negativity, even while distancing herself from it. A serious problem remains, however, if Kristeva's ultimately theoretical reading of the Hegelian concept can be sustained as a mere prelude to Marxist appropriations because this reading would undo the possibility of hermeneutical retrieval that this inquiry has endeavored to advance.[14]

Although the possibility of reading Hegel hermeneutically has been broached, we might consider how the philosopher's works would need to be interpreted if this possibility were to be more fully explored. A major stumbling block to this project is the tendency of many readers to separate Hegel's *Phenomenology of Spirit* from the later *Science of Logic*. The standard reading of "Absolute Knowledge," the concluding chapter in the former work, supports the view that Hegel considered his own philosophy to mark the "end of history" insofar as the ascendancy of the absolute is presented dialectically as having consolidated the human past in a single, unified consciousness. However, in my discussion of Proust, Hegel's final chapter was briefly mentioned as problematizing the claim that consciousness is constituted in a manner that allows reflection to be bound to an autonomous ego. We might also say that the phenomenological "we" is a sort of tipping point that adopts the standpoint of absolute idealism only to demonstrate how subjective consciousness is asked at this crucial moment to recognize the subject-object that forms the phenomenological narrative in its objective manifestation. Hence, in accordance with the hermeneutical interpretation provided by Paul Redding, we might say that the phenomenological observer "is asked to recognize or acknowledge itself as belonging to a concrete, objective historical community as one abstract moment of that community."[15] This nonstandard reading, however, would also be implicitly deconstructive insofar as it argued that only precarious unity is achieved when "Absolute Knowledge" emerges at end of the phenomenological process as a moment that preserves duality, rather than the final achievement of transcendental unity.[16]

Hegelian phenomenology cannot be interpreted adequately apart from logical considerations but provides only an early version of how the structure of recognition informs a movement that is irreducible to subjective consciousness. The third and final book of Hegel's *Science of Logic* is devoted to "Subjective Logic," which explores "The Logic of the Concept" through an exposition of the disjunctive syllogism. The first two books of the same work deal with the "Doctrine of Being" and the "Doctrine of Essence" respectively, but unlike those books, Hegel's thematic of the Notion (*Begriff*) in the final book argues against any attempt to ground the absolute in a vague definition or external form that would guarantee conceptuality on a contingent basis. To say, therefore, that the phenomenological "we" is no longer an outside observer who merely contemplates history from an external and presumably timeless vantage point is also to say that it exhibits a recognitive structure that is presented in logical terms when Hegel later expands on the idea of the disjunctive syllogism. And yet, even in this later argument, Hegel emphasizes that the absolute idea requires language to exhibit itself as a process of self-movement, thus underscoring the communicative aspect of recognition itself.[17]

The significance of language to the movement of the concept cannot be overestimated and clearly distances Hegelian thought from all "metaphysical" constructions that attempt to freeze this movement in oppositional frameworks that would limit meaning to what could be identified with the principles of the understanding. Bringing together the Leibnizian passion for concision and the psychological orientation of John Locke, Hegel's system represents "a global change in the object of philosophy" that enables a transition from the order of ideas to the order of words, thus suggesting the limitations of the moderns while also providing an alternative to the rule of representation:

To the concept of such order he will add his own great original contribution, that of narrative development, so that the Concept, like everything "true" in his sense, is not something existing in a static state to be inspected but develops itself dynamically, as the systematizing of a company of words which themselves, as utterances in time, are radically dynamic.[18]

The phenomenological prelude to this conceptual revolution is therefore necessary as a narratological exposition of what is recognized in the logical domain as a concretization that gives depth and meaning to an originary doubleness, the abstract form that later acquires the significance of memory. This does not mean, however, that the absolute idea is forever restricted to events that have already unfolded in time but simply that the phenomenological movement only discovers itself, in both tragic and fulfilling modes, as a version of recognition.

The crucial role of recognition in Hegelian logic and phenomenology also enables us to distinguish a new approach to ethics from what is more appropriately identified with that of Baruch Spinoza, who relies on a concept of substance that remains Cartesian in inspiration. According to this Cartesian model, the finite thinking subject is grounded as accidental in the more essential mode of substance. Hegel in contrast challenges the logic of essence as basically inadequate to the task of providing us with a genuinely postmetaphysical perspective on substance, which ceases in his thought to function as a limiting ground: "That is, 'substance' in itself is in no sense 'substantial', but rather is essentially self-negating."[19] This nonsubstantial notion of substance informs Hegel's reflections on ethical life as an expression of *Sittlichkeit*, a sphere that articulates the logical basis for negotiating the rights of individuals as particular in a communal matrix. In such a situation, the individual might be said to be immersed in a substance, but one that would allow "immediate determination" to be reinterpreted and thus perpetually revised in light of the difference between individual and normative concerns.[20] However, we might also say that Hegel's conception of ethical life unfolds *as if* it were perpetually open to contamination as well as to the work of reason precisely because it cannot be sealed off from a movement that constantly undermines the idea of a starting point, whether pure or simply imperfect, that otherwise might have grounded the evolving ethical narrative. Indeed, Kristeva's reading of Sophocles's *Oedipus at Colonus* shows how life can be understood in its inherent vulnerability as capable of recognizing its own weaknesses, even when a measure of heroism has become crucial to the life journey itself.

This is why the point of entry into the system of signs is more important than any static whole that is presented as the prior "meaning" of an evolving subject matter. In the case of literature, the movement toward increasing wholeness is an engagement with an intertext that only acquires meaning once it is abandoned and then rediscovered as the early version of what is subsequently taken up as late. The process through which the intertext is given a new meaning may be unconscious but it cannot for that reason be presented in an explanatory mode. On the contrary, the intertext is dispersed whenever it is reached as the goal of the journey, signaling back to the event of transliteration as coinciding with the temporal crossing of the event itself. At this moment, the past not only becomes present, but the present finds its way into the past to become divided internally; the past becomes a source of antagonism with any present that is separated from its development in time. However, what is then called the intertext is not only a more complex version of what came earlier but also what makes the present impossible, showing us that the past is the *form* of the present that gives the text its deeper significance. The form of this present is what in aesthetic terms enables the past to be recovered as negotiable, not only as late but as related to normative concerns.

The importance of normativity to whatever can be said about literature implies the need for an elaboration of sensuous contents, particularly when literary texts draw on the work of the imagination in engaging the reader in worldly projects that go beyond literature. Already in Kant, the aesthetic tradition is shown to be related to normative goals that are difficult to separate from how they are managed in an aesthetic context. But if this is indeed the case, we need to better understand how semiotics and aesthetics might be linked, rather than opposed as conflicting disciplines. Our task will be complicated due to the role of writing in semiotics as theorized by Derrida and Kristeva but only after its role has been revised by Heidegger and Blanchot in their respective discussions of art and literature. If writing can be conceived through semiotics and aesthetics is distinguishable but is not opposed to the movement of semiotics beyond an endless configuration of signs, then the possibility of linking the two disciplines is not intractable.

Thus, in confronting the challenge of reconfiguring what is different, we once again turn to Hegel for assistance in helping us develop an understanding of aesthetics that extends the post-Kantian insight that matters of art are not to be confused with matters of pure cognition.

SPACES OF THE IMAGINARY

Literature after Proust is largely concerned with providing the space within which the imaginary can present itself as the possibility of semantic variation, even when the aesthetic terrain upon which this occurs cannot be brought into view. The word "writing" has been deployed, starting with the discussion of Blanchot, not as a purely aesthetic term but as one that suggests how the opening of a world is indeed a textual event to the degree that it both assembles various narrative strains that constitute a totality but also indicates how this totality is rifted by forces that prevent us from reducing *world* to a structural concept.[21] The dual function of textuality in this opening allows us to transform Heidegger's philosophical intervention in "The Origin of the Work of Art" into Blanchot's literary poetics of space, which would not exclude aesthetics on principle. It also has been suggested that the survival of the aesthetic in Blanchot's adoption of Orpheus as a myth of appearances could be read in terms of Hegel instead of Heidegger. Without lapsing into naïve realism, Jean-Luc Nancy has provided a meditation on Hegel that takes this duality into account and might be considered in terms of Kristeva's early remarks on Hegel's kinship with Freud.

Nancy's specific discussion of Hegel's aesthetic theory in *The Muses* (1994) takes as its starting point the simple fact that there are many arts rather than one, and then explores the question of how unity can be assigned a philosophical role in this plural context. Nancy argues that this question is intimately linked to the issue of how aesthetics can be related to dialectics, which would seem to be at odds with the pluralizing tendencies implicit in *poesis* and *techné*, tendencies that become evident when we observe how different arts perform different functions in their entanglement with the life-world. Nancy notes that while Hegel privileges poetry in a manner that recalls Kant and perhaps looks forward to Heidegger, he does not pair poetry with music in a manner that would be metaphysical in the Platonic sense, allowing poetry to be dissolved in a movement of absolute sonority. Instead, Hegel argues that poetry is the polar opposite of architecture: It reduces sound to meaningless signs in contrast to the practice of transforming material into symbolic meanings. As a consequence, "poetry destroys the fusion of spiritual inwardness with external existence to an extent that begins to be incompatible with the original conception of art, with the result that poetry runs the risk of losing itself in a transition from the region of sense into that of the spirit."[22]

However, while validating its kinship with the two "romantic arts" of painting and music, poetry also functions as an inside to an quasi-material outside, constituting a possible "world" that is also interrupted *as sense* when it ceases to be unified on one plane and acquires density as light and color.[23] Nancy suggests how painting can perform a unique role in this case, not the mediatory one of bridging the opposition between the idea and its material embodiment but in retaining sense as what precedes the world and effectively interrupts it. When painting goes beyond world, as suggested through reading Heidegger's evocation of Vincent Van Gogh's peasant shoes as writing, it becomes a threshold that lies "between the intactness and touching of light and shadow. It offers access: sense itself, which is not the access to nothing but the access that infinitely accedes, ever further toward and into the night/the day, into the trace that divides and joins them."[24] And yet, in Hegel's argument, Heidegger's use of the poetic has been reversed because it employs writing as a way of marking sense (as painting), rather than as an evocation of being or truth. Moreover, although Nancy's reflections on touch indeed go beyond Hegel in many respects, they might be compared to Kristeva's remarks on the semiotic as what interrupts symbolization, thus enabling new formations to emerge in contrast to the various regimes that constitute the world during a given moment.[25]

For Nancy, the passage from poetry to painting also gives another meaning to Hegel's famous "end-of-art" thesis that would need to be reinterpreted in order to be more deeply affirmed. Hence, rather than interpret the thesis in a historicist manner as a narrative of art's long decline into cultural insignificance from classical times to the present, this same thesis might be read as a sign that art is always ending and that its end is therefore endlessly repeated whenever aesthetic interpretation maintains that art is no longer capable of sustaining the unified world that is promised when the arts are assumed to be in perfect accord, which of course is only imaginable in aesthetic terms when Greek sculpture momentary fused spirit and substance in bodily presentation. In the words of Nancy: "The end of art was always yesterday."[26] Such an end, nonetheless, bespeaks the ascendancy of aesthetics as an awareness that a certain world has ended and that sense exceeds this world, thus preserving in Hegelian fashion a counterthrust to the transcendental position of Kant and his many successors.

According to this reading, Hegel would be the name of the thinker who brings this world to an end and also the name of the theorist who inaugurates a model in which the semiotic (poetry) and aesthetic (painting) belong together as disjunctive expressions of what has been presented as a recognitive logic, rather than as an identitarian one, in the more formal context of the speculative idea. But such a reading would not be the familiar "humanistic" interpretation that seeks to harmonize the conflicting claims of poetry and painting in terms of their underlying kinship, which would be grounded in a positive assessment of human nature. Its strength, on the contrary, would reside in its faithfulness to a system of logic that was intended to capture the fluidity of life, the moment when thought ceased to be isolated but came to acknowledge its relationship to what enabled a world, even though it had not yet constituted one. The tension between the constituting and the constituted would be what prevented the semiotic from being separated from the symbolic as would occur if poetry, for instance, were turned into a mere object of connoisseurship or academic expertise. Moreover, this tension would also guarantee a perpetual openness on the side of constituted structures, so that the space of the imaginary would always be able to reconfigure sedimented cultural history, indicating its provisional nature in a system that always had a different future.

Our inquiry has been concerned with a series of writers who suggest disparate attempts to chronicle the dislocation of worlds due to melancholy, dejection, loss, and spiritual depletion. And yet, those same texts also point beyond themselves, not always on the level of the statement or in a manner that is evident from their organic composition, but rather in a manner that shows how the quest for origins is already always a path of signifying that can be read teleologically, apart from the issue of what this quest might have meant initially to the narrator who embarked on it. During the age of Romanticism, the French Revolution is perceived as a break, just as poetry begins to depart from mimetic systems that have the capacity to conceal the violence of history. The aesthetic possibilities of Romanticism are largely realized in Proust's work, which helps demonstrate how Friedrich Schiller's revision of Kant becomes a creative response to the French calamity but also looks forward to Hegel's dialectic of repetition as mnemonic retrieval, which presupposes the negation of a preconstituted ego. Blanchot's post-Hegelian aesthetics channels these same impulses and looks forward to both modernism and to the writers who evoke different trajectories that decenter and at least partially reconstitute the symbolic in fictional guises that would be hard to give a single and definitive name in the canon of cultural criticism. We have rediscovered Hegel in this movement but only after the Freudian contribution was encountered as a kind of spur to dialectics. At the same time, to view dialectics in this way is to redefine it, not so much as a teleology but as an archē that is less of an origin than a movement that is no longer distinct from a telos that resides in experience, so that finally, the sense that this movement draws near would be even more inclusive than the upsurge of the world.

NOTES

1. Walter Benjamin. "The Work of Art in the Age of Mechanical Reproduction," in *Illuminations* (New York: Schocken Books, 1968), 223–24.
2. Eva Geulen, "Under Construction: Benjamin's 'The Work of Art in the Age of Mechanical Reproduction'," in *Benjamin's Ghosts: Interventions in Contemporary and Cultural Theory*, ed. Gerhard Richter (Stanford, CA: Stanford University Press, 2002), 136.
3. Ibid., 137–38.
4. Benjamin acknowledges that the aura has the aesthetic significance of enabling the viewer to link art to a perceptual background. He even evokes a partial "defense" of the aura in the Artwork essay, thus complicating a narrative that otherwise would move inexorably from the world of tradition to the age of photography and film. There is an apparent contradiction between the experience of someone who views "a mountain range on the horizon or a branch which casts its shadow over you," and the desire of the masses to bring the object-world closer and thus to prefer the reproduction to the work itself. Geulen, "Under Construction," 222–23. This (re)formulation of the aura threatens to foreclose the progressive possibilities that Benjamin wants to attribute to film as an inherently emancipatory mode of cultural expression, but it also preserves a sphere that enables a critique of collective desire, particularly when the latter risks being commodified.
5. Geulen, "Under Construction," 239.

6. Shierry Weber Nicholsen, *Exact Imagination, Late Work* (Cambridge, MA: MIT Press, 1997), 216–17.

7. Kristeva argues that the drive to mark oppositions remains linked to a bodily exchange between mother and child but is not given a secure place until paternity imposes a triangular scheme on this dual relationship: "Neither the demarcating imperative nor the dejection that corresponds to it are a force of stabilization. The looming of abjection indicates destabilization—social and subjective." See Beardsworth, *Julia Kristeva*, 231. Hence, fluidity renders abjection intrinsically resistant to paternal organization and prevents paternity from assimilating it to more stable structures.

8. Ibid., 229.

9. Ibid., 242.

10. Benjamin's essay, "The Work of Art in the Age of Mechanical Reproduction," was composed during the years when Martin Heidegger's treatise, "The Origin of the Work of Art," acquired its initial form. Parallels between them are still worth exploring. Both authors are suspicious of philosophical aesthetics, however massively they depend on it as the starting point for arguments against subjectivity that are conspicuous in their respective reflections on film and poetry. Moreover, the role of the work of art and art itself are defined largely in opposition to aesthetic appropriations and underscore how the continuity of tradition is rifted when the fate of art is either traced back to a Greek temple or assumed to be contained in a modern photograph.

11. Kristeva, *Revolution in Poetic Language*, 214–16.

12. Hans-Georg Gadamer, "On the Scope and Function of Hermeneutical Reflection" in *Philosophical Hermeneutics*, ed. and trans. David E. Linge (Berkeley: University of California Press, 1977), 26–38.

13. Gadamer, *Truth and Method*, 167–69.

14. Kristeva's interpretation of "the atomistic subject of practice in Marxism" seeks to derive the later history of Marxism from Hegel's ultimate subordination of practice to theory, which becomes theological when it acquires a speculative form. See Kristeva, *Revolution in Poetic Language*, 198–201. This is akin to the antihermeneutical reading that was argued by Louis Althusser during roughly the same period. The difference is that for Althusser, unlike Kristeva, this became an argument that Marxism should not retain any aspects of the Hegelian legacy.

15. Paul Redding, *Hegel's Hermeneutics* (Ithaca, NY: Cornell University, 1996), 141.

16. This reading of Hegel would be profoundly different from the one that has been dominant in recent years, particularly among Continental philosophers. Another way of putting this might be to say that Hegel's philosophy always remains in some sense bound to the empirical, not only in remaining open to the possibility that the empirical sciences themselves might introduce data that requires the periodic revision of basic philosophical assumptions but also that dialectical logic itself does not exclude contingency, thus producing "deconstructive" effects in the citadel of knowledge. Nonetheless, this same interpretation is already to be found in Mure, *A Study of Hegel's Logic*, 314–31.

17. Ibid., 164. See also G. W. F. Hegel, *Science of Logic*, trans. A. V. Miller. (London: George Allen and Unwin, 1969), 825.

18. John McCumber, *The Company of Words: Hegel, Language, and Systematic Philosophy* (Evanston, IL: Northwestern University Press, 1993), 111.

19. Redding, *Hegel's Hermeneutics*, 183.

20. Ibid., 184.

21. Derrida, "Force and Signification," 3–30.

22. Cf. Hegel, *Aesthetics*, II:968.

23. The contrast between these two possibilities might be expressed historically in terms of the difference between Stephané Mallarmé and Arthur Rimbaud because the former argued that poetry invariably aspires to the conditions of music, whereas the latter was not averse to renewing the old adage, *pictura et poesis*, even if this adage came to justify a radically qualitative poetics that broke with mimesis as classically conceived. It is perhaps ironic that Rimbaud, who is often identified more strongly with the avant-garde, in sustaining the rapport between

poetry and the visual arts evokes one of the principle themes of aesthetic humanism that has argued, at least since Lessing, for a "conversation" between the two arts.

24. Nancy, *The Sense of the World*, 82.

25. A significant movement occurs in Nancy's thought between *The Inoperative Community* and *The Sense of the World* insofar as the former work describes myth as what literature overturns, just as the symbolic order testifies to an underlying coherence, whereas in the latter work, myth acquires a more positive role and contrasts with the more regulatory and restrictive function of symbolic arrangements. Kristeva's thinking also might be said to move, in its later phases, toward a view of the imaginary that has a potentially "mythic" significance, as implied in Nancy's more recent work.

26. Jean-Luc Nancy, *The Muses*, trans. Peggy Kamuf (Stanford, CA: Stanford University Press, 1996), 30.

Bibliography

Adorno, Theodor. *Aesthetic Theory*. Translated by Hullot-Kentor. Minneapolis: University of Minnesota Press, 1997.
Agamben, Giorgio. *Homo Sacer: Sovereign Power and Bare Life*. Stanford, CA: Stanford University Press, 1998.
Alpers, Paul. *The Poetry of the 'Faerie Queene.'* Princeton, NJ: Princeton University Press, 1967.
Arendt, Hannah. *The Human Condition*. Chicago: University of Chicago Press, 1958.
———. *Lectures on Kant's Political Philosophy*. Chicago: University of Chicago Press, 1992.
———. *On Revolution*. New York: Viking Press, 1975.
Aristotle. *The Ethics of Aristotle*. Translated by J. A. K. Thomson. London: Penguin Books, 1971.
Avineri, Shlomo. *Hegel's Theory of the Modern State*. Cambridge, UK: Cambridge University Press, 1994.
Bakhtin, M. M. *The Dialogical Imagination: Four Essays*. Edited by Michael Holquist. Translated by Caryl Emerson. Austin: University of Texas, 1981.
———. *Rabelais and His World*. Translated by Hélène Iswolsky. Cambridge, MA: MIT Press, 1968.
Barthes, Roland. *Image Music Text*. Translated by Stephen Heath. New York: Farrar, Straus and Giroux, 1988.
———. *Writing Degree Zero*. Translated by Annette Lavers and Colin Smith. New York: Hill and Wang, 1968.
Bartsch, Renate. *Memory and Understanding: Concept Formation in Proust's 'À la recherche du temps perdu.'* Amsterdam, the Netherlands: John Benjamins Publishing Company, 2005.
Beardsworth, Sara. *Julia Kristeva: Psychoanalysis and Modernity*. Albany: State University of New York Press, 2004.
Benjamin, Walter. "The Image in Proust." In *Illuminations*, 201–15. New York: Schocken Books, 1968.
———. "The Work of Art in the Age of Mechanical Reproduction." In *Illuminations*, 217–51. New York: Schocken Books, 1968.
———. "Theses on the Philosophy of History." In *Illuminations*, 255–66. New York: Schocken Books, 1968.
———. "On the Mimetic Faculty." In *Reflections: Essays, Aphorisms, Autobiographical Writings*, translated by Edmund Jephcott, 333–36. New York: Harcourt, Brace Jovanovich, 1978.

Berger, Harry. "A Secret Discipline: *The Faerie Queene*, Book VI." In *Form and Convention in the Poetry of Edmund Spenser*, edited by William Nelson, 35–75. New York: Columbia University Press, 1961.

Bhabha, Homi. "Signs Taken for Wonders: Questions of Ambivalence and Authority under a Tree outside Delhi, 1817." In *The Location of Culture*, 145–74. London: Routledge, 1994.

———. "The Postcolonial and the Postmodern: The Question of Agency." In: *The Location of Culture*, 245–82. London: Routledge, 1994.

Blanchot, Maurice, *The Book to Come*. Translated by Charlotte Mandell. Stanford, CA: Stanford University Press, 2003.

———. *The Infinite Conversation*. Translated by Susan Hanson. Minneapolis: University of Minnesota Press, 1993.

———. *The Space of Literature*. Translated by Ann Smock. Lincoln: University of Nebraska Press, 1982.

———. *The Work of Fire*. Translated by Charlotte Mandell. Stanford, CA: Stanford University Press, 1995.

Bloom, Harold. *The Anxiety of Influence: A Theory of Poetry*. Oxford: Oxford University Press, 1997.

———. *Shelley's Mythmaking*. Ithaca, NY: Cornell University Press, 1959.

Bradley, A. C. "Notes on Shelley's 'Triumph of Life'." *Modern Language Review* 9 (1914): 441–56.

Braithwaite, Edward Kaman. *Contradictory Omens: Cultural Diversity and Interrogation in the Caribbean* (Monograph 1). Mona, Jamaica: Savacou Publications, 1974.

Brontë, Charlotte. *Jane Eyre*. London: HarperCollins Publishers, 2011.

Brown, Stephen Gilbert. *The Gardens of Desire: Marcel Proust and the Fugitive Sublime*. Albany: State University of New York Press, 2004.

Buck-Morss, Susan. *Hegel, Haiti and Universal History*. Pittsburgh: University of Pittsburgh Press, 2009.

Butler, Judith. *Gender Trouble: Feminism and the Subversion of Identity*. New York: Routledge, 1990.

———. *Bodies that Matter: On the Discursive Limits of Sex*. New York: Routledge, 1993.

———. *The Psychic Life of Power: Theories of Subjection*. Stanford, CA: Stanford University Press, 1997.

Castiglione, Baldesar. *The Book of the Courtier*. New York: Anchor Books, 1959.

Cheney, Donald. *Spenser's Image of Nature: Wild Man and Shepherd in* The Faerie Queene. New Haven, CT: Yale University Press, 1966.

Clark, Timothy. *Derrida, Heidegger, Blanchot: Sources of Derrida's Notion and Practice of Literature*. London: Cambridge University Press, 1992.

———. *Embodying Revolution: The Figure of the Poet in Shelley*. Oxford: Clarendon Press, 1989.

Cohn, Robert. *The Poetry of Rimbaud*. Princeton, NJ: Princeton University Press, 1973.

Comay, Rebecca. *Mourning Sickness: Hegel and the French Revolution*. Stanford, CA: Stanford University Press, 2011.

Corneille, Pierre. *Oedipe* in *Oeuvres Complètes*, 3. Paris: Gallimard, 1987.

Dante. *Purgatorio*, xxvii–xxix. In *The Divine Comedy*, translated by Allen Mandelbaum, 512–21. New York: Alfred A. Knopf, 1995.

Dawson, P. M. S. *The Unacknowledged Legislator: Shelley and Politics*. Oxford: Clarendon Press, 1980.

Deleuze, Gilles. *Proust and Signs*. Translated by Richard Howard. New York: George Braziller, 1972.

de Man, Paul. "Image and Emblem in Yeats." In *The Rhetoric of Romanticism*, 145–238. New York: Columbia University Press, 1984.

———. "Reading (Proust)." In *Allegories of Reading: Figural Language in Rousseau, Nietzsche, Rilke, and Proust*, 57–78. New Haven, CT: Yale University Press, 1979.

———. *Resistance to Theory*. Minneapolis: University of Minnesota Press, 1987.

———. "Shelley Disfigured." In *The Rhetoric of Romanticism*, 93–123. New York: Columbia University Press, 1984.

———. "Wordsworth and Hölderlin." In *The Rhetoric of Romanticism*, 47–65. New York: Columbia University Press, 1984.
Derrida, Jacques. "Living On: Border Lines." In *Deconstruction and Criticism*, translated by James Hulbert, edited by Harold Bloom, 75–176. New York: Continuum, 1999.
———. "Plato's Pharmacy." In *Dissemination*, translated by Barbara Johnson, 61–171. Chicago: University of Chicago Press, 1981.
———. "Différance." In *Margins of Philosophy*, translated by Alan Bass, 1–27. Chicago: University of Chicago Press, 1982.
"Signature Event Context" in *Margins of Philosophy*, translated by Alan Bass, 307–30. Chicago: University of Chicago Press, 1982.
———. *Of Grammatology*. Translated by Gayatri Chakravorty Spivak. Baltimore, MD: Johns Hopkins University Press, 1976.
———. "Force and Signification." In *Writing and Difference*, translated by Alan Bass, 3–30. Chicago: University of Chicago Press, 1978.
———. "Freud and the Scene of Writing." In *Writing and Difference*, translated by Alan Bass, 196–231. Chicago: University of Chicago Press, 1978.
———. *Positions*. Translated by Alan Bass. Chicago: University of Chicago, 1981.
———. "At This Very Moment in This Work Here I Am." In *Re-Reading Lévinas*, edited by Robert Bernasconi and Simon Critchley, 11–48. London: Athlone, 1991.
Duffy, Edward. *Rousseau in England: The Context for Shelley's Critique of the Enlightenment*. Berkeley: University of California Press, 1979.
Ficino, Marsilio. *Marsilio Ficino's Commentary on Plato's Symposium*. Translated by Sears Reynolds Jayne. Columbia: University of Missouri Press, 1944.
Flaubert, Gustave. *L'Éducation sentimentale*. Paris: Gallimard, 1965.
———. *Madame Bovary*. Paris: Flammarion, 1986.
Foucault, Michel. *The Archaeology of Knowledge and The Discourse on Knowledge*. Edited by A. M. Sheridan Smith. New York: Pantheon Books, 1971.
———. *The Order of Things: An Archaeology of the Human Sciences*. New York: Routledge, 1989.
Fowler, Alistair. *Spenser and the Numbers of Time*. London: Routledge and Kegan Paul, 1964.
Freud, Sigmund. *Beyond the Pleasure Principle. The Standard Edition of the Complete Works of Sigmund Freud*, vol 18 of 24. Translated by James Strachey. London: Hogarth Press, 1925.
———. "Negation." In *The Standard Edition of the Complete Works of Sigmund Freud*, vol. 19 of 24. Translated by James Strachey. London: Hogarth Press, 1925.
Fry, Paul H. *Wordsworth and the Poetry of What We Are*. New Haven, CT: Yale University Press, 2008.
Frye, Northrop. *Fearful Symmetry: A Study of William Blake*. Princeton, NJ: Princeton University Press, 1947.
Gadamer, Hans-Georg. *Hegel's Dialectic: Five Hermeneutical Studies*. Translated by P. Christopher Smith. New Haven, CT: Yale University Press, 1976.
———. *The Idea of the Good in Platonic-Aristotelian Philosophy*. Translated by P. Christopher Smith. New Haven, CT: Yale University Press, 1986.
———. "On the Scope and Function of Hermeneutical Reflection." In *Philosophical Hermeneutics*, edited and translated by David E. Linge, 18–43. Berkeley: University of California Press, 1977.
———. *Truth and Method*. Translated by Joel Weinsheimer and Donald G. Marshall. New York: Crossroads Publishing, 1991.
Galperin, William H. *Revision and Authority in Wordsworth: The Interpretation of a Career*. Philadelphia: University of Pennsylvania Press, 1989.
Gardiner, Judith Kegan. "Good Morning, Midnight, Good Night Modernism." *Boundary 2* II.2 (1982): 233–52.
Genette, Gérard. *Figures of Literary Discourse*. Translated by Alan Sheridan. New York: Columbia University Press, 1982.
———. "Metonymie chez Proust." In *Figures* III, 42–63. Paris: Editions du Seuil, 1972.

Geulen, Eva. "Under Construction: Benjamin's 'The Work of Art in the Age of Mechanical Reproduction'." In *Benjamin's Ghosts: Interventions in Contemporary and Cultural Theory*, edited by Gerhard Richter, 121–41. Stanford, CA: Stanford University Press, 2002.
Gregerson, Linda. *The Reformation of the Subject: Spenser, Milton and the English Protestant Epic*. Cambridge, UK: Cambridge University Press, 1995.
Gregg, Veronique Marie. *Jean Rhys's Historical Imagination: Reading and Writing the Creole*. Chapel Hill: University of North Carolina Press, 1995.
Hackett, C. A. *Rimbaud: A Critical Examination*. New York: Cambridge University Press, 1981.
Hamilton, A. C. *The Structure of Allegory in* The Faerie Queene. Oxford: Clarendon Press, 1970.
Harris, H. S. "The Concept of Recognition in Hegel's Jena Manuscripts." In *Hegel-Studien Beiheft*, number 20, 229–248. Bonn, Germany: Bouvier Verlag, 1979.
Harrison, Nancy R. *Jean Rhys and the Novel as Woman's Text*. Chapel Hill: University of North Carolina Press, 1988.
Hartmann, Geoffrey. *Wordsworth's Poetry 1789 – 1814*. New Haven, CT: Yale University Press, 1964.
Hegel, G. W. F. *Aesthetics: Lectures on Fine Art*, 2 vols. Translated by J. M. Knox. Oxford: Clarendon Press, 1975.
———. *Phänomenologie des Geistes*. Frankfurt am Main: Suhrkamp Verlag, 1976.
———. *The Phenomenology of Spirit*. Translated by A. V. Miller. Oxford: Oxford University Press, 1977.
———. *The Philosophy of Right*. Translated by T. M. Knox. Oxford: Clarendon Press, 1965.
———. *Science of Logic*. Translated by A. V. Miller. London: George Allen and Unwin, 1969.
Heidegger, Martin. *Being and Time*. Translated by Joan Stambaugh. Albany: State University of New York Press, 1996.
———. *Hegel's Phenomenology of Spirit*. Translated by Parvis Emad and Kenneth Maly. Bloomington: Indiana University Press, 1988.
———. "*Der Ursprung des Kunstwerkes*." In *Holzwege, Gesamtausgabe*, 1–74. Frankfurt am Main: Vittorio Klostermann, 1977.
———. "The Origin of the Work of Art." In *Poetry, Language, Thought*, translated by Albert Hofstadter, 18–86. New York: HarperCollins, 2001.
Henry, Anne. *Marcel Proust: Theories pour une esthétique*. Paris: Klincksieck, 1981.
Hermann, Friedrich-Wilhelm von. *Hermeneutics and Reflection: Heidegger and Husserl on the Concept of Phenomenology*. Translated by Kenneth Maly. Toronto: University of Toronto Press, 2013.
Hough, Graham. *A Preface to* The Faerie Queene. New York: Norton Library, 1963.
Husserl, Edmund. *Cartesian Meditations: An Introduction to Phenomenology*. Translated by Dorion Cairns. Dordrecht, the Netherlands: Kluwer Academic Publisher, 1999.
———. *The Crisis of the European Sciences and Transcendental Phenomenology : An Introduction to Phenomenological Philosophy*. Translated by David Carr. Evanston, IL: Northwestern University Press, 1999.
———. *Logical Investigations*, Books I/II. Translated by J. N. Findlay. London: Routledge and Kegan Paul, 1970.
Iser, Wolfgang. *The Act of Reading: A Theory of Aesthetic Response*. Baltimore, MD: Johns Hopkins University Press, 1980.
Ishiguro, Kazuo. *An Artist of the Floating World*. New York: Vintage International, 1989.
———. *The Remains of the Day*. New York: Vintage International, 1993.
Iyer, Lars. *Blanchot's Vigilance: Literature, Phenomenology and the Ethical*. New York: Palgrave Macmillan, 2005.
Jacobson, Roman. "Two Aspects of Language and Two Types of Aphasic Disturbances." In *On Language*, edited by Linda R. Waugh and Monique Monville-Burston, 115–33. Cambridge, MA: Harvard University Press, 1990.
Jacobus, Mary. *Romanticism, Writing and Sexual Difference: Essays on* The Prelude. New York: Oxford University Press, 1989.

Kafka, Franz. *The Diaries 1910–1923*. Translated by Joseph Kresh and Martin Greenberg. Edited by Max Bod. New York: Schocken Books, 1990.
Kant, Immanuel. *Critique of Judgment*. Translated by J. H. Bernard. Amherst, NY: Prometheus Books, 2000.
———. *The Conflict of Faculties*. New York: Abaris Books, 1992.
Kristeva, Julia. *Black Sun: Depression and Melancholia*. Translated by Leon S. Roudiez. New York: Columbia University Press, 1987.
———. *Hannah Arendt: Life Is a Narrative*. Translated by Frank Collins. Toronto: University of Toronto Press, 2001.
———. "Freud and Love: Treatment and Its Discontents." In *The Kristeva Reader*, edited by Moril Moi, 238–71. New York: Columbia University Press, 1986.
———. *Tales of Love*. Translated by Leon S. Roudiez. New York: Columbia University Press, 1987.
———. *Powers of Horror: An Essay on Abjection*. Translated by Leon S. Roudiez. New York: Columbia University Press, 1982.
———. *Revolution in Poetic Language*. Translated by Margaret Waller. New York: Columbia University Press, 1984.
———. *Strangers to Ourselves*. Translated by Leon S. Roudiez. New York: Columbia University Press, 1991.
———. *Time and Sense: Proust and the Experience of Literature*. Translated by Ross Guberman. New York: Columbia University Press, 1996.
Lacan, Jacques. *Écrits*. Translated by Bruce Fink. New York: W. W. Norton and Company, 2006.
———. *Four Fundamental Concepts of Psychoanalysis*. Translated by Alan Sheridan. Edited by Jacques-Alain Miller. New York: W. W. Norton and Company, 1981.
Landy, Joshua. *Philosophy as Fiction: Self, Deception and Knowledge in Proust*. Oxford: Oxford University Press, 2004.
Lewis, C. S. *The Allegory of Love*. Oxford: Oxford University Press, 1932.
Lindenberger, Herbert. *On Wordsworth's Prelude*. Princeton, NJ: Princeton University Press, 1963.
Luckhurst, Nicola. *Science and Structure in Proust's 'À la recherche du temps perdu.'* Oxford: Clarendon Press, 2000.
Lyotard, Jean-François. *The Postmodern Condition: A Report on Knowledge*. Translated by Geoffrey Bennington and Bian Massaumi. Minneapolis: University of Minnesota Press, 1984.
Mallarmé, Stéphane. *Oeuvres complètes*. Edited by Bertrand Marchal. Paris: Gallimard, 1998.
Man, Paul de. "Wordsworth and Hölderlin." In *The Rhetoric of Romanticism*, 47–65. New York: Columbia University Press, 1984.
———. "Image and Emblem in Yeats." In *The Rhetoric of Romanticism*, 145–238. New York: Columbia University Press, 1984.
Marx, Karl. *Capital, Volume 1*. Translated by Ernest Mandel. New York: Penguin Books, 1990.
———. *The Civil War in France*. New York: International Publishers, 1940.
McCumber, John. *The Company of Words: Hegel, Language, and Systematic Philosophy*. Evanston, IL: Northwestern University Press, 1993.
———. *Understanding Hegel's Mature Critique of Kant*. Stanford, CA: Stanford University Press, 2013.
Merleau-Ponty, Maurice. *The Visible and the Invisible*. Translated by Alphonso Lingis. Edited by Claude Lefort. Evanston, IL: Northwestern University Press, 1968.
Miller, J. Hillis. *Fiction and Repetition: Seven English Novels*. Cambridge, MA: Harvard University Press. 1982.
Minoque, Valerie. *Nathalie Sarraute and the War of the Words*. Edinburgh, UK: Edinburgh University Press, 1981.
Mitchell, W. J. T. *Iconology: Inage, Text, Ideology*. Chicago: University of Chicago, 1987.
Montaigne, Michel de. "On Cannibals." In *Essays*. Translated by J. M. Cohen. New York: Penguin Books, 1976.

Mure, G. R. G. *A Study of Hegel's Logic*. Oxford: Clarendon Press, 1959.
Nancy, Jean-Luc. "Being Singular Plural." In *Being Singular Plural*, translated by Robert D. Richardson and Anne E. O'Byrne, 1–99. Stanford: Stanford University Press, 2000.
———. *The Experience of Freedom*. Translated by Bridget McDonald. Stanford, CA: Stanford University Press, 1993.
———. *The Inoperative Community*. Edited by Peter Connor. Minneapolis: University of Minnesota Press, 1991.
———. *The Muses*. Translated by Peggy Kamuf. Stanford, CA: Stanford University Press, 1996.
———. *The Sense of the World*. Translated by Jeffrey S. Librett. Minneapolis: University of Minnesota Press, 1997.
Nicholsen, Shierry Weber. *Exact Imagination, Late Work*. Cambridge, MA: MIT Press, 1997.
Nietzsche, Friedrich. *The Birth of Tragedy and the Case of Wagner*. Translated by Walter Kaufmann. New York: Vintage Books, 1967.
Pippin, Robert. *The Persistence of Subjectivity: On the Kantian Aftermath*. Cambridge, UK: Cambridge University Press, 2005.
Proust, Marcel. *À la recherche du temps perdu*, 7 vols. Paris: Éditions Gallimard, 1992.
Rancière, Jacques. "Aesthetics as Politics." In *Aesthetics and its Discontents*. Cambridge, UK: Polity Press, 2009.
———. *The Aesthetic Unconscious*. Translated by Debra Keats and James Swenson. Cambridge, UK: Polity Press, 2010.
———. *Dissensus: On Politics and Aesthetics*. Translated by Steven Corcoran. New York: Continuum, 2012.
———. *The Emancipated Spectator*. Translated by Gregory Elliot. New York: Verso, 2009.
———. *The Future of the Image*. Translated by Gregory Elliot. New York: Verso, 2009.
——— *Mute Speech*. Translated by James Swenson. New York: Columbia University Press, 1998.
Redding, Paul. *Hegel's Hermeneutics*. Ithaca, NY: Cornell University Press, 1996.
Rhys, Jean. *Good Morning, Midnight*. New York: W. W. Norton, 1982.
———. *Smile Pease: An Unfinished Autobiography*. New York: Harper and Row, 1979.
———. *Voyage in the Dark*. New York: Harper and Row, 1982.
———. *Wide Sargasso Sea*. New York: W. W. Norton, 1982.
Ricoeur, Paul. *Freud and Philosophy: An Essay on Interpretation*. Translated by Denis Savage. Delhi, India: Motilal Banardidass Publishers, 2008.
———. "The Question of the Subject: The Challenge of Semiology." In *The Conflict in Interpretations: Essays in Hermeneutics*, edited by Don Idhe, 236–66. London: Athlone Press, 2000.
———. *Interpretation Theory: Discourse and the Surplus of Meaning*. Fort Worth, TX: Texas Christian University Press, 1976.
———. *Time and Narrative*, 3 vols. Translated by Kathleen McLaughlin and David Pellaver. Chicago: University of Chicago Press, 1985.
Rilke, Rainer Maria. *Duino Elegies*. Translated by J. B. Leishman and Stephen Spender. New York: W. W. Norton and Company, 1963.
———. *The Notebooks of Malte Laurids Brigge*. Translated by Stephen Mitchell. New York: Vintage International, 1990.
Rimbaud. Arthur. *Illuminations. Collected Poems*. Translated by Martin Sorrell. Oxford: Oxford University Press, 2001.
Ross, Kristin. *The Emergence of Social Space: Rimbaud and the Paris Commune*. Basingstoke, Hampshire: Macmillan Press, 1988.
Rousseau, Jean-Jacques. *Les Confessions de J.-J. Rousseau*. Edited by George Sand. Paris: Charpentier, 1811.
Rousseau, Jean-Jacques. *The Confessions*. New York: Penguin Books, 1953.
Sarraute, Nathalie. *Tropismes*. Paris: Éditions de Minuit, 1957.
Schelling, F. W. J. *System of Transcendental Idealism*. Translated by Peter Heath. Charlottesville: University of Virginia, 1978.

Schiller, Friedrich. *On the Aesthetic Education of Man*. Translated by Elizabeth M. Wilkinson and L. A. Willoughby. Oxford: Clarendon Press, 1982.
Schürmann, Reiner. "Heidegger's 'Being and Time'." In *On Heidegger's "Being and Time,"* edited by Steven Levine, 56–131. London: Routledge, 2008.
Shelley, Percy Bysshe. "On Life." In *Percy Bysshe Shelley: The Major Works*, edited by Zachary Leader and Michael O'Neill, 633–36. Oxford: Oxford University Press, 2003.
———. *The Triumph of Life*. In *Percy Bysshe Shelley: The Major Works*, edited by Zachary Leader and Michael O'Neill, 604–21. Oxford: Oxford University Press, 2003.
Shen, Fu. *Six Records of a Floating Life*. Translated by Leonard Pratt and Chiang Su-hui. New York: Penguin Books, 1983.
Sidney, Sir Philip. *The Defense of Poesy*. *Sir Philip Sidney: Selected Poetry and Prose*. Edited by Robert Kimbrough. Madison: University of Wisconsin Press, 1983.
Spenser, Edmund. *Spenser: Poetical Works*. Edited by J. C. Smith and E. de Selincourt. London: University of Oxford Press, 1969.
———. *A View of the State of Ireland as it Was in the Reign of Queen Elizabeth*. Dublin: Printed for Lawrence Flin and Ann Watts, 1763.
Spivak, Gayatri Chakravorty. *A Critique of Postcolonial Reason: Toward a History of the Vanishing Present*. Cambridge, MA: Harvard University Press, 1999.
———. "Three Women's Texts and a Critique of Imperialism." *Critical Inquiry* 12, no. 1 (1985): 243–61.
Starobinski, Jean. *Jean-Jacques Rousseau: Transparency and Obstruction*. Translated by Arthur Goldhammer. Chicago: University of Chicago Press, 1988.
Tetreault, Ronald. "Shelley: Style and Substance." In *The New Shelley: Later Twentieth-Century Views*, edited by G. Kim Blank, 15–33. New York: St. Martin's Press, 1991.
Thody, Philip. *Marcel Proust*. London: Palgrave Macmillan, 1987.
Tonkin, Humphrey. *Spenser's Courteous Pastoral: Book Six of The Faerie Queene*. Oxford: Clarendon Press, 1972.
Ulmann, Stephen. *Style in the French Novel*. Cambridge, UK: Cambridge University, 1957.
Voltaire. *Oedipe, tragédie*. Paris: Hachette Livre: Paris, 2018.
Warren, Mark. *Nietzsche and Political Thought*. Cambridge, MA: MIT Press, 1991.
Watanabe, Jiro. "Categorial Intuition and the Understanding of Being in Husserl and Heidegger." In *Reading Heidegger: Commemorations*, edited by John Sallis, 109–117. Bloomington: Indiana University Press, 1993.
Weber, Samuel. *Return to Freud: Jacques Lacan's Dislocations of Psychoanalysis*. Translated by Michael Levine. New York: Cambridge University Press, 1991.
Whitehead, A. N. *Science and the Modern World*. New York: Free Press, 1967.
Williams, Arnold. *Flower on a Lowly Stock: The Sixth Book of The Faerie Queene*. Ann Arbor: University of Michigan Press, 1967.
Williams, Robert. *Recognition: Fichte and Hegel on the Other*. Albany: State of University of New York Press, 1992.
Wind, Edgar. *Pagan Mysteries in the Renaissance*. New York: Norton Library, 1968.
Wordsworth, William. *The Prelude, or Growth of a Poet's Mind*. Edited by Ernest de Selincourt. Oxford: Oxford University Press, 1970.

Index

Agamben, Giorgio, 113, 124, 131n29
Adorno, Theodor, 4, 16n12, 72n40
Althusser, Louis, 169n14
Arendt, Hannah, 17n31, 72n40, 113
Ariosto, Ludovico, 28, 33n31
Aristotle, xvi, 16n12, 20, 21–22, 32n5, 95n3, 114n2
Auerbach, Erich, xiv
Augustine, 29–30

Barthes, Roland, 99, 102, 107, 115n9
Bergson, Henri, 103
Baudelaire, Charles, xvii, 78, 81
Baumgarten, Alexander G., 29
Benjamin, Walter: and aesthetics, xviii, 94; and the dialectical image, 44, 54n10; and Heidegger, 100, 169n10; "The Image of Proust" ("Zum Bilde Prousts"), 91; and memory, 78; "On the Mimetic Faculty" ("Über das Mimetische Vermögen"), 90–91; and the origins of language, 16n12; and reproducibility, 150–153, 155, 157, 168n4; and semiotics, 90–92, 97n46, 154; and trauma theory, xix, 53n7, 78, 91, 149, 153, 154; "The Work of Art in the Age of Mechanical Reproduction" ("Das Kunsterk im Zeitalter seiner technischen Reproduzierbarkeit"), 100, 150–153, 169n10
Bhahba, Homi, 123, 125–127, 131n35

Blanchot, Maurice: and aesthetics, 103–104, 157–158; and criticism, xviii; and Derrida, 111; and Gadamer, xviii, 107–110, 113, 116n35, 158, 161; and Hegel, xviii, 99, 102, 109–110, 111–112, 113–114, 166, 168; and Heidegger, xviii, 99–102, 103, 104, 110–111, 112, 155–167, 157–158; and history, 109–110, 158; and Kafka, xviii, 105, 158; and Lévinas, 102, 115n7; and Mallarmé, 105, 108, 110, 158; and Merleau-Ponty, 103, 110, 158; a new beginning, 113; and reversal, 18n40, 99, 101–102, 104, 115n7; and Rilke, 105–106, 158; *The Space of Literature* (*L'Espace littéraire*), xviii, 99–100, 102–111, 113, 115n7, 157–158; and writing, xviii, 99, 110–113, 165–166
Bloom, Harold: and Blake, 58–59; and Bradley, 58, 59, 60, 71n13; and Dante, 58–59, 60; and de Man, 61–62; and mythmaking, 58; and non-aesthetic reading, 63–64; and repetition, 53n4; and "The Triumph of Life", 57–61; and Wordsworth, 60, 61–62. *See also* Shelley
Boethius, 25
Boiardo, Richard, 28
Botticelli, Sandro, 27, 33n19
Braithwaite, Edward, 121
Brönte, Charlotte, 122, 123, 124, 125, 126

Burke, Edmund, 86
Butler, Judith, 154–155
Byron, George Gordon, Lord, 123

Castiglione, Baldassare, 21
Cervantes, Miquel de, 44–45
Chaucer, Geoffrey, 39
Clark, Timothy, 60, 64, 110
Coleridge, Samuel Taylor, 47, 51, 54n12, 54n15
Collins, William, 52n2
Comay, Rebecca, 72n41, 97n45, 97n46
Corneille, Pierre, 75

Dante, 47, 58–59, 60, 64–65, 69–70, 156
Deleuze, Gilles, 96n18
de Man, Paul: and ideology, 135, 147n4; linguistic reading, xviii; and Proust, 81–86, 96n25, 97n37, 157; and Romantic tradition, 71n16; and "The Triumph of Life", xvii, 57, 61–63; and Wordsworth, 47, 54n15, 54n17. *See also* Shelley and Proust
de Quinsey, Thomas, 123
de Saussure, Ferdinand, 17n32, 82, 107
Derrida, Jacques: and community, 113; "Différance", 111; and Freud, 97n46, 97n47; and linguistics, 107; and the logos, 112–113; and the metaphysics of presence, 159; and the *pharmakon*, 132n42; and translation, 71n25; and writing, 111–113, 165–166. *See also* Blanchot
Descartes, René, 54n12, 100, 114n4
Dilthey, Wilhelm, 41–42, 53n6

Eliot, T. S., 119

Fichte, Johan Gottlieb, 55n18
Flaubert, Gustave, xvii, 79
Foucault, Michel, 31, 32n2, 33n31, 107
Frege, Gottlob, xv, 3
Freud, Sigmund: and aesthetics, 8–10, 73–74, 75–77; *Beyond the Pleasure Principle* (*Jenseits des Lustprinzip*), 53n7, 97n53; and causality, 76; and Hegel, xvi, xix–xx, 1–2, 7, 9–10, 16n12, 55n20, 90, 153, 168; and identification, 50–51; and Kristeva, xix, 1–2, 5, 7–8, 10, 160; and linguistics, 3, 9–10, 160; "Negation", 2, 16n3; and negativity, 2–3, 10, 16n3, 16n7, 153–154; and repetition, 53n7, 90, 97n46, 97n53; and trauma theory, xvii, xviii, xix, 8, 42–43, 68, 70, 71n25, 72n41, 91, 92, 122, 149, 150–153, 153, 154, 160; and the unconscious, 4, 160. *See also* Benjamin, Kristeva and Lacan
Frye, Northrup, 58

Gadamer, Hans-Georg: and aesthetics, 97n41; and classical hermeneutics, xviii, 107–110, 116n35; and experience, 53n6; and "fusion of horizons", 115n28; and language, 114n1, 130n1; and life, 55n19; and the origin of hermeneutics, 161–162; *Truth and Method* (*Wahrheit und Methode*), 53n6, 55n19, 97n41, 107–110, 114n1, 115n28, 116n35, 133–135, 147n2; and "world literature", 133–135, 140, 147n2
Genette, Gerald, 81, 82, 83, 97n48, 157
Giotto, 82, 84–85, 97n37
Gray, Thomas, 52n2
Gregg, Veronique, 121–122

Habermas, Jürgen, 151, 161
Harrison, Nancy, 126
Hartman, Geoffrey, 47, 54n13
Hegel, G. W. F.: and the absolute idea, 13, 51, 89–90, 151, 162–163; *Aesthetics* (*Vorlesungen über die Äesthetic*), 18n42, 95n3, 115n10; and aesthetics, xii–xv, xvi, xviii–xx, 14–15, 48, 54n15, 57, 73, 88–89, 91, 105, 110, 115n10, 147, 148n34, 149, 152, 157, 158–159, 165–168; and Benjamin, 151–153; canonical readings, xv–xvi, 7, 88, 94; and community, 113–114; contractual view of marriage, 129, 132n45; and critique of pure present, 111, 127, 152; and dialectics, xvi, 9–10, 11, 13–15, 82, 112, 168; and disinvestment, 14, 94, 158; and "end-of-art" thesis, xiii, 15, 18n42, 152, 167; and ethics, xix, 15, 132n45, 144–147, 159, 164; and the figural, xiv–xv, 13, 14–15, 51, 55n20, 89, 114, 117, 160; and forms of the ego,

Index

xv–xvi, 13–14, 18n40, 49–50, 51, 162–163; and hermeneutics, 161–164, 169n16; and history, xiv, 4, 16n12, 48, 99, 109–110, 146; immanence of the logos, 74–75; and life, 38–50, 55n19; and Kant, xi–xiii, xiii–xiv, xv, xvi, xix, 7, 52, 53n5, 54n15, 66, 89, 102, 131n34, 132n45, 144–147, 151, 159, 167, 168; and Lacan, xv, xix, 3, 5–6, 16n10; language and logic, 51–52, 131n41, 163–164; and metaphor, 96n12; and narrative, 94–95, 95n3; and negativity, 1–2, 18n44, 68, 112, 153–154, 164; lordship and bondage, 132n46; non-classical reading, xii–xiii, xvi–xvii, xviii, xix–xx, 157; and phenomenology, 15, 22; *Phenomenology of Spirit* (*Phänomenologie des Geistes*), 18n40, 88–90, 97n45, 132n46, 162; and "philosophy of reflection", 54n17; *Philosophy of Right* (*Grundlinien der Philosophie des Rechts*), 132n45, 148n34; and Platonic tradition, 19, 22, 33n19; and Marx, xv, xix, 82, 148n32, 158–159, 160, 162, 169n14; and Merleau-Ponty, 98n64; postwar readings, 99; and recognition, 163–164, 167; and Schiller, xii–xiii, 66, 168; *Science of Logic* (*Wissenschaft der Logik*), 162–164; and semiotics, xiv–xv, xix–xx, 1, 5–6, 13–15, 154, 162; state and politics, 140, 148n32, 159; and "totalizing" thought, 159; and tragedy, 7–8, 74–75. *See also* Heidegger, Kristeva and Nancy

Heidegger, Martin: and aesthetics, 102, 158, 166, 169n10; art and world, xviii, 100–102, 103, 104, 110–111, 157–158, 166–167; *Being and Time* (*Sein und Zeit*), 100, 102, 114n2–114n4; and Hegel, 14, 18n40, 166–167; *Hegel's Phenomenology of Spirit*, 18n40; and hermeneutics, 107; and Nietzsche, 16n14; "The Origin of the Work of Art" ("Der Ursprung des Kunstwerkes"), xviii, 100–102, 147n2, 166–167, 169n10; and phenomenology, 22, 100, 114n1–114n4; and repetition, 53n4; and reversal, 99, 102, 104, 166–167; and writing, 101, 110, 165–166, 166–167. *See also* Blanchot

Husserl, Edmund: and "anonymous" subjectivity, 102, 114n6; and categorial intuition, 114n1; and life, 55n19; and Spenser's narrative, 22, 26–27

Hölderlin, Fredrich, 75

Ingarden, Roman, 107
Ishiguro, Kazuo: art and ideology, 135–140, 148n15; *An Artist of the Floating World*, 19, 153, 156-60; and aesthetics, 133, 135, 139–140, 146–147, 148n34, 159; ethics and politics, 133, 139–140, 140–141, 148n22, 149, 159; and the Hegelian legacy, xix, 140, 148n32, 159; and hermeneutics, 133–135, 140, 147n2; *Remains of the Day*, xix, 133, 140–147; and semiotics, 135, 137; and Shen Fu, 136, 137

Jacobi, Friedrich Heinrich, 55n18
Jacobson, Roman, 81
Jauss, Hans Robert, 107
Joyce, James, 119, 130n10

Kafka, Franz, 105, 158
Kant, Immanuel: and aesthetics, xi–xv, xvi–xvii, xix, 29, 33n27, 37, 48, 53n3, 53n5, 54n17, 55n24, 59, 66, 68, 76–77, 86–89, 97n41, 131n34, 165, 166, 167; *Critique of Judgment* (*Kritik des Urteilskraft*), xi xii, 33n27, 37, 41, 53n3, 53n5, 55n24, 67–68, 72n40, 86, 144, 146; and ethics, 44, 68, 132n45, 140, 141, 144–147, 148n32, 159; and the French Revolution, 67–68, 72n40–72n41, 168; and idealism, 2, 7, 15, 17n15, 38, 71, 95n4, 98n54, 167; *Philosophy of Law*, 132n45; and Romanticism, 66; and Schiller, xii–xiii, 86–88; and Vaihinger, 89. *See also* Hegel

Kierkegaard, Søren, 53n4
Kristeva, Julia: and abjection, xv–xvi, 6–8; and aesthetics, xv–xvi, xviii, 8–10, 14–15, 74, 157; and Hegel, xvi, xix–xx,

1–2, 3, 7–8, 9–10, 13–15, 16n4, 96n12, 112, 162, 169n14; and metaphysics, 16n14, 18n40; and narcissism, 3–4, 16n10, 50–51, 120, 121; and poetics, xv, 3, 9, 10, 11, 77, 94, 95n8, 96n12; *Powers of Horror* (*Pouvoirs de l'horreur*), xv–xvi, 6–8; and psychoanalysis, xvi, xix, 1–8, 50–51, 55n20, 73, 93, 149, 153–154, 155, 160, 169n7; *Revolution in Poetic Language* (*La Révolution du langage poétique*), xv, 1–3, 4–6, 8–10, 13–15, 18n42, 18n44, 112, 160, 169n14; and semiotics, xv–xvi, xix, 1–10, 8, 13, 14–15, 90, 93, 96n18, 153–155, 165; *Tales of Love* (*Histoires d'amours*), 3–4, 16n10. *See also* Freud and Hegel

Lacan, Jacques, xv, xix, 3–4, 5–6, 90, 153–154, 160
Landy, Joshua, 85, 96n35
Lévinas, Emmanuel, 102, 112, 115n7
Lewis, C. S., 28, 33n26
Lyotard, Jean-François, 125, 126, 131n34

Mallarmé, Stéphane, xviii, 79, 105–106, 108, 110, 158, 169n23
Marx, Karl, xv, xix, 9–10, 11, 17n31, 82, 128, 132n43, 139, 148n32, 149, 158, 160, 162, 169n14
McCumber, John, 132n45, 148n32, 164
Merleau-Ponty, Maurice, 93–94, 98n64, 103, 107, 157, 158
Miller, J. Hillis, xviii, 91–92, 94
Milton, John, 40, 43–44, 53n4–53n5, 58–59
Montaigne, Michel de, 24
Mure, Geoffrey, 144–145, 169n16

Nancy, Jean-Luc, 104, 112, 113, 115n17, 166–167, 170n25
Newton, Isaac, 43
Nietzsche, Friedrich, 4–5, 12, 16n7, 16n14, 17n17, 72n34, 75, 88, 95n4, 96n18, 106

Ovid, 120

Peirce, Charles Sanders, 13, 137

Plato, xii, xiv, xvi, 4, 5, 15, 16n12, 16n14–17n15, 19, 20, 22, 27–28, 29, 29–31, 32n3, 33n22, 33n26, 49, 58, 60, 61, 61–62, 67, 80, 86, 88, 96n18, 98n54, 114n2, 132n42, 155, 166
Plotinus, 33n19
Poulet, Georges, 81–82
Proust, Marcel: and aesthetics, xvii–xviii, 73, 77–80, 88, 90–95, 96n35, 98n64, 156–157; and Benjamin, 78, 90–92, 94; and creativity, 85; and Flaubert, 79; and de Man, 81–86, 96n26, 97n37, 157; and Genette, 81, 82, 157; and Hegel, xix, 88–90, 94–95, 95n3, 97n46, 162–163; *In Search of Lost Time* (*À la Recherche du temps perdu*), 73, 79–80, 80–86, 92–95, 96n17, 96n19, 96n35, 97n37, 97n48, 98n54, 98n64, 156–157; and linguistic disjunction, 82–83; and Kristeva, 74, 77, 90, 93, 94, 96n12, 96n18, 157; and literary history, xvii–xviii, 73, 77, 79–80, 114, 156–157, 158, 165; Mallarmé, 79; and Merleau-Ponty, 93–94, 98n64, 103, 157; and Miller, xviii, 91–92, 94; and psychoanalysis, 73, 90–92, 93, 97n47, 97n53; and Ranciére, xvii–xviii, 73, 77–81, 86, 88, 92, 94, 95n8, 96n18, 156–157; and Schelling, 95

Rabelais, François, 17n15
Ranciére, Jacques, xvii–xviii, 69, 73, 73–81, 86–88, 92, 94, 95n3, 95n8, 96n18, 156–157, 160
Redding, Paul, 163
Rhys, Jean: and aesthetics, 117, 118–119, 125–127, 127–128, 130, 130n1, 131n34–131n35, 158–159; early novels, 117–119; discourse as political, 129–130; and ethics, 127, 128–130; *Good Morning, Midnight*, 118–119, 130n10; and the Hegelian legacy, xix, 117, 127, 129, 131n41, 132n45–132n46; and *Jane Eyre*, 122, 123, 124, 125, 126; and myth of natural authority, 122–123, 124; and nature as myth, 121, 125; and *pharmakon*, 128–129, 132n42; and polylogue, 120; rethinking the postmodern, 125–127,

131n34–131n35; and repetition, xix, 122, 129, 158; and semiotics, 117, 118, 119, 121–122, 123, 129; *Voyage in the Dark*, 118, 130n1; *Wide Sargasso Sea*, xix, 117, 120–130, 158–159; and "zone of indistinction", 124, 127, 131n29
Ricoeur, Paul, 2, 16n4, 16n7, 64, 71n29
Rilke, Rainer Maria, xviii, 105–106, 111, 158
Rimbaud, Arthur, xvi, 11–13, 17n32, 169n23
Robespierre, Maximilien, 69
Ross, Kristin, 17n32
Rousseau, Jean-Jacques, xvii, 57, 57–70, 72n36–72n37, 72n40, 156
Rousset, Jean, 112
Ruskin, John, 80, 84

Sarraute, Nathalie, 118, 130n2
Schelling, Friedrich Wilhelm, 55n18, 95
Scott, Sir Walter, 123
Shen, Fu, 136, 137
Schiller, Friedrich, xii–xiii, 66, 76–77, 86–88
Schleiermacher, Friedrich, 41–42, 53n6, 161
Schopenhauer, Arthur, 75, 88, 95n4
Shaftesbury, Anthony Ashley Cooper, Third Earl of, 86
Shakespeare, William, 39
Shelley, Percy Bysshe: and aesthetics, xvi, 57, 63–65, 66, 67–68, 69–70, 156; and Blake, 58–59; and Bloom, 57, 57–61; and Bradley, 58, 60, 61; and Clark, 60, 64; and Dante, 58, 60, 64–65, 69–70; and de Man, 57, 61–63; and the Enlightenment, xvii, 57, 60, 65, 66, 68–59, 70; and ethics, 57, 63; and Hegel, xix, 68–69; and the French Revolution, xvii, 60, 68–69; and Rousseau, xvii, 57–70; "The Triumph of Life", xvii, 57–70; and Virgil, 59; and Wordsworth, 60, 61–62, 150
Spenser, Edmund: and aesthetics, xvi, 19, 24–26, 29, 30–31, 33n22; and Aristotelian virtue, 20, 21–22, 30, 32n5; "Book of Courtesy" (*Faerie Queene* VI), 19, 20–31; and Botticelli's "Primavera", 27, 33n19; and discourse, 19, 29, 32n2, 33n31; ethical and political aspects, 19, 20–22, 26, 29, 31, 149; historical background, xvi, 19, 20, 32n1; ideal and real, 26–27; and neo-Plotinian allegory, 22–25, 27–28, 33n26; and phenomenology, 22, 23, 26–27; and Platonic cosmology, 20, 27–28, 30, 32n3; and Protestant hermeneutics, 29–30; and sixteenth-century epistemology, 31; religious aspects, 23–24; and Renaissance pastoral, 24, 25–26, 27, 28, 32n15; and Romance tradition, 22; and Sidney, Sir Philip, 25, 28; and the Three Graces, 25–26, 27–29
Spivak, Gayatri, 120, 122, 124, 128, 132n42
Sophocles, 7–8, 164

Tasso, Torquato, 28, 33n31
Tertullian, xiv
Thompson, James, 52n2

Ullmann, Stephen, 81, 157

Van Gogh, Vincent, 100–101, 111, 166
Virgil, 47, 59
Voltaire, 75, 95n3

Weber, Max, 151
Whitehead, A. N., 65
Wolff, Christian, 29
Wordsworth, William: and aesthetics, xvi, 35, 35–38, 44, 54n15, 54n17, 55n24, 156; and Blake, 53n8; and Bloom, 53n4, 61–62; and Coleridge, 47, 51, 52, 54n12; and the dialectical image, 44, 54n10; and de Man, 47, 54n16; and division in life, 49–50; and ethics, 36, 37, 43, 50–51, 52n2; and the French Revolution, xvi, 45–48, 155–156; and Hartmann, 47; and Hegel, xvi, xix, 51, 52, 54n15, 55n24; and hermeneutics, 41–42, 53n6, 156; and the literary canon, 39; and Kant, xvi, 37, 47, 48, 51, 52, 53n5, 54n15, 55n24; and Milton, 40, 43–44, 53n4; and performativity, 38–41, 156; *The Prelude*, xvi–xvii, 35, 35–52; and psychoanalysis, 50–51,

53n7, 55n18, 150; and semiotics, 48–52, 55n20
Wittgenstein, Ludwig, xi

Yeats, William Butler, 54n16
Yorck, Graf, 49–50

www.ingramcontent.com/pod-product-compliance
Lightning Source LLC
Chambersburg PA
CBHW021849300426
44115CB00005B/81